Managing Telecommunications and Networking Technologies in the 21st Century: Issues and Trends

Gerald Grant
Carleton University, Canada

IDEA GROUP PUBLISHING
Hershey • London • Melbourne • Singapore

Acquisition Editor:	Mehdi Khosrowpour
Managing Editor:	Jan Travers
Development Editor:	Michele Rossi
Copy Editor:	Elizabeth Arneson
Typesetter:	Tamara Gillis
Cover Design:	Deb Andree
Printed at:	Sheridan Books

Published in the United States of America by
    Idea Group Publishing
    1331 E. Chocolate Avenue
    Hershey PA 17033-1117
    Tel: 717-533-8845
    Fax: 717-533-8661
    E-mail: cust@idea-group.com
    Web site: http://www.idea-group.com

and in the United Kingdom by
    Idea Group Publishing
    3 Henrietta Street
    Covent Garden
    London WC2E 8LU
    Tel: 44 20 7240 0856
    Fax: 44 20 7379 3313
    Web site: http://www.eurospan.co.uk

Library of Congress Cataloging-in-Publication Data

Managing telecommunications and networking technologies in the 21st century : issues and trends / Gerald Grant [editor]
    p. cm.
  A collection of 13 papers by various researchers.
  Includes bibliographical references and index.
  ISBN 1-878289-96-9 (paper)
  1. Telecommunicaiton. 2. Internetworking (Telecommunication) I. Grant, Gerald, 1956-

HE7631 .M36 2001
384'.068--dc21
                                           2001016578

British Cataloguing in Publication Data
A Cataloguing in Publication record for this book is available from the British Library.

NEW from Idea Group Publishing

- ❏ **Developing Quality Complex Database Systems: Practices, Techniques and Technologies/** Shirley Becker, Florida Institute of Technology/ 1-878289-88-8
- ❏ **Human Computer Interaction: Issues and Challenges/**Qiyang Chen, Montclair State University/ 1-878289-91-8
- ❏ **Our Virtual World: The Transformation of Work, Play and Life via Technology/**Laku Chidambaram, University of Oklahoma, and Ilze Zigurs/1-878289-92-6
- ❏ **Text Databases and Document Management: Theory and Practice/**Amita Goyal Chin, Virginia Commonwealth University/1-878289-93-4
- ❏ **Computer-Aided Method Engineering: Designing CASE Repositories for the 21st Century/**Ajantha Dahanayake, Delft University/ 1-878289-94-2
- ❏ **Managing Internet and Intranet Technologies in Organizations: Challenges and Opportunities/**Subhasish Dasgupta, George Washington University/1-878289-95-0
- ❏ **Information Security Management: Global Challenges in the New Millennium/**Gurpreet Dhillon, University of Nevada, Las Vegas/1-878289-78-0
- ❏ **Telecommuting and Virtual Offices: Issues & Opportunities/**Nancy J. Johnson, Capella University/1-878289-79-9
- ❏ **Managing Telecommunications and Networking Technologies in the 21st Century: Issues and Trends/**Gerald Grant, Carleton University/1-878289-96-9
- ❏ **Pitfalls and Triumphs of Information Technology Management/**Mehdi Khosrowpour/1-878289-61-6
- ❏ **Data Mining and Business Intelligence: A Guide to Productivity/**Stephan Kudyba and Richard Hoptroff/1-930708-03-3
- ❏ **Internet Marketing Research: Theory and Practice/**Ook Lee,University of Nevada Las Vegas/1-878289-97-7
- ❏ **Knowledge Management & Business Model Innovation/**Yogesh Malhotra/1-878289-98-5
- ❏ **Strategic Information Technology: Opportunities for Competitive Advantage/**Raymond Papp, Quinnipiac University/1-878289-87-X
- ❏ **Design and Management of Multimedia Information Systems: Opportunities and Challenges/** Syed Mahbubur Rahman, Minnesota State University/1-930708-00-9
- ❏ **Internet Commerce and Software Agents: Cases, Technologies and Opportunities/**Syed Mahbubur Rahman, Minnesota State University, and Robert J. Bignall, Monash University/ 1-930708-01-7
- ❏ **Environmental Information Systems in Industry and Public Administration/** Claus Rautenstrauch and Susanne Patig, Otto-von-Guericke University Magdeburg/ 1-930708-02-5
- ❏ **Strategies for Managing Computer Software Upgrades/**Neal G. Shaw, University of Texas, Arlington/1-930708-04-1
- ❏ **Unified Modeling Language: Systems Analysis, Design and Development Issues/** Keng Siau, University of Nebraska-Lincoln, and Terry Halpin, Microsoft Corporation/ 1-930708-05-X
- ❏ **Information Modeling in the New Millennium/**Keng Siau, University of Nebraska-Lincoln, and Matti Rossi, Helsinki School of Economics/ 1-878289-77-2
- ❏ **Strategies for Healthcare Information Systems/**Robert Stegwee, Ernst & Young, and Ton Spil, University of Twente/ 1-878289-89-6
- ❏ **Qualitative Research in IS: Issues and Trends/** Eileen M. Trauth, Northeastern University/ 1-930708-06-8
- ❏ **Information Technology Evaluation Methods and Management/**Wim Van Grembergen, University of Antwerp/1-878289-90-X
- ❏ **Managing Information Technology in a Global Economy** (2001 Proceedings)/Mehdi Khosrowpour/1-930708-07-6

Excellent additions to your library!

**Receive the Idea Group Publishing catalog with descriptions of these books by calling, toll free 1/800-345-4332
or visit the IGP Web site at: http://www.idea-group.com!**

Managing Telecommunications and Networking Technologies in the 21st Century: Issues and Trends

Table of Contents

Preface

These are exciting and challenging times for the fields of telecommunications and networking. They are exciting because we are witnesses to an explosion in technological developments in almost all aspects of the fields. "Convergence" is now the watchword when speaking of telecommunications and networking. The coming together of telecommunications and computing technologies portends a future of ubiquitous, high-bandwidth multimedia communications. Such a scenario was almost undreamed of a few years ago. However, developments in wireless telecommunications, fiber optics, along with advances in Internet-related technologies have opened new vistas for growth in modern communications (Adam, 2000). These times are challenging in that these same developments in technology emanate from a variety of technological paradigms and are occurring at a furious pace. It is therefore difficult to know which technologies will survive the almost inevitable shakeout that must occur.

The battle to survive and dominate is fierce. Incumbent telecommunication and networking technology and service providers are working vigorously to retrofit their existing networks to supply next-generation broadband services. Digital subscriber line (DSL) and cable modem technology have been developed to leverage the existing telephone and cable television networks. These technologies, while effective in the short term, suffer from a variety of shortcomings that make it difficult for widespread deployment to occur rapidly and cost effectively. DSL requires relatively clean circuits to carry data at high speeds. However, the copper wires in the telephone system suffer from high levels of electromagnetic interference. This means that circuits have to be rigorously tested before they can be used. This makes deployment expensive.

Cable modem service has an advantage over DSL in that the cable networks are simpler and they can carry more information. However, cable has its own drawbacks. It is a shared network, which means that all nodes in a neighborhood must share the same high-speed connection. This means that speed and service can degrade depending on how many people are using the service at a particular point in time. Cable modem service also suffers reliability problems.

Gigabit Ethernet (now 10-Gigabit Ethernet) over dense wave division multiplexed (DWDM) fiber is challenging the hegemony of DSL and cable modems and has the potential to deliver much higher bandwidth and cheaper, more reliable broadband access to consumers. There is explosive growth in fiber-optic technology. Coupled with fiber-optic technology, Ethernet networks can have links of tens of kilometers (Fishburn, 2000). Using Ethernet allows network service providers to move away from more expensive and complex technologies (Phillips & Redifer, 1999). This means that the cost of deploying fiber-based last-mile technology could be even cheaper than that of retrofitting the current telephone and cable networks for high-speed service.

Mobile wireless access promises to be a substantial telecommunications growth area. Increased demand for mobile services is being driven by a number of factors.

On the business side, there is a growing need to connect increasingly mobile workers to backbone networks to provide data input and get updated business information. On the consumer side, businesses are working to provide consumers with access to information at their fingertips such as stock quotes, travel, shopping, and entertainment information. Although mobile wireless appears conceptually simple, it is difficult to implement mainly because of the mobility aspect. A variety of approaches are being suggested to deal with the problems associated with providing highly reliable mobile services. Developments in 3G mobile standards currently underway will "provide increased capacity, data capability, and a far greater range of services using an innovative radio access scheme and an enhanced core network. (Rees, 2000).

The explosive growth in the development of alternative telecommunications and networking technologies has largely been spurred by the significant regulatory changes enacted by governments around the world. In the monopolistic environment that pervaded the old telecommunications industry there was little incentive to move quickly to bring new technologies and services online, since incumbent operators wanted to recoup their investments from already deployed technology. Following the wide-ranging deregulation of the telecommunications industry in North America and parts of Europe, a wide variety of service and equipment providers began delivering radically new products and services to the market.

Although much of the Americas and Europe enjoy a highly deregulated industry, this is not the case in other regions of the world. Many governments are still very cautious about how best to approach deregulation of the telecommunications industry. This caution reflects their unwillingness to allow their local industry to be dominated by bigger foreign players. These countries face a conundrum, however, since the expansion of their telecommunications capabilities requires massive injection of capital, which is most likely to come from foreign investors. The "digital divide" between industrialized and less industrialized regions will continue to grow if ways to benefit from the growth in telecommunications and networking technologies are not found. For this to happen, an appropriate regulatory scheme must be found.

Deploying broadband and wireless technologies poses significant challenges, especially in community and cross-cultural settings. Those engaged in deploying new technologies must recognize and attend to the diverse needs, abilities, and cultural complexities if communities and business organizations are to benefit from the new technologies.

Organization of the Book

It is impossible, in one book, to address all the issues and trends relating to telecommunications and networking. The issues are diverse and wide-ranging. This book is intended to make a small contribution to understanding some of the technologies, issues, and challenges in telecommunications and networking in the early part of the 21st century.

We have divided the book into three sections. In the first section, there are six chapters that focus on current developments in telecommunications and networking technologies. These chapters present us with insights into the evolution of current technologies and their potential impact on the telecommunications industry as well as organizations and individuals. The four chapters in the second section discuss international experiences in telecommunications and networking infrastructure development. These chapters remind us that while there are significant developments taking place in the telecommunications fields, all regions and countries in the world are not benefiting equally from these. There are numerous political, social, legal and technological challenges that need to be addressed. Section three contains three chapters that highlight challenges and impacts of implementing telecommunication and networking technologies to address specific organizational or community issues.

In Chapter 1, Brennan et al. provide an overview of current developments in Intelligent Networks standardization and evolution. The tremendous increase in demand and the commercial potential for integrated multimedia communications have spurred significant interest in leveraging current and future telecommunications infrastructure for delivering converged services. The Intelligent Network (IN) is seen by many as the foundation service delivery platform of the future. The chapter describes the standardization efforts being pursued by various groups. The IETF's PINT and SPIRITS working groups are working on protocols and architectures that will further the internetworking between IP and IN. The Parlay Industry working group (comprising such players as BT, Seimens AG, IBM, Lucent, etc.) is concerned with specifying object-oriented service control APIs designed to support all major middleware technologies and that are independent of the underlying communications infrastructure. The goal is to develop an IN infrastructure that will make the provisioning of telecommunication services seamless and effective. An integrated Intelligent Networks/CORBA infrastructure provides the basis for more open and distributed implementation of IN services as well as facilitating increased interconnection with Internet-based services and private databases. While no one of these approaches in IN standardization predominates, technological developments in IN will continue to accelerate.

Bill St. Arnaud, in Chapter 2, proposes a research program leading to the deployment of a Gigabit Internet to the Home (GITH) network that bypasses the traditional voice- or cable-based networks. The proposal is based on the premise that IP services will dominate in the future. Therefore, a "last mile" solution built from the ground up to support IP services will be best positioned to meet the demands for integrated communication services in the future. A GITH network would allow for the competitive provisioning of communication services based on the principle of equal access. This network would primarily be an optical network applying dense wave division multiplexing (DWDM) technology. This would allow it to be highly flexible and scalable. The building of a GITH network will be an undertaking of the size and scale of previous telecommunications infrastructure projects and will require partnership between governments and the private sector. While the costs involved in implementing such a network are immense, the projected long-term benefits will be significant.

The widely deployed wireless communication facilities in many countries (originally designed to provide voice services) increasingly are being used to provision data services. Both technology and the increased deployment of mobile applications are pushing the need for wireless data. More and more companies are attempting to connect their mobile workers to networked enterprise applications through a variety of communication links. These links have different capacities and apply diverse protocols and technologies, making the process complicated. Wireless mobile devices are expected to constitute a significant portion of the client devices accessing enterprise networks. However, these devices are limited in their capacity to handle computationally intensive applications. These limitations will continue into the future because functionality requirements of mobile applications are expected to expand. The challenge faced by those deploying mobile applications is how best to manage the complex environment and computational intensity presented by wireless mobile. In Chapter 3, Thomas Kunz presents a promising solution: a new architecture for adaptive mobile applications based on mobile code.

Both Chapters 4 and 5 deal with space and time dimensions of mobile wireless networks. Chapter 4, by Paulraj and Sampath, provides a broad overview of the concepts behind "smart antennas." They describe the four main leverages of smart antennas: array gain, diversity gain, interference reduction, and multiplexing. They conclude by outlining a number of industry trends in the commercialization of space-time processing technology.

In Chapter 5, André Brandão proposes space division multiple access (SDMA) as a "promising technique useful for increasing capacity, reducing interference, and improving overall wireless communication link quality." While SDMA is not conceptually new, the technique is difficult to apply in wireless mobile environments. The chapter provides a discussion on SDMA and intelligent antennas, conceptually illustrating how the technologies work. Technical difficulties and lack of commercial applications aside, Brandão challenges the reader to apply a business perspective concerning wireless communications akin to that adopted by Marconi almost a century ago. With wireless mobile computing expected to grow exponentially, the current difficulties with deploying the technology should not prevent further research and development efforts about SDMA and intelligent antennas.

Chapter 6 by Lance Pickett and Kathy S. Lassila discusses issues related to the deployment of virtual private networks (VPN) by organizations wanting to increase access to enterprise networks by mobile workers and to provision new mobile services, cost effectively and securely. Virtual private networks allow firms to leverage the public Internet, by using variety of software and hardware technologies to create a secure environment for remote network access. The chapter discusses the technologies and issues relating to VPNs and concludes with a look at future trends in VPN deployment.

The second part of the book shifts the focus away from specific technologies and focuses the reader's attention on a number of international standardization and public policy issues surrounding the deployment of telecommunication services. This international perspective is important because it alerts the reader to the fact that development and application of telecommunication technologies are not universally comparable. Efforts relating to the standardization of telecommunications technologies as well as public policies relating to the application of those technologies significantly affect their diffusion.

To begin part two, Zixiang Tan discusses the international efforts leading to standardization of wireless communications. Internationally accepted and applied standards are essential for global diffusion of wireless communications technologies. However, the history of wireless communications demonstrates the highly competitive nature of the standardization process. Tan explores this history, highlighting the issues and challenges faced in first generation (1G) and second generation (2G) standardization efforts. The current efforts by the ITU to guide the development of third generation (3G) wireless communication standards (referred to as IMT-2000) are characterized by an intense mix of international cooperation and competition. The author concludes by suggesting that with the ITU's IMT-2000, global wireless communications may have moved into an era of "de-standardization," where multiple standards are expected to exist yet work co-operatively.

For most of the time since the invention of the telephone, telecommunications services have been operated and governed as a monopoly enterprise. In many countries, even today, the telecommunications industry is highly regulated and telecommunications service provision remains in the hands of a few entities. This is particularly the case in many less emerging and less developed countries. The 1980s and 1990s have witnessed significant moves in Europe and North America to deregulate the telecommunications industry and open it to full competition. The United Kingdom and the United States are examples of two countries that took a somewhat radical approach to telecommunications reform. Other countries followed more gradual approaches. Gao and Lyytinen, in Chapter 8, provide insights into the Chinese approach to telecommunications reform. China's gradual process is viewed as appropriate given the economic, political and social circumstances.

Although now part of China, Hong Kong's telecommunication industry has advanced further in its telecommunications reform process than mainland China. The effect of deregulation has been the introduction of fierce competition in the telecommunications market. By the end of 1999, over 148 external telecommunications service licenses had been issued. One of the consequences of introducing new service providers into a market is the varying levels of service quality. In Chapter 9, Xu Yan and James Y. L. Thong report on an experiment to test the quality of international direct dial (IDD) services in Hong Kong in the deregulated environment. The findings from the experiment suggest that quality of IDD services is probably the most enduring determinant of competitive success in deregulated market although price is important in the early stages. One implication of the study is that regulators should consider introducing facilities-based competition early in the reform process as incumbent operators will tend to create an artificially high barrier for new entrants, thus denying consumers the full benefits of deregulation.

Fola Yahaya's chapter on *new connectivity options for information infrastructure development in Sub-Saharan Africa* introduces the reader to some of the issues faced in developing information infrastructure in Africa. The author highlights the many projects, planned or underway, to radically develop the continent's telecommunications and networking infrastructure. These include satellite and submarine cable projects as well as projects focusing on wireless local loop. Most of the most publicized projects are being proposed by external parties, particularly private telecommunications consortia, hoping to capitalize on what is perceived to be a high pent-up demand for telecommunication services. Given the high involvement and power of external parties the author suggests that public policy must play a pivotal role in determining the most beneficial route to pursue. Since there is no quick or universal solution to challenges in developing information infrastructure in Africa, choices as to which connectivity solution is best should only be made after careful and in-depth analysis.

Part three of the book focuses on the impacts and challenges of implementing telecommunications and networking technologies in particular settings. This section begins with Venkatesh's case description of the issues and challenges in implementing broadband networks for community-based organizations in the state of New York. The state-funded program described in the case was designed to bridge the digital divide between economically advantaged and disadvantaged areas of the state. Venkatesh highlights a number of issues relating to the deployment of broadband networks including "last mile" access, integration of software applications, and challenges in acquiring technical support services. One of the key findings is that know-how barriers are pervasive in the context of broadband networks and that these barriers increase in smaller organizations. The author suggest the use of application prototypes to help network owners develop an understanding of the proposed technology before adoption decisions are made.

In another case study from New York State, Dawes and Oskam describe efforts to create an Internet-based GIS Clearinghouse for the state in keeping with the statewide information policy. The state has instituted a policy for sharing of data, including GIS data. The New York State Library plays a pivotal role in this program. The provision of online services for accessing GIS data is a key objective of the clearinghouse.

A number of issues arise when communications technology is being applied in a variety of cultural settings. In the final chapter, Chapter 13, the authors compare efforts to adopt cellular phones in France and the United States. The results of the study show that culture plays a major role in explaining the different results from adopting cellular phone technology.

Conclusions

The telecommunications and networking field is experiencing tremendous growth in technologies and services. This is at the same time exciting and challenging. It is exciting because the new developments open the potential for many new advanced products and services. They are challenging because of the complex nature of the technologies themselves and the environments in which they are being deployed. This book presents some insights into these issues and developments.

References

Adam, J. (2000, September/October) Internet everywhere. *MIT Technology Review*, Retrieved from the World Wide Web: http://www.techreview.com/articles/oct00/adam.htm.

Fishburn, M. (2000, August) *10 Gigabit Ethernet: Testing challenges ahead. Telecommunications Online*. Retrieved from the World Wide Web: http://www.telecoms-mag.com/issues/200008/tcs/10gigabit_ethernet.html.

Philips, J. and Redifer, G. (1999, January) *Long-haul networking: The case for GigE+DWDM, Telecommunications Online*. Retrieved from the World Wide Web: http://www.telecoms-mag.com/issues/199901/tcs/state6.html.

Rees, G. (2000, September) The quiet wireless revolution, Telecommunications Online. Retrieved from the World Wide Web: http://www.telecoms-mag.com/issues/200009/tci/the_quiet_wireless.html.

Part One:

Developments
in Telecommunications
and
Networking Technology

Chapter I

Intelligent Networks: A Discussion of Current Developments

Rob Brennan, Brendan Jennings, Conor McArdle
and Thomas Curran
Teltec Ireland

INTRODUCTION

Recent years have seen a huge increase in the prevalence of desktop computing in homes and businesses worldwide. This has been fuelled, to a large extent, by the success of the Internet, which has clearly demonstrated the immense commercial potential of multimedia communications services. Exposure to the Internet has raised customer expectations of the service features that should be offered by the public telecommunications infrastructure, principally that they support a mix of media types and allow easy customization. Additionally, users expect that these services will be available on-demand, regardless of their location or the capabilities of their terminal equipment. Whilst the main technological components required to realize this vision are available, there remains a significant challenge in deploying them in a manner that is both cost effective and that can continue to meet the demands of a volatile marketplace.

As the level of interconnection between fixed, mobile, Internet and enterprise networks increases, a key component in ensuring their ongoing success will be the availability of a common platform for the development and delivery of communications services. Of course a key requirement for operators who intend enhancing their service delivery capabilities is that existing systems are leveraged as much as possible rather than replaced outright. Many see the Intelligent Network (IN), which is today the prevalent means of providing services based on manipulation of voice call setup, as a starting point for the service delivery platform of the future. Currently a number of groups are proposing short-to medium-term evolutionary paths for IN that aim at overcoming limitations of existing systems. In this article we discuss some of these initiatives, show that taken together they may provide the basis of a flexible and open architecture, and identify a number of common trends and outstanding issues.

In the next section we outline the basic elements of the IN as it exists today. We then discuss some of the technical and commercial limitations that are currently driving the development of IN. The following three sections summarize Internet/information technology and PSTN (Public Switched Telephone Network) integration standardization work carried out by the IETF (PINT/SPIRITS), the Parlay consortium (Parlay) and the OMG (IN/CORBA Interworking) respectively. The final two sections identify important common trends in the development of IN and some issues for which immediate solutions are not apparent.

THE INTELLIGENT NETWORK

The IN provides the PSTN (Public Switched Telephone Network) with the infrastructure to provide advanced services such as freephone (1-800) and number portability. The Intelligent Network came into being in the mid-1980s as a way of decoupling telecommunications service logic from the call switching functions of exchanges. This facilitated centralized service processing functionality, eased the deployment of new services and reduced the escalating complexity of exchanges. IN standardization has taken place in ANSI, the ITU and ETSI. Unfortunately this distribution of standardization effort and the proprietary enhancements to IN by vendors have created a plethora of non-interworking IN solutions. Within geographical regions, for example, the US or Europe, there is sufficient agreement on standards that interworking is possible and, at least nominally, the ITU standard forms the basis for international interworking.

The basic IN model involves a distributed functional architecture which contains functional entities which are collectively responsible for handling any calls which use more sophisticated services than traditional call routing by dialed digits. Figure 1 shows the functional entities, their relationships and how these entities are typically grouped into platforms in a network. All

Figure 1. The IN architecture

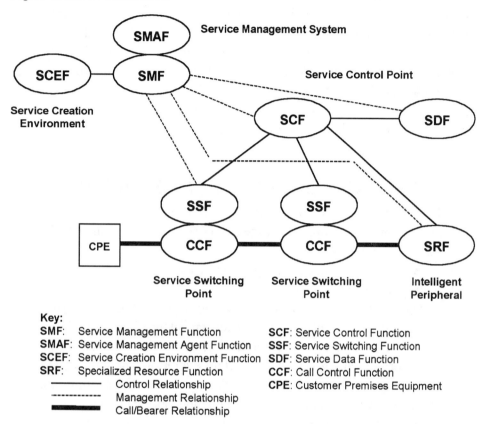

control relationships are normally supported by signaling transported over the reliable SS.7 (Signaling System Number 7) packet data network.

Each function plays a role in the completion of calls which require additional processing to be routed through the network. The CCF takes care of the routing of normal calls through the PSTN and detects when an IN session should be initiated, for example, by examining dialed digits. For an IN call the CCF gives control to the colocated SSF, which starts an INAP (Intelligent Network Application Protocol) session with the SCF to request any special handling instructions for this call. Normally the SCF will then respond with a destination address (number) to which the call should be routed. Many variations on this basic scheme are possible, involving the SCF querying a database (the SDF) or instructing the SSF to connect the call to a recording playback device in a SRF. The SCF may also instruct the SSF on specific billing arrangements to be used when dealing with this call. Supporting entities provide functionality such as service creation (SCEF) and service management (SMF, SMAF).

IN has been structured into a number of modular extensions called Capability Sets (ITU-T, 1997). The first Capability Set (CS-1) was standardized in 1993 and is widely deployed (although often with proprietary extensions). CS-2 has also been standardized and is available from many equipment manufacturers. CS-3 really only exists as a standard at this time and work on CS-4 has begun. Each Capability Set extends the IN model and INAP protocol to deal with more sophisticated services while remaining within the original IN architectural framework.

DRIVING FORCES FOR IN EVOLUTION

Development of the IN concept has been motivated mainly by:

- a need for a reduction in the time from service conception to deployment in PSTN networks,
- a desire to free network operators from dependence on particular equipment vendors, and
- a wish to enable the provision of services by third party providers.

The degree to which existing IN systems meet these goals may be debated; however, IN is clearly a commercial reality, with an ever-increasing penetration of IN services and growing demand for ever more sophisticated features that can be customized by the end user. Deregulation of telecommunications markets globally will result in a more open environment in which third party service providers will seek access to the public network infrastructure. These trends point towards a growing necessity to overcome some of the constraints of existing IN platforms.

1. *Inherent Limitations*

The majority of IN implementations are still based on the CS-1 standards, which limit IN service logic to control of (voice) call setup in response to triggers[1] activated at network switches. For some time there has been a clear need to extend the capabilities of IN to allow control of calls throughout their duration and to introduce support for multiparty, multi-connection calls, possibly involving the exchange of multimedia data. It should be noted that ITU-T IN CS-2 does go some way towards realizing this goal. In addition, the manner in which IN services are deployed and accessed should be made more open – for example service logic should be accessible from Internet terminals and contain components residing in both SCPs and Internet nodes. Trigger deployment in switches is also currently a problem area as service deployments can require upgrades of switch software.

2. *Service Development and Deployment*

As alluded to above, a key motivation for IN was to reduce the time between service conception and full-scale deployment in the public telephony network. Whilst IN has succeeded in cutting this time lag it is evident that even faster service deployment is required today to satisfy rapidly changing customer demands. However the necessary improvement may be hard to achieve in the short term as methodologies and tools for service creation and validation have not yet matured to support the degree of automation required for rapid development. To a large degree this is due to the complexity and time-consuming nature of service validation in general and the difficulties associated with detection of unwanted interactions between services in particular. In addition, service components are generally not developed with reusability or customizability in mind; thus, development times for new services may be unnecessarily lengthy. Finally, generic service deployment and management are still not mature technologies. This means that portability of service logic from one IN platform to another (even within one manufacturer's range of platforms) is very time-consuming and uneconomical for all but the most basic services.

3. *Vendor/Technology Independence*

Stringent reliability and performance targets for telephony services have meant that fault-tolerant equipment and specialized software have been necessary for the realization of IN platforms. Variations in versions of the communications protocols and service logic mean that in many cases the task of getting equipment from different vendors to interoperate properly is very difficult. These factors contribute greatly to the difficulties for smaller vendors and third party service providers who wish to enter the IN market. Many see the implementation of IN elements using middleware solutions such as CORBA as offering the potential to overcome these difficulties by making service logic independent from underlying hardware/software architectures and communications protocols.

4. *Openness*

A key barrier to the development of IN into a truly open service environment is the lack of standardized interfaces for service creation, management and deployment that can be used by nonspecialists to develop IN services using commercial software development methods and tools. These open interfaces may even be tailored for the use of end users wishing to create/customize services to meet their own needs. An additional limitation is a lack of facilities for brokerage of service components that would promote dynamic reuse of IN software. However this would require significant enhancements to present IN equipment, which, as discussed above, tends to be very proprietary in nature.

5. *Integration of Services for Packet Networks*
Currently IN is focussed on delivering services for the PSTN and more recently the PLMN (Public Land Mobile Network). Operators and customers realize that new services delivered by packet networks (such as the Internet) which are integrated with the PSTN and PLMN represent vast potential for growth. From the consumer's point of view, standard telephony services (which are currently provided by IN) should be available in the new domain; from the operator's point of view, the currently installed base of IN equipment should be leveraged to provide these services. The current incompatibility of the closed telephony network and the open environment of the Internet must be addressed.

Consideration of the limitations discussed above leads to the view that the key requirements for future development of IN are that customers can access a wider variety of services in a wider variety of ways and that they can customize existing services or even create new ones as simply, quickly and cost effectively as possible. This requires operators to have more efficient and open service creation, deployment and management facilities that are integrated into IN service platforms.

PINT/SPIRITS

This section discusses two working groups of the IETF (Internet Engineering Task Force), PINT and SPIRITS, which are developing complementary protocols/architectures for interworking between the IN and IP-based devices. PINT essentially deals with services initiated in the IP network and SPIRITS deals with services initiated in the PSTN/IN.

The PINT (PSTN/Internet Interworking) working group is part of the IETF Transport Area and was created in 1997 to address how Internet applications can request and enrich telecommunications services. It has published an informational RFC on existing practices in this area and version 1 of the PINT protocol as a proposed standard (IETF, 2000a).

The PINT protocol enables the invocation of telephony services from terminals in an IP-based network environment. More specifically a host in the IP network forwards a service request to a PINT server, which relays the request to the relevant PSTN network resource, for example, a node imple-

Figure 2. IETF PINT architecture

menting a Service Control Function (SCF), that then executes the requested service, possibly reporting service session status back to the originating IP terminal. Version 1 of the PINT protocol focuses on a small number of "milestone" services, namely Request to Call, Request to Fax and Request to Hear Content. The protocol is specified as a profile for use of the IETF standard Session Initiation Protocol (SIP) and specific extensions to SIP and the associated standard Session Description Protocol (SDP).

While the overall aim of the PINT initiative is to enable integration of Internet resources and telephony services in broad terms, it will effectively standardize access from the Internet to the IN Service Control Function. It will also enable development of novel services that execute partially in the Internet domain and partially in the traditional telephony domain. Another consequence is that due to the reuse of standard IETF protocols and methodologies the solution it will provide will be very lightweight in nature. Importantly, the PINT protocol fits into the existing SIP architecture for Internet-based media session control, which will be significant in the future if (as this author expects) SIP forms the basis for IP Telephony. From a broader business perspective important factors pointing towards the likely success of PINT are the fact that the IETF standards process is proven in producing timely, flexible, scalable and extensible protocols and that nearly every major telecommunications equipment vendor and operator participates in the process. In addition, PINT is being actively considered by ITU-T SG11 for inclusion in the IN CS-4 functional architecture.

A potentially significant drawback of the PINT work is that no standard API will be defined as part of the IETF process. This will either lead to an emergence of a de facto standard API or a multitude of vendor-specific implementations with resultant porting difficulty for code to run on different products. Indeed as seen with past IETF standards, the lack of specification rigor may mean that it will take several years of vendor implementation experience before a high level of interoperability is achieved. In terms of interoperability we also note that interworking between the PINT gateway and the SCF is currently unspecified although it is potentially a useful interface (it may be considered by ITU-T SG11).

From a more holistic viewpoint, it can be argued that PINT is quite limited in scope–it prevents IP hosts from participating directly in call control. Because such a capability would greatly enhance the possibilities for hybrid Internet/IN services the IETF has started the SPIRITS (Service in the PSTN/IN Requesting an Internet Service) working group (IETF, 2000b), which is addressing the use of Internet resources by SCFs during service execution.

The SPIRITS architecture has not yet been finalized but Figure 3 illustrates the working group consensus at the time of writing. It is generally felt within the working group that any SPIRITS protocol will be based on extensions to SIP and/or PINT. By combining PINT and SPIRITS in one architecture, services such as ICW (Internet Call Waiting) will be able to be implemented in an interoperable way. It is also noteworthy that SPIRITS is more explicit in its interaction with IN equipment, specifying that it is intended to interact with ITU-T IN SCFs, whereas PINT only defines an

Figure 3. IETF SPIRITS draft architecture

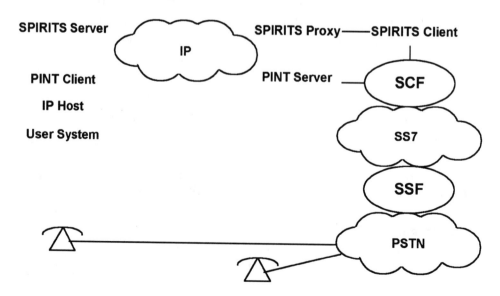

abstract "executive system" controlling the telephony network.

One concern about the SPIRITS work is that consensus has been hard to reach within the working group and hence progress to date has been slow. At the time of writing, these issues seem to have been dealt with and the pace of work seemed to be accelerating. Whatever the progress of IETF work on SPIRITS, a number of commercial implementations of ICW based on SIP extensions are already available.

A final factor worthy of consideration is that PINT/SPIRITS competes, albeit indirectly, with other initiatives such as SIGTRAN (addressing transport of SS.7 protocols over IP) within the IETF and external initiatives like ETSI TIPHON, which is also addressing integration of IP Telephony and IN.

Parlay

The Parlay Industry working group was formed in April 1998 to specify an open API for telecommunications service control. Version 1 of the specification was issued in late 1998. The consortium has grown in member-

Figure 4. Parlay architecture

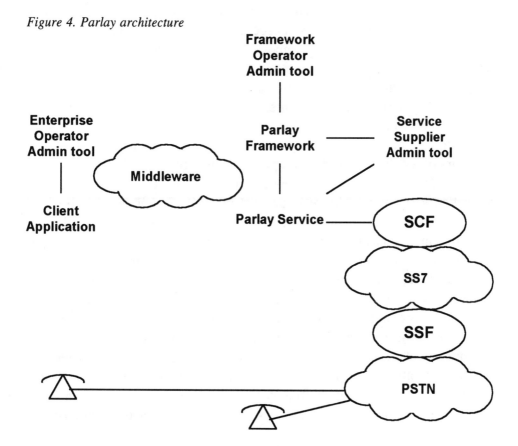

IBM and Lucent Technologies. The current version of the Parlay specifications is 2.1 (Parlay Industry Group, 1999) and the consortium is now focussed on refining the specifications to make commercial implementations a reality.

The Parlay group aims to specify object-oriented service control APIs that are independent of underlying communications technologies (PSTN, wireless and IP networks). The APIs are specified in UML and are designed to support all major middleware technologies (DCOM, CORBA, Java Platform). The technical goals of the group include:
- encouraging CTI (Computer Telephony Integration),
- allowing enterprises, IT systems to access, control and configure traditional telephony IN services,
- providing a unified abstract service control interface for heterogeneous media network types (PSTN, wireless, and Multimedia over IP (MoIP)), and
- specification of value-added framework services such as online brokerage and billing mechanisms.

Business goals include creating a market for third party service providers, enabling services that are more customized to individual enterprise needs, enabling smaller IT companies to develop telecommunications services and allowing network operators to sell access to their IN infrastructure.

The API is structured into framework interfaces and service interfaces. Framework interfaces provide the support infrastructure for Parlay components to work together. Service interfaces deal with the interactions related directly to service execution. The interfaces are grouped into Parlay Interface Sets, each of which describes the allowed interactions between a pair of Parlay components while those components are playing a particular role. A summary of the Parlay interfaces is provided in Table 1.

The Parlay API enables a new generation of customer or third party controlled services which are integrated into IT systems such as e-mail, customer information databases, etc. These services will use directly the telecommunications operators' IN capabilities without the need for wasteful call routing through PBXs for redirection into the operator network. It is envisaged that it will promote a rapid development of tailored services which allow use of general purpose IT systems, thus reducing costs and increasing the availability of tailored services to small- to medium-sized enterprises. The support of a large number of telecommunications equipment vendors, major network operators and vitally the dominant enterprise IT solutions providers indicates potential for a rapid proliferation of this technology. Careful consideration of existing IN capabilities ensures that the API provides an easy evolution path from the traditional IN. Novel features of the API such as

Table 1. The Parlay interfaces

Framework Interfaces	
Trust & Security Management	Enables initial contact, mutual authentication, access to other framework interfaces, activation of services, signing of service agreements.
Service Discovery	Allows an application to list the service types supported by this framework, view service properties, search for services based on their properties, and register new services.
Integrity Management	Provides support for registration/reporting of the load levels of framework, services or client applications. Allows the request of diagnostic functions or performance management statistics. Provides coarse time synchronization between entities.
Service Factory	Allows framework to notify service of new authorized client application ("user"), allows service to supply a unique service manager instance for that user.
Service Subscription	Allows enterprise applications to sign contracts about service usage with the framework provider and to authorize specific client application instances to be service users.
Service Interfaces	
Connectivity Manager	Allows an application to be developed to configure virtual circuits with selectable QoS levels on an IP based network.
Call Control	API to create applications that use centralized call routing or services that span PSTN, Mobile, & MoIP networks. This includes two-party calls, N-party calls and conference calls.
User Interaction	Allows an application to send and receive information to or from a user.
Messaging	Exposes limited functionality for store and forward messaging systems for voice and e-mail messaging.
Mobility	Presents mobile user location information through API to be used to develop applications for network services.

Note: Some capabilities of an interface may not be exposed in a specific
Parlay Interface Set.

online service brokering and framework interfaces for essential supporting functionality such as billing combine to make a very complete solution. The API supports the current business and regulatory drivers towards third party service providers and the reselling of operator IN functionality.

There are of course limitations to the work that the Parlay group has done so far. It is important to note that the current version (2.1) of the API includes areas that are for further study. This includes many of the OA&M features that make the solution so attractive. It is unlikely that there will be any clear winner of the current competition for dominance of the middleware marketplace, especially in the problematic domain of real-time service control. The technology independent approach of the consortium guards against this but will provide interoperability problems as multiple vendors claim Parlay compliance but only support one (or a subset) of the possible middleware implementation mechanisms. Of course the nonspecific middleware approach also guarantees that while Parlay may be implemented with any technology, it is unlikely to be optimal as compromises must be made to ensure cross-technology support. Being middleware based and the size of the planned API ensure that Parlay may be, fairly or unfairly, viewed by the marketplace as a heavyweight solution. It is also apparent that the promise of an abstract service control interface for heterogeneous connections is not fully realized in the current specifications. There will be problems for future development in this area as very dissimilar call control mechanisms (such as SIP and INAP) are integrated under one API. The result may well be that only very basic call control may be exerted over such connections or that specialized sub-APIs are required to access the powerful features of the underlying technologies, thus reducing the benefits of the abstraction promised by the Parlay solution.

IN/CORBA Interworking

The Common Object Request Broker Architecture (CORBA) is a software architecture, defined by the Object Management Group (OMG), that enables software objects to interact with each other despite their location, type of host computer, or programming language. Improved system scalability, increased software reuse, ease of distribution, implementation language independence and object-orientation are seen as the main benefits of adopting CORBA for large-scale application development. In September 1998 the Telecoms Domain Task Force of the OMG produced a specification focussed on interworking of CORBA-based systems with telecommunications signaling systems, such as IN and mobile systems. This standard resulted from a joint submission by AT&T, GMD FOKUS, Nortel, IONA Technologies and Teltec Ireland, in collaboration with Alcatel, Deutsche Telekom, Ericsson Telecommunications, Humboldt University, Object Oriented Concepts Inc., and Telenor. The resulting standard has since been adopted by the OMG (OMG, 1999). An introduction to the standard may be found in Mitra and Brennan (1999).

(OMG, 1999). An introduction to the standard may be found in Mitra and Brennan (1999).

The primary technical motivation for the IN/CORBA interworking specification is to provide mechanisms for interworking of the existing service infrastructure, which uses Transaction Capabilities (TC) for communication, with CORBA-based service objects, which use an Inter-Object Request Broker Protocol (IOP) for communication. The specification defines a framework for the design of CORBA-based TC-User Applications, such as IN, which may communicate, via a gateway, with legacy TC-Users such as Service Switching Points (SSPs). An additional part of the specification allows interworking between "islands" of CORBA-based systems using the existing SS.7 infrastructure as a transport network for CORBA messages between, for example, switches that expose CORBA interfaces and CORBA objects providing service logic.

Middleware technologies like CORBA are increasingly seen as the appropriate infrastructure for future service networks due to the inherent technological advantages brought to bear by distributed, object-oriented

Figure 5. OMG IN/CORBA interworking

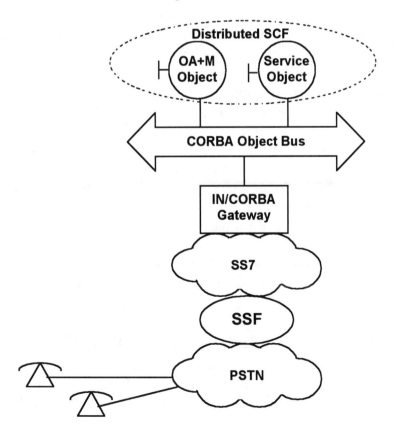

network information model, and a proposal has been submitted to the ITU-T in an attempt to develop international standards for CORBA-based network management interfaces (ANSI T1, 2000). In a similar manner, the CORBA interfaces provided by the IN/CORBA interworking specification provide standardized interfaces which allow more open and distributed implementations of IN service control programs. Also, the common CORBA approach to management and service provisioning allows a more integrated network and less cumbersome service management. IN/CORBA also facilitates increased interconnection capabilities with external resources such as the Internet and private databases. The approach has the added advantage of providing a homogeneous interface for any SS.7 protocol stack implementation. This independence reduces technology lock-ins, allowing service creation that is independent of proprietary SS.7 protocol stack implementations. OMG standards also have the desirable feature of fast standardization and short time to market. As the specification enables implementation of both CORBA-based IN and MAP systems, it may also provide a common ground for fixed-mobile convergence. Leverage of existing, off-the-shelf CORBA services, such as security, naming, messaging and notification, can also help to accelerate application development.

Although the IN/CORBA approach presents many possibilities for the future of IN, there are some associated drawbacks. In order to maintain generality, the solution is quite low-level and does not provide support specifically for IN service development. CORBA still has shortcomings when expected to operate in a highly fault-tolerant, real-time environment as is expected of telecommunications systems, indeed these issues are not addressed directly by the IN/CORBA interworking specification. From a more general viewpoint, since CORBA standardization is controlled by an IT industry body rather than a telecommunications body, it may be difficult to impose telecommunications systems requirements on standards which are based on an architecture for implementation of more general purpose distributed systems. However, the Realtime Platform Special Interest Group within the OMG has begun development of a series of standards, which will eventually allow the purchase of off-the-shelf CORBA products that are suitable for these tasks. Currently, a number of specialized, proprietary solutions are available for use in this application domain.

Common Attributes of IN Evolution Paths

Although it is impossible to predict exactly how the current standardization efforts will impact the Intelligent Network of the future, the scenarios presented here do point towards some overall technological and business trends. This section attempts to identify those key trends that will have a far-reaching impact on service providers, network operators and service subscribers.

From the viewpoint of the emerging standards, one of the key features in current thinking is the use of generic middleware technologies such as CORBA. Middleware will be used for the provisioning of distributed service logic in an open-market environment and also for providing a platform for leverage of resources, such as the Internet, which are largely isolated from the current Intelligent Network. Conversely, the use of middleware and generic protocols also opens the network to access to and from other domains. The trend of standardizing fine-grained middleware interfaces allows for the possibility of smaller, more manageable standard software components making up an overall service architecture. This in turn allows a more open marketplace with opportunities for many independent service vendors and third party service providers, whose presence makes it easier for operators to minimize technology lock-ins.

An alternative point of view sees simple, extensible IETF and W3C (World Wide Web Consortium) protocols and standards as the common glue that binds these domains together. It may be argued that the sum of these technologies, for example, XML and HTTP (as found in the W3C SOAP protocol), is equivalent to existing middleware solutions such as CORBA. With this approach the attractions of minimalist standardization, apparent simplicity, wide availability of implementations and knowledgeable staff must be offset against current architectural holes in the infrastructure, real complexity of building hybrid systems that combine multiple "simple" architectures and lack of compatibility with traditional telecommunications design methodologies.

Standardization of bridging interfaces is also a common trend that allows a merging of currently isolated enterprise, public and private service networks such as PBX, Intranet, Internet and existing INs. This will enable more complex and flexible services to be offered. Access by differing terminal equipment will be more easily coordinated and interact to provide the subscriber with more powerful interfaces for service subscription, access and configuration.

A general trend found in current standards work is the use of generic IT software solutions for acceleration of the development cycle, allowing sophisticated service provisioning, increasing the size of the recruitment pool of knowledgeable staff and lowering costs by avoiding specialist solutions. This has the effect of allowing service execution to be distributed across many domains, allowing reuse of existing service networks in new ways and allowing

This has the effect of allowing service execution to be distributed across many domains, allowing reuse of existing service networks in new ways and allowing access to services by different users with different terminals than originally intended.

Figure 6 describes pictorially how, based on the technologies discussed here, different elements of existing and future technologies may combine to

Figure 6. Common attributes of IN evolution paths

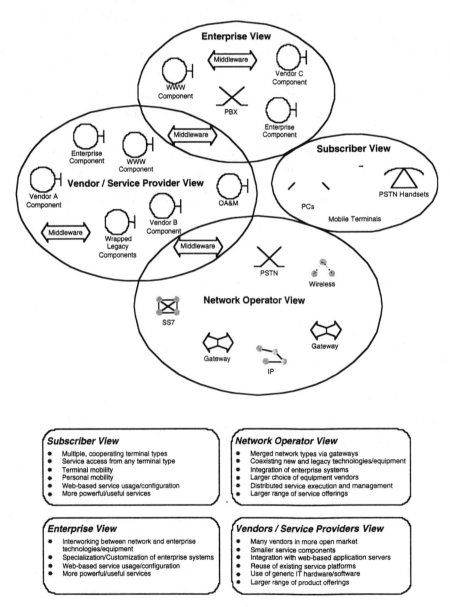

IN Evolution Challenges

The future direction of IN development is uncertain, as even the subset of possible approaches discussed in this article suggests. As there are common themes that run through the various technologies, there are common pitfalls and deficiencies to be contemplated. In this section some of the more pressing issues are discussed.

1. *Difficulty of Specification*

   A common pitfall for evolution technologies is the specification of an enhanced service architecture which is dependent upon other technologies which are not yet mature enough to be deployed (and hence may never be deployed due to other market forces). All of our chosen technologies are specified by IT or communications technology fora that depend upon rapid implementation and wide-ranging industrial participation for specification adoption. However, only IETF PINT is unhindered by dependencies on middleware technologies which may delay deployment of either Parlay or OMG IN/CORBA interworking solutions. Of course IETF PINT has a much more limited scope and this will also be a key to its rapid implementation and deployment. Technical difficulties with any proposed change in the existing IN architecture will not always be immediately apparent from specifications – actual implementation experience is always required.

2. *Nonfunctional Requirements of Telecommunications Systems*

   Performance and reliability will always be key attributes of telecommunications systems that are not traditionally present in enterprise IT systems. There are several facets of the technologies presented in this paper which are impacted by this. Service logic distribution, a common attribute of all of these systems, involves a communications and processing cost which will have to be justified in terms of the added capabilities or other savings. TCP/IP networks are generally envisaged as the transport for the protocols supporting the new technologies and it is well known that they are currently less well suited to telecommunications demands in terms of predictability, congestion avoidance and reliable fault recovery than the well-established SS.7 family of protocols used for traditional signaling applications (Bolotin et al., 1999). Finally middleware solutions have not yet proved themselves capable of the high availability requirements (minutes downtime per year) of the telecommunications service network.

3. *Fragmentation of Standardization Activity*

Maintaining and expanding network elements based on one or more families of network protocols has always been a major effort for operators and vendors. However we now have a situation where the number of design ideologies is expanding from the traditional telecommunications (e.g., ITU-T) view to include data communications (IETF) and distributed object technology (CORBA/Java/DCOM). This brings with it differing approaches to protocol design that may have to be accommodated within one product. This will increase training costs for staff and reduce the number of common software elements in a network element. Of course the overall vision for evolution will also be split amongst differing bodies with the likely result of a gradual decline in the size of evolutionary steps. Hopefully this will lead to a more dynamic environment where gradual change is more normal and advances may more easily be introduced into the network. Alternatively more and more processing power, bandwidth and development effort may be devoted to maintaining backwards compatibility and interworking between almost compatible solutions.

4. *Convergence With IP Solutions*

Every standardization effort discussed in this article includes, at least in some form, an integration of IN and IP solutions. As can be seen from even this limited selection, there are many ways in which this convergence can be achieved. The reality is that most approaches will not survive in the long term; one or more clear winners are likely to emerge. It is even possible that pervasive IN-MoIP integration will not occur. There are many in the Internet community who believe that throwing off the shackles of traditional telecommunications systems such as IN is part of the new departure offered by protocols such as SIP. For them, to bind MoIP to IN would stifle the potential for unforeseen service developments in the MoIP world. Thus it is more likely that centralized solutions such as IN will be the servants rather than the masters of future IP terminals. The reality is that at least some level of IN/MoIP integration is made necessary by the large installed base of traditional telephony equipment.

5. *Opening the IN Services Plane*

Traditionally IN SCP systems have had to deal with service requests originating from SSPs across a well-engineered SS.7 network-a relatively well-controlled environment. All of the architectures featured in this article include the possibility of new types of service requests arriving through other channels, probably carried on an IP network. If this is coupled with user service customization traffic arriving via a WAP gateway (an application with huge growth potential), quite a different operating environment is created for service execution nodes. How will this traffic be managed? What mechanisms will be used to prioritize different types of requests? In order to answer these questions and others, the necessary architectural elements will have to be put in place before these systems are viable in an operational environment. Undoubtedly proprietary solutions will be available first, but this development probably requires some rethinking of the current IN model and surely some standardization will be necessary to provide seamless inter-domain solutions.

6. *A Brave New World*

Finally, the very act of opening up operator networks will have a profound effect on issues such as security, dimensioning, network planning, fault management and network integrity. Traditionally closed worlds, operator networks will be forced to evolve to include complex gateway functions which both protect the network and monitor external usage for legal and accounting purposes. Although similar situations can occur today in the case of inter-provider agreements, the scale of the problem will be enormously magnified if and when any small- to medium-sized enterprise or individual can have such an arrangement with a provider. Large-scale issues of network strategy are also looming. Many operators are currently both transport and service providers. Is this the best way to sustain growth? Ease of IT integration and the proliferation of data network access for individuals will force operators to provide a more dynamic environment. This interconnected world will provide challenges for today's hierarchical management systems and thus requires new solutions to be put in place.

CONCLUSION

The world of IN standardization and evolution is changing. There are many disparate bodies involved in the work; a mix of both traditional telecommunications and information technology solutions will soon be widely deployed. There will be both successful and unsuccessful specifications but there are several underlying trends in the IN evolution path that will be present in future systems. Due to the energy being put into new technologies and their ability to open new markets, it is likely that the pace of change will continue to accelerate.

REFERENCES

ANSI T1. (2000). *Working document for draft standard ANSI T1.2xx-2000, framework for CORBA-based telecommunications management network interfaces* (T1 Committee Document No. T1M1.5/2000-029R1c). American National Standards Institute.

Bolotin, V., Coombs-Reyes, J., Heyman, D., Levy, Y., & Liu, D. (1999). IP traffic characterization for planning and control. In P. Key & D. Smith (Eds.), *Teletraffic science and engineering, 3a* (pp. 425-436). Amsterdam: Elsevier.

IETF (2000a). *The PINT Service Protocol: Extensions to SIP and SDP for IP Access to Telephone Call Services*. (IETF Document number RFC2848). The Internet Engineering Task Force.

IETF (2000b). *SPIRITS charter* [online]. Available: http://www.ietf.org/html.charters/spirits-charter.html. (August 29, 2000).

ITU-T. (1997). *Recommendation Q1221: Introduction to Intelligent Network Capability Set 2*. International Telecommunications Union.

Mitra, N. & Brennan, R. (1999). Design of the CORBA/TC Interworking Gateway. In Han Zuidweg et. al., (Eds.), *Lecture Notes in Computer Science Vol. 1597 Intelligence in Services and Networks*, pp 84-100, 1999. Berlin: Springer.

OMG. (1999). *IN/CORBA Interworking*. (OMG document number /dtc/99-12-02). The Object Management Group.

Parlay Industry Group, *Parlay 2.1 Specification* [online]. Available: http://www.parlay.org/specifications/index.html. (August 29, 2000).

ENDNOTE

1 A trigger determines when a call being processed at the SSF/CCF should interact with a SCF.

Chapter II

Gigabit Internet to Every Home and School: A Conceptual Overview

Bill St. Arnaud
CANARIE, Canada

ABSTRACT

One of last great impediments to wide-scale and rapid deployment of the information society is the "last mile" issue. This chapter outlines some of the issues and history of the last mile problem and proposes a research and development program leading to early deployment of extreme high speed Internet access to schools and libraries (GITS), which will then underpin an architectural framework for high speed Internet access to the home-Gigabit Internet to the Home (GITH). The proposed strategy calls for the deployment of a third residential network service operating in parallel with existing telephone and cable delivery mechanisms and thereby avoiding the regulatory and technical hurdles of integrating traditional telephone and cable services into one common delivery mechanism.

INTRODUCTION

In recent years there have been major advances in the speed and capacity of Internet backbone networks such as the CANARIE optical Internet,

CA*net 3.[1] These networks offer a dramatic increase in bandwidth and quality of service for new advanced multimedia applications. As well, with the advent of innovative competitive service providers such as Qwest,[2] Level 3,[3] and Frontier,[4] there has been a significant reduction in prices commensurate with the development of these new service offerings.

While there have been dramatic changes in backbone capacities and the number of service providers, high speed local access to the home and individual businesses has been considerably slower to develop. Solving the "last mile" problem is one of the grand challenges facing the research community, government and industry. The realization of a Gigabit Internet to the Home (GITH) network will truly allow the wide-scale deployment of new high speed multimedia services and the ultimate realization of the information society.

The advent of low-cost high bandwidth to the home may usher in a new world of applications where the network, in effect, becomes the computer. Currently, there are few traditional applications that require bandwidth to the home in excess of a few megabits per second. But the same story was true for the personal computer, where 15 years ago there were few applications that required more than kilobytes of memory and all the data could be easily stored on a single floppy disk. It is now difficult to conceive of operating a PC with anything less than 32 Mbytes of memory and a 2 gigabyte drive.

It is expected that high bandwidth applications will follow a similar evolutionary path once high bandwidth is routinely available at low cost to the home, school and office. Schools, libraries and universities are currently the some of the biggest consumers of Internet service. Schools in particular have a pressing demand to increase their Internet capacity. Most schools are poorly served with low speed data lines. As multimedia instruction, educational streaming video and other services become increasingly popular, the demand for higher speed Internet access will be insatiable.

As will be described further in this chapter, there are many last mile access technologies including wireless, satellite, xDSL and cable modem services. While the capital cost of GITH to the home may be substantially greater than these alternatives, its life cycle costs are significantly smaller. The biggest single cost component of GITH is the installation of the fiber itself, whether it is in the ground or on poles. Governments and large utilities have the resources to raise money for 20- to 30-year life cycle infrastructures such as roads, bridges and hydro facilities. As such, government again can play a key role in the early deployment of a GITH network by leveraging its capability to easily raise infrastructure money for the deployment of such a network. One possible model would be for government to initially underwrite the infrastructure costs of deploying Gigabit Internet to the home and school and pay down the construction bond or loan by leasing or selling access to either the fiber or conduit on a shared condominium basis.

HISTORICAL PERSPECTIVE

When fiber systems were first deployed in backbone networks it was widely expected that fiber would be quickly deployed to the home. Fiber-to-the-home (FTTH) had a number of attractive benefits, particularly to the telephone company in that its intrinsic bandwidth provided a future proof network, low maintenance cost and no susceptibility to electrical interference.

The Japanese government probably has the most ambitious plans to wire up every home in Japan with fiber. In pursuit of this goal considerable research work has been undertaken in Japan in developing high density optical "ribbons," which can support the connection of hundreds of individual fibers from homes to central offices. In North America FTTH was slower to be adopted because of the concern by the carriers of the high cost of trenching the fiber. The inability of fiber to carry electrical current, which means DC voltage would not be delivered to the home to ensure operation of the phone in the event of a power outage, was also seen as a hindrance to wide-scale deployment.

Instead, throughout the late 1980s and the early 1990s a number of telephone and cable companies initiated broadband to the home trials. These trials focused primarily on video on demand and home shopping services. These trials focused on a number of architecture models including Fiber to the Curb (FTTC), Fiber to the Building (FTTB), Hybrid Fiber Coax (HFC) and Switched Digital Video (SDV). Just about every one of these trials was a failure as there seemed little consumer demand for such services.

Despite the initial failures in these earlier trials a number of telephone companies have undertaken a new initiative called FSAN–Full Service Access Network Initiative. FSAN encompasses the network requirements of the various FTTx schemes and is intended to be a full-service technology that not only offers high speed Internet delivery to the home but also provides basic telephony and video on demand services. However, in light of the insatiable demand for Internet services to the home and the prospect that all future advance multimedia services would be most likely delivered over the Internet, the telephone and cable companies have begun offering high speed Internet via cable and xDSL (Digital Subscriber Line) modems. This is a significant departure from the original FSAN concepts. In addition to the different FTTx approaches, a number of companies are also looking at using wireless technologies for addressing the last mile problem.

These access technologies will be explored in more depth in the following sections. But suffice it to say, there are two underlying assumptions to all of these approaches. Firstly, that a few megabits of bandwidth may be sufficient for future advanced applications and secondly, a single service provider will be delivering that bandwidth.

Cable and xDSL Modems

In the past few years, developments in signal processing capabilities have enabled the traditional copper wires and TV coaxial cable to support data communications at rates up to 5 Mbps. Future versions of this technology promise to deliver data rates approaching 50 Mbps. These technologies are generically called xDSL or cable modem services. While these technologies may serve as a transition strategy, they suffer from a number of limitations. They, essentially, are trying to modify and adapt infrastructure that was designed for another purpose. Cable modems use an underlying infrastructure that was designed to deliver one-way video to the home, and DSL modems use infrastructure originally constructed to deliver two-way voice communication to the home. Because these technologies are trying to make a "silk purse out of a sow's ear," there are a number of technical challenges that remain unresolved in terms of scalability and serviceability. For the cable modem, the challenge is increasing the bandwidth and minimizing the return channel noise on most cable systems. For xDSL deployments, the challenge is extending the service reach beyond 5 kilometers and minimizing the cross talk interference between adjacent copper pairs.

A considerable amount of research is going into solving these problems, but the solutions involve a increasing amount of technical complexity within the modems themselves and at the servers in the central office or head end. As a result the costs are likely to remain high for the customer premises modem, particularly compared to a relatively simple Ethernet interface that is now readily available for most home computers. Another fundamental limitation to cable and xDSL modem services is that customer channels are multiplexed together and the data rates are highly asymmetric. So while the wire speed of cable or xDSL modem service may be in the order of 1-10 Mbps, the actual effective throughput may be considerably less and will vary depending on how many other simultaneous users are accessing the service. More importantly because of the highly asymmetrical nature of cable modem or xDSL service it will be difficult for a home, school or small business to be a data exporter rather than a data consumer.

Cable and xDSL modems in the short term may provide relative high-speed access to the home. In the long run, both technologies have fundamental limitations and will not be suitable for higher bandwidth applications and services, particularly those that require high data volumes originating from the home or school or involve real-time interactive video. High-quality real-time interactive video, for example, requires anywhere from 13 to 40 Mbps of bandwidth. xDSL and cable modems simply do not have this throughput capacity at the present time or in the foreseeable future.

The other challenge with cable and xDSL modems is providing competitive equal access. Neither technology was originally designed for competitive access by other service providers, and it is proving quite costly and technically complex to retrofit such capability. Competitive equal access in the cable and telephone industry relies on multiple ISPs peering at a single Point of Interconnection (POI), at the incumbent's operator facilities at the head end or at the central office. This Internet traffic is redirected to the ISP. There is no physical interconnection between the facilities of the ISP and of the cable company or telephony company operator, that is, the ISP never gets physical access to the spectrum of the incumbent CATV or telephone service operator.

Wireless Local Loop

Wireless access has been suggested in a number of forms including unlicensed spread spectrum, wireless optical, infrared, micro-cellular telephony, and broadband microwave such as local multipoint communication services (LMCS). While wireless access may be optimum for remote and rural areas, the high cost of roof access, the lack of line sight access, disruption from extreme weather and interference from other radio-emitting sources will present serious challenges in obtaining full coverage in urban locations. Ultimately wireless access may also be limited in the amount of usable bandwidth particularly at high data rates. While it is quite conceivable to have wireless data rates up to 100 Mbps, it will be quite another challenge for wireless to scale to Gigabit Ethernet speeds. However, as a transition technology to GITH it may serve as a useful mechanism to circumvent the costs of the last 100 meters, particularly in low-density service areas.

FSAN – FTTx Technologies

In the past couple of years a group of telecommunications network suppliers, operators and manufacturers has undertaken an international initiative to create the required specifications for fiber access systems that will support a full range of integrated narrowband and broadband services. This initiative is called the Full Service Access Network – FSAN.[5] The FSAN initiative encompasses a number of different fiber strategies including Fiber to the Curb (FTTC), Fiber to the Cabinet (FTTCab), Fiber to the Building (FTTB), Hybrid Fiber Coax (HFC) and ultimately Fiber to the Home (FTTH).

Although it was recognized that different carriers would adopt different strategies, sufficient similarities exist in the requirements for these future networks to suggest that significant benefits can be achieved through adopting a common set of requirement specifications. This in turn would presumably drive down costs through high volume production of a common set of technologies that meet the FSAN specifications.

The FSAN committee has recommended an ATM Passive Optical Network (APON) as the most promising approach to achieve large-scale full-service access network deployment that could meet the evolving needs of network users. The FSAN strategy also assumes a single service provider solution for the mile. Presumably ATM virtual circuits could be set up to connect the home to separate service providers, but that would still necessitate a common carrier to provide the local infrastructure. Many aspects of FSAN have a striking similarity to the early days of ISDN as a comprehensive full-service solution.

A RADICAL NEW CONCEPT FOR THE LAST MILE ISSUE

In many ways, the last mile issue parallels recent developments in backbone networks. Until recently, it was assumed that backbone networks would be a shared facility supporting a number of different services such as telephony, video and data services. The carriers and equipment manufacturers have expended great resources in developing and deploying SONET/ATM networks to support this concept of delivery of multiple services. However, it has become increasingly evident that the Internet is the network technology of choice for a wide range of services to consumers and is going to be the vehicle for delivering the information highway. As a consequence of the predominance of the Internet and its associated phenomenal growth, the deployment of backbone networks that are dedicated solely to the carriage of Internet traffic is now conceivable.

This is the premise of CANARIE's CA*net 3 optical Internet. It is the first Internet network in the world that is being built from the ground up to support, first and foremost, Internet traffic. By eliminating the need for a multiservice network, a much simpler and cost effective Internet network can be deployed. Given the growth of the Internet, it would only seem natural that perhaps the same model could be extended to the last mile as well. Rather than trying to build multiservice, integrated high-speed networks to support voice and video, it would be perhaps easier and cheaper to deploy a last mile network that is solely dedicated to carrying Internet traffic.

With the rapid development of IP Telephony and IP Video it would be only a matter of time before these services migrated to such a network as well. However, there is also a clear trend that the traditional telephone and cable TV networks may move to new modes of operation. Voice telephony is rapidly moving to the wireless environment and cable TV may be more efficiently delivered via Direct Broadcast Satellite. In a few years it is quite conceivable that the old copper and coax plant may become obsolete as their traditional host services are delivered by more efficient transport technology. The only "wired" terrestrial service that may remain will be Internet service and this is another compelling reason why it probably does not make sense to try to integrate these traditional services with Internet delivery. The GITH concept described in this document therefore follows Occam's rule of network design - "The simplest network design is likely the most effective network design."

A residential network dedicated to carrying Internet traffic would be in effect a third independent residential network running in parallel to existing telephone and cable TV networks. The computer, or more likely a LAN hub that interconnects to a home-based LAN, will be the principle appliance in the home that would connect to this network. The GITH network would connect directly into the high speed Ethernet port of the computer or similar device, which would then route the traffic within the house. There would be no need for telephone interface devices or expensive digital set-top boxes to segregate and deliver multiple services.

As in the backbone, residential Internet networks could be built from the ground up to carry, first and foremost, Internet traffic. Internet delivery therefore would not be a kludge of existing transport technologies as currently being deployed in the cable and DSL modem services. More importantly an independent residential Internet network would not be encumbered with delivery of legacy services particularly in dealing with complex regulatory and technical issues such as 911 services, number portability, voice splitters, battery backup, digital to analog conversion, etc. Such a green field deployment would also allow for new network architectures and regulatory environments that support competitive equal access as a first principle rather than a as a retroactive service requirement.

A competitive equal access service environment has a number of technical as well as business advantages. Back in 1964, Paul Baron, one of the early Internet visionaries, produced a series of articles proposing the idea of packet switching networks. He was working at a time when there was considerable worry about destruction of the US communications infrastructure by enemy action. He proposed a network design that is fundamentally the Internet as we know it today. He showed that when reliability was measured end-to-end, a distributed network with multiple different connections would exhibit very high reliability even in the face of the failure of a number of the switches or links in the network. Therefore, if homes have multiple separate connections to different service providers, less expensive, reasonably reliable switches and routers may offer just as reliable a network to the customer as is possible with today's networks that are made up of components with 30-year life cycle reliability.

Multiple network paths are quite common in backbone networks, which partly contributes to the high reliability of the Internet, despite the router reset button being the most commonly used network management tool for network operators. Currently most homes and businesses have only a single point of connection to their local service provider and therefore do not enjoy the same network reliability as multi-connected backbone networks. A competitive access service environment, however, extends the concept of multiple routes possibly right down to the individual home. A house could be conceivably be multi-homed to several different service providers via direct fiber connections or logical switched paths. Each path may not have the reliability of a traditional telecommunications network, but the combination of multiple separate paths would result in a local access architecture that may have a greater reliability and redundancy than today's traditional telephone or cable company networks.

A competitive access network also will allow ISPs to offer specialized services. For example some ISPs may specialize only in e-mail delivery, while others may offer guaranteed video services, caching services or news feeds. Enron in the United States, for example, is deploying an optical Internet that only delivers highly reliable video feeds from Internet video distribution companies such as Real Video. ISPs and large companies purchase this service at local point of presence for delivery to the end customer. The same concept has already been established for caching, news feeds and satellite multicast where companies specialize in different service areas. A GITH network allows this concept to be scaled and deployed to a much larger market.

A POSSIBLE ARCHITECTURE
FOR A GITH NETWORK

The following section describes some potential architectural possibilities for a GITH network. A considerable amount of research and development will be required to further define the most appropriate architecture of a GITH network. However, the following architectural concepts are premised on the design principles described in the previous section, particularly that of a competitive equal access service deployment. The new optical Internet backbones being deployed by CANARIE and some carriers point to a technology solution that also may scale very cost effectively for the last mile in terms of a GITH network. Optical Internets like CA*net 3 have had to address many of the same design constraints that currently face the designers of a GITH network. By building on the technology and lessons of CA*net 3 and other similar networks it is conceivable that wide-scale economical deployment of GITH is possible in the next few years.

Optical Internets like CA*net 3 are characterized by a number of unique network attributes:

1. The use of individual wavelengths on a DWDM fiber to significantly increase fiber capacity and to allow for traffic engineering in the direction and the number of wavelengths;
2. The use of GigaPOPs to serve as an interconnection between multiple backbone networks and the set of locally served institutions and to provide route diversity between network nodes in case of network failure and/or congestion;
3. The use of high performance routers to statistically multiplex data streams to reduce "state" in the network rather then establishing circuit-oriented connections;
4. The use of a simple, low-cost framing protocol such as Gigabit Ethernet to transport the data; and
5. The use of Multi Protocol Label Switching to provide logical paths.

These solutions developed for a high speed backbone network may equally apply to a GITH network. Instead of a GigaPOP, a Neighborhood Competitive Access Interconnection Point (NCAIP) may provide the same functionality at a much smaller scale by providing simultaneous access to multiple service providers. DWDM technology may be augmented by other access technologies such as Passive Optical Networking (PON) technology, shared Gigabit Ethernet coax, wireless access and ultimately dedicated fibers to each and every home in a neighborhood. And finally high performance routers in the GigaPOPs would be replaced with routers on a chip, called routing pucks, in the neighborhood service pedestal. These technologies are described in more detail in the following sections.

Neighborhood Competitive Access Interconnection Point

The Neighborhood Competitive Access Interconnection Point (NCAIP) is the architectural linchpin of a GITH network. It is at this point individual drops from households access different competitive service suppliers, and conversely competitive service providers would have equal access to individual customers. One of the key regulatory issues is that the NCAIP be designed first and foremost like a GigaPOP which serves as a "customer or third party controlled" interconnection point between the customer and multiple competitive service providers. The NCAIP, in effect, replaces the telephone central office and the cable head end as the principle interconnection facility for competitive access to the customer.

Like a GigaPOP, an NCAIP may be distributed or hierarchical in design. For example an NCAIP could be a simple shared gigabit Ethernet coax cable linking a number of homes to a single interface on a routing puck in a neighborhood pedestal. The routing puck would then interconnect to a number of separate service providers through individual dark fibers, dark wavelengths or logical switched paths. It is important to point out that the routing puck is considered part of the NCAIP and would be under a customer or third party control independent of the competitive service provider's own routers and switching technology.

Figure 1. A possible GITH configuration

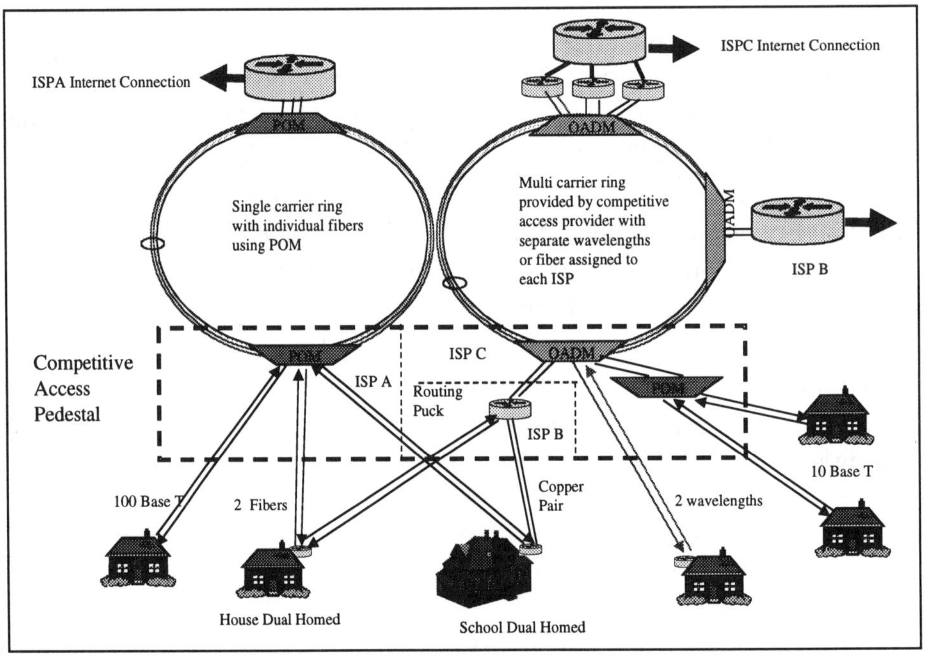

Another example of a distributed NCAIP would be the use of Passive Optical Network (PON) technology to interconnect 8 to 16 homes over a single fiber back to a routing puck at a main serving node at a neighborhood pedestal and/or more centrally located node where the individual PON channels would interconnect to a larger routing puck, perhaps even a router. The topology and architecture of NCAIP will vary depending on penetration and speeds of access. It is conceivable that in some situations there may be competitive serving NCAIPs and the customer would have multiple independent connections to different NCAIPs.

DWDM in the Metro Area and to the Home

A number of companies have announced municipal area DWDM network products. Currently these products can support up to 64 WDM channels, each capable carrying 2.5 Gbps of data up to 80 km with no electrical or optical re-amplification. It is expected that in the next few years these systems will soon support 100s if not 1000s of wavelengths. Most of these DWDM systems can be deployed on existing fibers in metro areas today. More importantly, as no repeaters are required, they provide for complete data transparency, which can be used to deliver different types formatted data on the individual wavelengths. A 64-channel, metro DWDM fiber ring can provide up to 150 pair wise connections depending on how many wavelengths can be reused. Each one of these channels can support a dedicated Gigabit Ethernet or an OC-48 connection. DWDM multiplexers will also soon be directly incorporated into router interfaces, thereby eliminating the need to have a separate physical interface for each DWDM channel. It is the physical interfaces that drive up the cost of any local access telecommunications systems.

It is expected that the cost of DWDM technology will drop dramatically as its capacity increases over the next few years. It is conceivable that local access service providers will be able to connect homes in a neighborhood with a single fiber and assign one or more DWDM channels to each home. The fiber could also interconnect different competitive NCAIPs and individual wavelengths could terminate on different NCAIPs. DWDM mesh concepts developed in optical Internets like CA*net 3 can be equally applied to a DWDM access network. Individual DWDM channels can be routed or cross-connected through different fiber routes.

Currently DWDM technology suffers from relatively high cost as it requires temperature compensated lasers to work effectively and hence DWDM will remain a costly proposition for the next few years, at least for the last 100 meters. A major area of research is to develop and manufacture low-cost and stable DWDM components. However, in the local access DWDM environment, lasers and interface equipment can ultimately be made cheaper because power, dissipation, density, and signal spread requirements are significantly less stringent than in the metro or long-haul network implementations due to the very short distances.

Passive Optical Networking

A complementary, and initially less expensive, technology compared to DWDM may be Passive Optical Networking (PON). Recently, considerable research work has gone into developing passive optical components that couple low-cost fiber from the home to dedicated wavelengths or fibers in a curbside optical multiplexer. PON technology allows for a number of households to share the same physical fiber back to a centrally located NCAIP or connect to a single interface port in a neighborhood routing puck. By using CDMA, TDMA or FDMA signaling and modulation of a simple, low-cost broadband laser, shared data rates up to several 100 Megabits are possible.

The FASN initiative proposes to develop a new protocol based on ATM for the delivery of PON services. But in many ways Gigabit Ethernet is already a well established and proven PON technology. Gigabit Ethernet can easily reach distances of 20 km in bi-directional mode, and in collision avoidance mode it can work quite effectively up to a 1,000 meters. More importantly, a GITH network built on Gigabit Ethernet can benefit from the price curve reduction of high volume manufacturing for Gigabit Ethernet in the LAN and enterprise market.

Gigabit Ethernet on a shared fiber or coax cable does suffer from one limitation in that it is a shared medium. Data for one home would be received by all homes on the same shared fiber and therefore would be susceptible to security problems. A number of techniques have been developed to address this problem including Gigabit Ethernet switching and the use of encryption. It is not clear whether PON technology will also suffer from the same limitation.

The Routing Puck

One of the most significant design issues of earlier FTTx networks was the assumption that the networks would be "connection" oriented, eventually leading to wavelength to wavelength routing across multiple network clouds from source to destination. Any connection-oriented network introduces "state" conditions so it can create and maintain considerable information and status on the number and duration of connections. A "connectionless" oriented network like the Internet maintains very little state and is therefore much simpler to implement and manage. With the increasing availability of high performance routers that can work at wire speed, statistical multiplexing of connections makes increasing sense and decreases the complexity of managing and maintaining "state" on thousands of simultaneous connections. A number of semiconductor companies are developing routers on a chip for the local access market. Soon a router on a chip may be standard equipment on most PCs, following a similar evolutionary path of adding layer 2 devices such as Ethernet and Fast Ethernet connections on new personal computers.

Rather than backhauling signals to a central office or head end from PON or DWDM multiplexers, it might make more sense to make the connections directly to a high speed router on a chip in a local neighborhood pedestal. Using DWDM or PON from the customer premises also minimizes the number of physical interfaces. This combination of integrated DWDM or PON with a routing chip is hereafter referred to in this document as a "routing puck." A routing puck is somewhat of a combination of a layer 2 switch and a layer 4 logical switched router. It should provide for very simple and fast high speed forwarding at layer 2 and yet allow a subscriber to be part of separate address spaces of different service providers by supporting logical switched paths between the subscriber and a competitive access service provider. The logical switched paths would be an integral part of the routing puck and yet can be configurable to map to separate physical paths such as an individual fiber or wavelength or a virtual path like a MPLS label switched path. Similarly the routing puck can be interconnected to other routing pucks further upstream by use of a dedicated fiber, dark wavelengths and/or virtual paths.

Statistical Multiplexing

It is proposed that a GITH network will principally be a statistical multiplexed Internet network. As such, a key requirement is to provide consistent mixing ratios at every level of hierarchy in the network. This is a problem that currently plagues xDSL and cable modem deployments. Initially when these systems are deployed there are few customers connected and consequently performance and throughput is excellent. As more customers are added to the network, congestion increases. Multiplexing of larger data streams further upstream in the network also complicates this problem. To circumvent this, carriers have proposed the use of virtual circuits with defined bandwidth parameters. However a number of university and business customers have developed packet loss and latency requirements in their service level agreements. Development of similar specifications and measurement techniques may be required for GITH networks. This way customers will always be assured the same level of service regardless of the type of multiplexed connection and the number of multiplexed layers in a hierarchical network.

By defining GITH service in this manner, rather than defining the type or size of a connection, as is currently offered in telecommunication networks, a NCAIP operator can change the multiplexing mechanism as required to scale the network from a few connections in a neighborhood to a highly dense access network. Figure 2 illustrates a very sparse mode architecture. In this example a dedicated fiber is connected directly to individual schools and perhaps a few homes in a neighborhood. The individual fiber connections are terminated at a routing puck that may be several kilometers distant from the customer premises. By first connecting schools, governments may be able to accelerate the deployment of an infrastructure service providers can later use for connecting individual homes.

As the neighborhood density increases with connections to individual homes the NCAIP operator may elect to install a Gigabit Ethernet hub or a routing puck in a neighborhood pedestal as shown in Figure 2. In that case the single dedicated fiber may become a shared medium for several houses in the neighborhood. As long as the statistical multiplexing ratio remains the same then the customer should not notice any difference in throughput or congestion from the original dedicated fiber configuration. As network access density increases, eventually individual wavelengths or fibers may be assigned to each neighborhood routing puck, or ultimately to each home in the neighborhood as shown in Figure 3.

Figure 2. Very sparse mode GITH

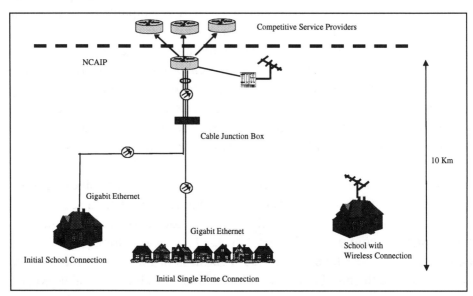

Figure 3. GITH sparse mode network

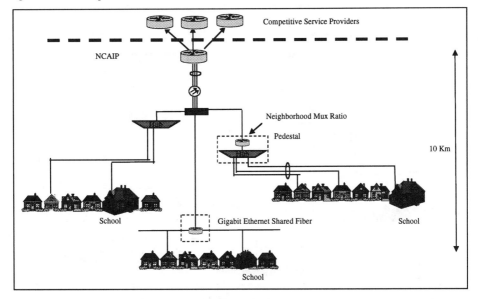

Minimizing State

"State" is one of the most costly attributes of any network. State requires that network elements and management systems maintain knowledge about a specific relationship or connection that has been established between elements across a network. Every time state is introduced into a network, additional computing and network management resources must be brought to bear to keep track of the number and quantity of different connections and also mechanisms for the initiation and termination of state on an individual connection.

Most telecommunication networks are considered to be either "stateless" or "stateful." A cable TV system, for example, is considered to be a "stateless" network, as there is no *a priori* relationship established between the receiver and the transmitter prior to transmission. The data is sent across the network to all recipients regardless of whether they are able to receive it or not. A telephone system on the other hand is a "stateful" network, where every relationship requires the *a priori* establishment of state before the connection can be established.

The Internet at its most basic level is a "stateless" network. IP packets operate much like TV signals on a cable system in that they are unidirectional (unicast) and can be transmitted without a prior relationship being established between the sender and receiver. But one of the most powerful features of the Internet is a set of protocols called TCP packets that allows "state" to be established over an effectively stateless network. One of the fundamental

Figure 4. GITH dense mode architecture

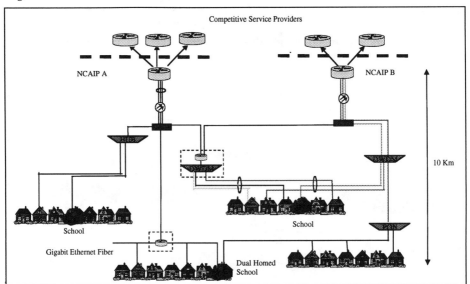

reasons why the Internet is so successful today is that it can support both stateless and stateful relationships between network elements. This means that the network can be operated at very low cost and with "state" only introduced where and when it is needed. Most other network architectures, particularly ATM networks, require "state" regardless of whether it is needed or not and this ultimately drives up the cost of the network.

There are three kinds of state in a network – "topology," "network" and "client-to-client" state. Topology state is essentially to keep track of and identify the many possible routes and destinations in a network, in other words, routing. Network state is involved in allocating network resources for a specific connection, and client-to-client state is the relationship or connection between clients attached to the network. TCP and SS7 are typical client-to-client state protocols and operate independently of the underlying network. SS7, for example, determines if the destination phone is busy and, if not, initiates a ringing sequence and then, upon an off-hook condition, signals for a network state connection across the network.

TCP operates in a similar manner to SS7 but it does not initiate a request for network state. The Internet is considered a best efforts network and to date there has been no effective way of initiating network state in the Internet. However, techniques such as RSVP have been proposed to introduce "network state" in the Internet. These network state protocols are still untested and many experts believe that they will not scale. Instead techniques that introduce simpler types of network like "differentiated services," frequently referred to as "Diff Serv," have been proposed. Diff Serv only introduces state at the edge

Figure 5. Optical Regional Advanced Network as a pilot for GITH

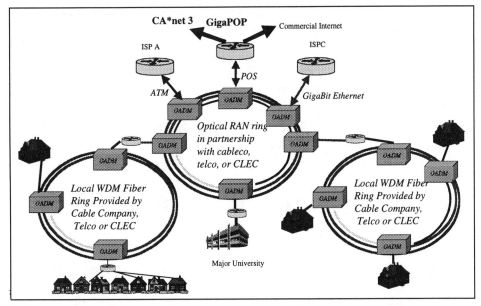

of the network to prioritize but does not establish state across the network. One of the advantages of a GITH network over alternate FTTx technologies, particularly those that assume the use of ATM style networks, is that a GITH network can be operated like the Internet with minimal "state." This significantly simplifies the network design and ultimately its operational and capital cost.

Network engineers have long realized that there is a set of converse technologies to "state" that can deliver the same performance objectives without the processing and management overhead of using state. For example the need for "network" state can be minimized through the use of additional bandwidth or through the use of distributed storage such as caching. End-to-end state can be minimized by retransmitting data sessions many times over or storing copies of the data locally, and routing state can be minimized by using pre-configured networks and/or intelligent packets. A data network that only delivers broadcast video streams may not need client state, but require network state to guarantee the delivery of the video stream. On the other hand, a bank transaction network may require client-to-client state in order to guarantee the delivery of a financial transaction, but may require little network state as the transaction itself is only a few bytes in bandwidth.

The choice and balance of whether to use network protocols that employ state or its converse are largely dependent on the types of applications and services carried on the network and the associated cost in deploying the appropriate "state" protocol. The beauty and power of the Internet is that, unlike most other networks, it can support any balance and mix of state or its converse. The Internet does not presuppose any form or application type and therefore has much greater flexibility and scalability in adapting to future applications and services.

Consequently, with the advent of low-cost DWDM technology, it may be cheaper and easier to provide high bandwidth to each and every home in a neighborhood rather than introducing state into the network. Most likely a balance will have to be maintained between the requirements for network state and the provisioning of bandwidth.

THE BUSINESS CASE FOR A GITH NETWORK

Researchers at Bellcore provide an economic analysis of the costs of traditional telephony and different FTTx services (http://began.com/broad3.htm). Past FTTH studies have concluded that the costs of connecting every home with fiber could be anywhere in the range from $1500-$3000. This is 2 to 3 times the cost of installing a residential telephone line, which is about $900-$1200, or a cable TV connection, at $600-$900 per residential subscriber.

This earlier FTTH economic analysis assumed an architecture closely modeled on either today's telco "fan" or cableco's tree and branch architecture with every home connected by an individual fiber to a central office or head end. But even the newer Hybrid Fiber Coax (HFC) systems remain relatively expensive, at $1200-$1500 per subscriber. On the other hand, since a GITH network does not have to deliver legacy services and it can aggregate traffic locally via a neighborhood routing puck, the costs of such a network may be substantially less then other FTTx approaches.

According to the Bellcore study, in a typical copper wire system of today about 25% of the capital costs are local access. The balance of the costs is in central office switching and inter-city trunks. The Bellcore study indicates that anywhere from 25% to 60% of the cost of a HFC system is the distribution network and local access. As with today's telephone system, the bulk of the costs of a HFC system is in the switching facilities in the central office and transport trunks. The distribution and access costs of a HFC system are approximately $750 per subscriber, while the telephone switching and interface costs are in the order of $500. It is expected that a GITH network would more closely model a TV cable system, where most of the costs are in the access and distribution. In a TV cable system only 6% of the costs are in the head end. As a rough approximation it is expected that a GITH network would have the access and distribution costs similar to those of a HFC system and head end costs typical of a cable TV system. The only extra cost element would be extending fiber all the way to the home. The Bellcore study estimates that the cost to upgrade the local access to fiber would be $50-$100 per subscriber.

A GITH network with Fiber to the Home would therefore likely cost about $750 for the basic distribution plant and access, plus an additional increment $100 for fiber to the home and (6% of cable subscriber cost of $600 is for the head end) a very small $36 for a total of approximately $900-$1000 per subscriber. It is important to note these cost figures are based on the costs of existing technology. With the advent of lower cost PON and DWDM technology it is expected that these costs will drop even further.

It is conceivable that a GITH system could be deployed for less cost than existing HFC systems. It may even be cost effective compared to xDSL or cable modem systems. These systems have a capital cost of about $500 per subscriber. But DSL and cable modem systems have a much shorter life cycle due to the rapid obsolescence of the technology. The main cost components of a GITH system on the other hand are made up of much longer life cycle cost items, in particular, the actual fiber and its installation either in the ground or on poles. So, although the capital costs of a xDSL or cable modem system may be half of GITH system, the longer life cycle of the latter means that a GITH can be amortized over much longer period, anywhere from 20 to 30 years.

A basic rule of thumb used by telecom companies is that for every $1 of network investment cost, annual revenue would need to be $.40 to recover the original capital investment over 10 years time. Assuming the telco revenue numbers are reasonable, the annual cost per subscriber of a GITH system would be in the order of $400 per year, or $40-$50 per month. However, given the largest component of the cost is the actual trenching and installation of conduit, those costs can be amortized over a much longer time frame, up to 30 years, which could reduce the cost down to $200-$250 per year, or $20-$25 per month. Currently the biggest demand for HFC systems is Internet access, so it would seem to make more sense to deploy a competitive access GITH system rather than deploying a full-service FTTx system.

In many ways the deployment of a GITH network would parallel the rollout of the second parallel residential network–cable TV. In the early days of cable TV, enterprising entrepreneurs deployed low-cost cable systems for the reception of cable TV independent of the expensive and complex schemes proposed by the carriers at that time. (Ever since the 1964 World's Fair in New York City, the world is still waiting for video dial tone.) Public utility companies, CLECs and incumbent telephone and cable companies could all be independent competitive service providers. Utility companies in particular may have an advantage of being a competitive service provider due to their already large established infrastructure in most urban areas. A third residential network for delivery of Internet service exclusively would provide a similar environment for entrepreneurs to deploy new Internet networks and exciting new high speed Internet services in parallel with the proposed xDSL and cable modem deployments. This would immediately allow for at least three different modes of competitive access. Perhaps where such residential high speed Internet networks were deployed, regulators might also be inclined to give relief to cable and TV companies to provide equal access to their cable modem and xDSL services.

With GITH, the local access market may evolve similar to the backbone infrastructure market. In this market telecommunications companies such as Ledcor and Qwest were established to specialize and define different niches for themselves in the telecommunications food chain, rather than trying to be comprehensive, total solutions service providers. It is abundantly clear that governments and regulators have a important role to play in the evolution of this concept of a third residential network for high speed Internet service to the home. Fair and equitable competitive marketplace is a fundamental driver for early adoption by the consumer and rapid reduction in price for any new technology. This basic tenet of competition has been demonstrated, repeatedly, in other areas of new technology development. As such, governments and regulators must insure that incumbent carriers and cable companies are required to provide access to their fiber or wavelength distribution system until such time as there are multiple separate fiber service providers in a neighborhood. This is already happening in the business sections of many Canadian cities, where the local cable company and telephone company are independently deploying fiber, but it may take considerably longer in suburban areas.

Governments can also help stimulate the early deployment of a GITH network by funding the connection of schools, libraries and universities to a GITH network as the first early adopters. By mandating an open architecture that is extensible for delivery to every home and perhaps underwriting the long-term capital costs of at least putting the conduit in the ground, as well as the deployment of condominium fibers and NCAIP pedestals, it is quite conceivable that a national GITH network could be deployed in the next few years.

The history of the Internet to date has been one where bandwidth growth has always exceeded forecast planning. If advanced high bandwidth applications develop as quickly as similar memory hogging applications have developed for the PC, then the need for high bandwidth to the home may come upon us sooner than expected. Clearly, high speed fiber to the home is the ultimate answer, particularly for high bandwidth multimedia Internet applications. Fiber to the home is the ultimate future proof technology. A third residential network dedicated to high speed Internet access and predicated on competitive equal access may allow for the rapid deployment and early adoption of the new infrastructure.

GIGABIT APPLICATIONS TO THE HOME

One of the main challenges to articulate the need to build a GTTH network is the lack of definable applications. Few applications today, even on high speed backbone networks, require bandwidth in excess of a megabit per second. We can only speculate at what may be some of the future applications that will drive the demand for such bandwidth but the following examples may give us some early indications of the early potential for high speed applications.

DVD Video

The latest generation of low-cost digital video cameras allows the transmission of a high-quality real-time video transmission directly from the camera when connected to a computer. The real-time video stream can then be redistributed over the Internet. However its data rate is in excess of 40 Mbps per second. It is expected that this data rate may be reduced to that of motion JPEG with more efficient compression schemes, but still remain in excess of 20 Mbps. DVD cameras are the latest hot consumer product and should quickly displace the older analog home cameras in a few years.

Mega E-mail Attachments

It is quite amazing that despite all the talk about advanced multimedia applications e-mail still remains the most popular application on the Internet. Users are not only sending large text documents as e-mail attachment but they are now sending video and audio clips as well. With the advent of large disk drives that can support gigabytes of data it is quite conceivable that even large movie and audio CDs can be sent as a regular e-mail attachments. With current Internet bandwidth to the home it can take several hours or days to receive such an attachment. But in a GITH network it would be possible to deliver such attachments in seconds.

DWDM Caching

Terabit DWDM networks are, in effect, large storage devices. The bandwidth delay product of a nationwide terabit network is in the order of several hundred megabytes if not gigabytes, assuming a 100 ms transit delay.

The challenge for traditional servers in such a large bandwidth network is the need to maintain that much data in the server outbound queue waiting a receipt of the first ACK from the recipient machine. One possible solution to continually transmit large files such as hit movies is to have them constantly in transit, circulating in the network. Rather than establishing a client-to-client connection, the network is treated like a dynamic cache that may be seamlessly integrated with more traditional static caching data.

Multimedia Push and Always On Applications

There has been much talk about how xDSL and cable modem services are "always on" services. The next logical step is to have "always on" applications. A 5,000 channel universe is probably not the ideal example of a futuristic application, but does point to the possibility where it might be easier to "broadcast" popular channels without requiring state to each home, regardless of whether they were requested or not, and allow the establishment of multicast "state" connections for less popular TV stations.

Future "TV" stations may be a mixture of data, broadcast and multimedia services. Rather than "pulling" these services as is commonly done today, in a GITH network it might be just as cost effective to continually "push" the more popular multimedia services to the GITH consumer.

Home Caching

Home caching is a simple extension of the multimedia push concepts described previously, but combined with a hierarchical caching network. Hierarchical caching networks that support streaming video and other services are now being deployed across most Internet networks. Hierarchical caching significantly improves "perceived" network performance and throughput. Hierarchical caching is a classic example where large storage can be used to minimize state in the network.

CONCLUSIONS AND NEXT STEPS

The building of a GITH network may equal some of the other great infrastructure deployments of this century such as electrification of the nation and providing basic telephony as an essential service to every home in the country. These large infrastructure deployments were not possible without a clear and strong partnership between industry and government. In these past deployments industry was granted an exclusive monopoly in exchange for a commitment to provide ubiquitous service to all communities throughout the country. A GITH network, however, is premised on competitive equal access and will require the defining of a new set of relationships between industry and government.

It is hoped that this paper will be the first step in a series of discussions that, in partnership with NRC, OPCOMM and other organizations, will lead to a research program that will explore the technical and regulatory parameters of such a program.

Already we have early examples of some Gigabit Internet to the Schools in places like Spokane, Washington, and other cities in the United States. In Spokane a unique partnership was formed between the local power utility and the Spokane school district to deliver dark fiber to the 160 or so schools and community colleges in the Spokane area. Each of the schools is being connected with dark fiber and a10/100 connection to a neighborhood Gigabit Ethernet switch. Although the initial connection is a 10/100 Mbps Ethernet connection, it can be easily upgraded to Gigabit speeds for a small one-time upgrade charge on the switch. Because the basic connection service is dark fiber, rather than managed bandwidth, the upgrade path to higher and higher speeds is simple and economic.

Early field trials might be possible with the Optical Regional Advanced Networks that are being deployed as part of the CA*net 3 optical Internet program. These are extending connectivity to some lead institutions such as schools, universities and community access sites in the next year or two. Schools and universities have pressing needs for increasing Internet bandwidth. By serving their requirements first, governments might be able to leverage their investment in the educational sector to accelerate the early deployment of an infrastructure that eventually results in Gigabit Internet to every home and school.

REFERENCES

Chung, TW, Coulter, J, Fitchett, J, Mokbel, S, & St. Arnaud, Bill, "Architectural and Engineering Issues for Building an Optical Internet", September 1998, http://www.canet3.net/c3/c3arch.html.

Reddy, R., "A gigabit National Grid/Fiber to the Home Initiative", June 1997, http://www.rr.cs.cmu.edu/ndg/gndg-ftth.html.

ACKNOWLEDGMENTS

The author wishes to acknowledge the contributions and helpful comments made by the following individuals in the writing and editing of this chapter: TW Chung and Sam Mokbel.

ENDNOTES

1 http://www.canet3.net/.
2 http://www.qwest.com.
3 http://www.level3.com.
4 http://www.frontiercorp.com.
5 http://www.labs.bt.com/profsoc/access/Default.htm.

Chapter III

Adaptive Mobile Applications: Experience With an Approach Based on Mobile Code

Thomas Kunz
Carleton University, Canada

INTRODUCTION

The convergence of two technological developments has made mobile computing a reality. In the last few years, developed countries spent large amounts of money to install and deploy wireless communication facilities. Originally aimed at telephone services (which still account for the majority of usage), the same infrastructure is increasingly used to transfer data. The second development is the continuing reduction in size of computer hardware, leading to portable computation devices such as laptops, palmtops, or functionally enhanced cell phones. Given current technology, a user can run a set of applications on a portable device and communicate over a variety of communication links, depending on his/her current location. For example, the user can access the wired corporate LAN at 10 Mbps or higher in the office. Roaming in the building, connectivity is provided by an indoor wireless LAN at 1-2 Mbps. Outdoors, connectivity is provided by cellular wireless-IP networks, providing bandwidths of a few tens of kbps. Furthermore, the sets of services available in each location will generally differ.

Similar discrepancies will also persist in future wireless networks, such as the ones under study by the International Telecommunication Union (2000) and the European Union's ACTS program (ACTS, Mobility, 1997). Unlike second-generation cellular networks, future cellular systems will cover an area with a variety of nonhomogeneous cells that may overlap. This allows the network operators to tune the system layout to subscriber density and subscribed services. Cells of different sizes will offer widely varying bandwidths: very high bandwidths with low error rates in pico-cells, very low bandwidths with higher error rates in macro-cells. Again, depending on the current location, the sets of available services might also differ. It is generally argued that applications should "adapt" to the current environment, for example, by filtering and compressing data or by changing the functionality offered to the user, see Badrinath, Acharya, & Imielinski, 1994; Welling & Badrinath, 1997; Zenel & Duchamp, 1997. Some researchers even argue that all future applications, not just the ones intended for execution on mobile devices, will have to be able to adapt to changing requirements and changing implementation environments on time scales from microseconds to years (Kavi, Browne & Tripathi, 1999). Our research addresses this problem by proposing an approach to application adaptivity based on code mobility. This chapter explains the basic concept underlying our approach, describes our proposed architecture, and explains our initial experience in developing this architecture.

The alternative to adaptive applications is multiple functionally identical or similar binaries, tuned for specific environments. This is an inferior solution, for a number of reasons. The user of a portable device has to install and maintain multiple applications, which is a drain on the limited storage capabilities typically found on those devices. It also potentially results in different user interfaces and causes high software development overheads when developing the "same" mobile application multiple times. Finally, it forces the user to identify the current execution conditions and select the "right" application.

Our work is based on offloading computationally intensive application components to more powerful servers in the access network. Ideally, this "load sharing" between a portable device and more powerful machines would occur transparent to the user, at runtime, taking into account the currently available resources in the execution environment. To realize this goal, a support infrastructure is required to monitor the available resources, to decide how best to utilize these resources, and that deals with user mobility. The following sections will motivate our approach, introduce a suitable architecture, and explain what experience we collected to date in realizing various components of this architecture.

MOBILE APPLICATIONS

To define a suitable architecture, we first identified categories of applications a mobile user is most likely to execute on his mobile device. Due to the existing limitations of portable devices (limited computational power, disk space, screen size, etc.), we claim that portable devices should not be considered general-purpose computers. Even though portable devices will become increasingly powerful, they will never match the computational power and facilities available on typical desktop machines. Similarly, while the wireless technology will improve, providing more and more bandwidth to the end user, wired network technology will advance as well, with the result that wireless networks will remain, in the near to medium future, orders of magnitudes slower. Therefore, mobile computing will always be characterized by a scarcity of resources, relatively speaking. In our opinion, an end user will execute applications in one of the following six categories in such an environment:

- Stand-alone applications such as games or utilities;
- Personal productivity software (word processors, presentation software, calendars);
- Internet applications such as e-mail, WWW browsers, multiuser calendars, or telnet;
- Vertically integrated business applications (field installation and services, security);
- New "location-aware" applications: tour planners, interactive guides;
- Adhoc network and groupware applications.

The first category was originally of little interest to us, since these applications do not involve communication. However, the main idea underlying our architecture is to transparently support resource-constrained portable devices by powerful proxy servers. We are therefore currently exploring how to generalize this idea to support stand-alone applications as well.

Applications in the second category will be used on multiple platforms: A user will have a version of his/her favorite word processor executing on a laptop as well as on the more powerful desktop in the office. This requires the exchange and synchronization of documents between the machines. Depending on the prevailing view of available network connectivity, two possible approaches are imaginable. Windows CE and MS Office exemplify a first solution. A user works on a document at either the laptop or the desktop, synchronizing multiple versions only infrequently and in a controlled environment. A second solution assumes that connectivity is more pervasive, allowing access to "authoritative" copies of a document on demand. This solution will require client-server applications to allow access to remote documents in the presence of highly variable communication links.

The Internet applications constitute a very interesting and challenging category. Mobile devices are often considered as the "on-ramp" to the Internet. Consequently, a user will want to execute the client side of typical Internet applications on his portable device, communicating with servers in the existing Internet infrastructure. This is not as straightforward as it may seem at first glance. The Internet developed as a wired network, connecting powerful computers over relatively high-speed communication links. The assumptions underlying the design of many Internet clients reflect this view of the world. They are therefore not particularly well suited to a mobile environment. For example, the communication protocol of choice is TCP, which is known to behave poorly in the presence of wireless links with their corresponding high bit-error rates. Client applications typically assume that they have sufficient bandwidth, memory, and computational power at their disposal, which is equally questionable. Given the huge amount of money invested in the current infrastructure, it is unrealistic to expect that the whole Internet will change to accommodate mobile users overnight. In particular, servers deployed worldwide will not change in the near future. To facilitate access to the Internet, only the client side of the application can be adapted to function well in the dynamic and resource-constrained mobile environment. Our approach is primarily intended for applications in this category.

Vertically integrated business applications are often structured as client-server applications. Furthermore, the back ends (servers) have to support both existing wired desktops and wireless mobile devices. One example is a bank, where the back office has to support account managers in branch offices as well as mobile customer service representatives. Therefore, the clients executing on the portable devices face challenges similar to those faced by traditional Internet clients. They have to adapt to the limitations of the portable device in a dynamically changing execution environment. To facilitate the deployment of mobile applications, solutions should be transparent to the servers. Due to these similarities, we believe that our approach applies equally well to this group of applications.

The location-aware applications exploit the fact that a user is mobile. Possible examples include travel guides, which might display the shortest path from a user's current location to the closest/cheapest/best Italian restaurant, or applications that allow a user to print a document on the closest color postscript laser printer. To the extent that these applications utilize the existing Internet (discovering and accessing nearby resources, for example), our work can be of value here as well.

Applications in the final category arise out of the mobility of a number of users, for example, the meeting of a number of researchers or managers, each equipped with a portable device. Users might want to establish ad hoc networks to exchange documents (the newest version of the transparencies for the invited talk) or to execute groupware applications to update a shared business plan. Since these applications will not, to a large extent, be limited by the need to interact with an existing infrastructure, the proposed approach is probably not directly relevant to them. Similar to stand-alone applications, we are however exploring how to generalize our ideas to support ad hoc network applications.

THE CLIENT-PROXY-SERVER MODEL

Most application categories discussed above comprise client-server applications. An application on a mobile device or desktop workstation provides some functionality to the end user in conjunction with server(s) in the Internet. Examples are the WWW browsers that retrieve documents from servers around the world, or clients that connect to FTP servers to upload or download files. Our architecture is based on an extension of this traditional client-server model to a client-proxy-server model. Figure 1 shows the relevant components.

The mobile devices execute the client, which provides the user interface and some part of the application logic. In all wireless technologies, a mobile device communicates with the fixed network through a base station, which is

Figure 1. The client-proxy-server model

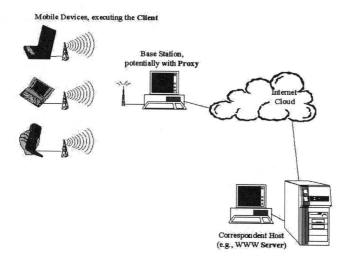

the access point for all devices in a cell. Through some switching fabric, the base station provides connectivity with other hosts in the network, such as a WWW server or an SMTP server. The third component of our model is the proxy, a component of the application that executes in the wired network and supports the client. One possible location for the proxy is the base station. In general, any computer on the communication path between client and server can host the proxy. Logically, the proxy hides the "mobile" client from the server, who thinks it communicates with a standard client (i.e., a client that executes on a powerful desktop directly connected to the wired network). The application logic of the "standard client" is split between the mobile client and the proxy to adapt to the dynamic wireless environment and to address the limitations of the portable device. For example, the proxy could execute on a powerful workstation with large amounts of memory and disk space. This would make the proxy an ideal candidate to manage large caches or to perform computationally intensive tasks such as interpreting an MPEG video stream and turning it into a pixmap. Where bandwidth limitations over the wireless link are of major concern, the proxy could provide filtering and compression functions.

To avoid suboptimal communication paths, the proxy must migrate within the fixed network, following the user. "Migrating" the proxy can mean either that the proxy moves physically from machine to machine, or that a system of proxies exists, and only relevant state information is passed during a hand-over. The two approaches are complementary, and the best choice depends upon the details of a given situation. Other issues raised by user mobility are:

- How should the proxy migration decision be made (based on what information, using what algorithm)?
- Given that we expect a large number of mobile users, how does the approach scale? For example, what happens if a sizeable subset of users decides to head to the same shopping mall at noon, checking stock options over the WWW while having lunch?

COMPARISON TO RELATED WORK

The idea of using a proxy in the wired network to support a mobile device is well known. In fact, most wireless WWW browsers, among others, use one or more proxies to support their operation in a low-bandwidth environment (Chang et al., 1997; Gessler & Kotulla, 1994; Han et al., 1998). However, our approach is more concerned with adaptability, flexibility, and mobility than work published in the literature, as explained below.

Adaptability

Existing proposals often install a proxy that filters and/or compresses data for a specific application. This filter is either enabled or disabled. Examples are filters to turn color in-line images into lower-resolution grayscale images or to convert postscript into ASCII text, or e-mail readers that provide the "subject" line of a mail message only, avoiding the transmission of the main message body over a slow link. In the scenario of the introduction, the environment changes dynamically, depending on the user's behavior and that of others. We therefore foresee the need to make the proxies more dynamic, to adapt more closely to changes in the environment. Examples are changing the resolution and/or color of an in-line image only when necessary and changing the resolution incrementally. Another example could be to allow an e-mail reader to read the body of small e-mail messages but to avoid downloading large messages. To enable this more fine-grained adaptation, a mechanism is needed that provides the mobile application with information about the environment, including device information, information about the wireless link, infrastructure information like reachable servers or services, and location-related information.

Adaptation decisions need to take information about multiple resources into consideration. For example, high available bandwidth might favor a shift from the proxy to the mobile. However, the mobile might be running low on power, arguing for a shift from the mobile to the proxy. Similarly, certain adaptation options might not be feasible in environments that lack the appropriate infrastructure. Previous research tended to focus on one resource only: Othman and Hailes (1998) and Rudenko, Reiher, Popek, and Kuenning (1998) focus on power consumption; Maass (1997) on location information; Hodes, Katz, Servan-Schreiber, and Rowe (1997) on local services; and Bolliger and Gross (1998) and Zenel and Duchamp (1997) on the network characteristics.

A completely different approach would be to design the division of labor between mobile client and proxy for the worst case only, which would provide consistent functionality across all environments. We consider such a solution less than desirable, for at least two reasons. First, whenever possible, a user should experience the best service achievable. Normalizing to the lowest common denominator often unnecessarily deprives the user of full service and functionality. Second, a proxy server will, in general, support many mobile users. To the extent that the individual portable devices can contribute to better client functionality, they should be encouraged to do so. Otherwise, even a powerful proxy server might be overloaded, resulting in poor performance for all applications.

Flexibility

Most existing proxy solutions operate at the protocol level. They intercept messages and reduce the data sent over the wireless link by filtering less important data and utilizing compression algorithms. As discussed in Chang, et al., 1997), while data compression and filtering improve the perceived performance of web browsers, they are not sufficient. Support for new types of operations, such as browsing while disconnected and/or asynchronous browsing, is needed in a mobile environment. The research in Chang, et al., 1997), (Le, et al., 1994) is based on a static client-proxy-server architecture, where the division of labor between client and proxy is determined and fixed at design time. Both papers, however, emphasize that a more flexible, dynamic, adaptation based on mobile code should be explored in the future.

Our approach is aimed at more general proxy solutions. As mentioned above, we envision mobile applications where the proxy can overcome some of the limitations of the portable device by maintaining a cache or performing CPU-intensive interpretation of the data stream. Offloading some of the application logic to a proxy comes at a cost. We therefore want to shift parts of the client logic only when necessary (to conserve battery power or reduce network bandwidth, for example). This again argues for a dynamic, adaptive proxy design, with the added complexity of moving not only data, but also code.

Mobility

A third major difference from previous work is that we plan to address issues of mobility. Nearly without exception, existing solutions address the situation where a mobile host continually interacts with a fixed host over the same wireless link. In fact, Zenel and Duchamp (1997) claim that the issue of proxy migration is beyond the current state-of-the-art. Given that "migrating" the proxy does not necessarily mean that we physically migrate the proxy, we disagree with this statement. We are investigating how to create a proxy infrastructure, perhaps connected with or related to the concept of Intelligent Networks in telephony, which was devised for fast deployment of new services in a network. "Migrating" the proxy would then take the form of a handoff between two proxies. There are three salient issues to be addressed here.

- What information should be collected (and how to collect it) to make "migration" decisions?
- What are good decision algorithms, based on this information?

• How does the solution scale to a metropolitan or regional coverage area?

ARCHITECTURE

To achieve truly adaptive applications, we need to design and implement a number of components. Figure 2 gives an overview of the relevant pieces and how they interact. In this architecture, we distinguish two proxies, a *high-level* proxy and a *low-level* proxy, similar to Zenel and Duchamp (1997). They play distinctive roles and require different mechanisms for their implementation.

A central piece of infrastructure is the environment monitor. The client application needs to be informed of changes in the environment. This can be achieved by a daemon process on the mobile device, monitoring relevant environment parameters and notifying the application through registered callback functions. To avoid interruptions of the client logic, these callback functions could execute in a separate thread, for example, communicating with the rest of the mobile client through shared state. An application must register with this daemon, inform it of environment parameters it is interested in and the conditions under which it wants to be notified, and provide appropriate call-back functions. To obtain reliable information about the wireless link, the client-side daemon might interact with a similar daemon on the other end of the wireless link.

The mobile device will execute the user interface and parts of the client application logic. Other parts of the client logic execute on a dedicated proxy server, which is a powerful machine in the fixed network. Ideally, the proxy

Figure 2. Proposed architecture

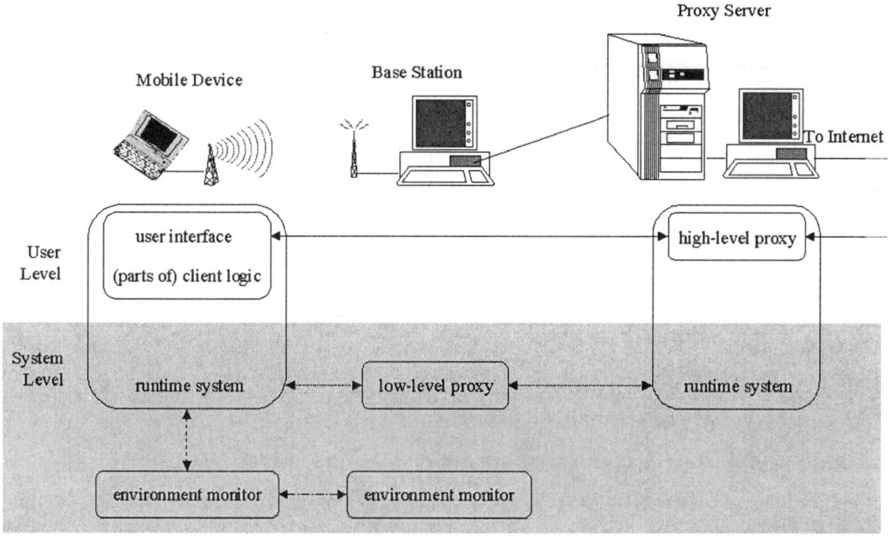

server should be close to the base station. The high-level proxy communicates with the server, transparently hiding the fact that the server communicates with a mobile client. Since the high-level proxy will execute parts of the application code, it will exist at the user level.

The application logic is divided between the mobile client and the high-level proxy. This division of labor changes over time, depending on the current environment. In previous work, we designed and implemented a number of applications that registered with the monitor and made decisions about the most appropriate adaptation, based on the feedback received from the monitor, see, for example, Kunz and Lo (1999) and Whalen (1997). To facilitate the development of adaptive mobile applications, we plan to factor the partition algorithms out into the runtime system. Each client application will be designed concentrating on the functional aspect only. To enable dynamic partitioning, the application may register certain information with the runtime system. It is up to the runtime system to connect with the monitor and to combine the information registered by the application with the feedback received from the monitor to make partitioning decisions.

We have started implementing this architecture as follows. The mobile device and the proxy server both execute a Java virtual machine. The client application consists of a number of objects, communicating via method invocation. Upon creation, each object may register with the runtime system. The registrations are of the form "Execute on mobile if bandwidth greater than X" or "Execute in same location as object O." A default policy handles objects that did not explicitly register and provide specific information. For example, a default policy links object size to bandwidth and/or available memory. Objects exceeding a threshold size execute on the proxy server, otherwise they execute on the mobile host. The runtime system monitors the relevant parameters and initiates object migration if necessary. Object migration is achieved by a mobile code technology based on Java (Objectspace Voyager), though we are currently also implementing our own mobile code toolkit based on Java to allow for a more heterogeneous set of portable devices (Objectspace only provides support for a limited number of computing platforms).

A low-level proxy supports the communication between client and high-level proxy. One example of such a low-level proxy is SNOOP (Balakrishnan, Seshan, Amir & Katz, 1995). The low-level proxy operates at the data, network, and/or transport layers. Protocols at these layers are typically provided as part of the operating system protocol stack, so for maximal efficiency we expect the low-level proxy to become part of the operating system. The low-level proxy supports communication over the wireless link, so we envision that the low-level proxy will execute on a host that directly connects to the wireless link. There are only two choices: the mobile device and the base station. Given the restrictions of the mobile device, the logical place for the low-level proxy is the base station. However, a low-level proxy might also be split between the mobile device and base station, to provide symmetric support for communication to and from the mobile device.

Most published low-level proxies work under the assumption that the low-level proxy is transparent to higher-level communication. Another useful extension of the proxy approach is to extend the capabilities of the higher-level protocols. In previous work Kidston, 1998; Lioy, 1997), we identified services such as prioritizing competing TCP connections or keeping TCP connections alive in the presence of spurious disconnections. In this case, the existence of the low-level proxy cannot be kept transparent to the client. In fact, the client needs an interface to request such enhanced services and to provide the proxy with necessary information. As far as possible, this functionality should be hidden in the runtime system, invisible to the application logic implemented by the programmer.

EXAMPLES

To give an indication of how the architecture may support adaptive mobile applications, this section briefly describes designs for a number of potential applications.

MPEG Filter

We are completing the implementation of a transparent MPEG filter that operates as part of the low-level proxy (Lin, 2000). It selectively drops frames of various types depending on the current network conditions. This is achieved transparently to the application through the use of a second, lower-level filter (Kidston, 1998) that adjusts the TCP protocol headers to mask the removal of data. This preserves the end-to-end semantics of the TCP stream, even though the two endpoints have divergent views about the amount of data exchanged.

MP3 Player

Recently, we finished the design and implementation of an adaptive MP3 player (Omar, 2000). In contrast to the MPEG filter, the MP3 player does not actively modify the data stream and is unaware of the execution environment. Our runtime system monitors the currently available resources (link bandwidth, CPU speed, battery power) and transparently decides to move the computationally complex MP3 decoder (a set of communicating objects) to the proxy server under certain conditions. Our experiments show that improvements in application performance and reductions in battery power consumption of over 90% are possible. These gains can be achieved when executing the MP3 player on a slow PDA, connected to the access network over a relatively fast wireless link, for example, a Windows CE PDA connected via WaveLAN. However, for low bandwidth wireless links or fast portable devices, such as a laptop, it is more beneficial to execute the complete application on the portable device. Contrary to our expectations, and the results reported in Omar and Kunz (1999), we did not find a trade-off between application performance and power conservation. Further investigations are necessary to determine whether this is true for many different applications or only specific to our MP3 player.

WWW Browser

A possible design for a WWW browser uses the high-level proxy as a data filter. The client registers with the monitor, asking to be informed of changes in the bandwidth. In a high-bandwidth environment (for example, when the user is working in the office), the high-level proxy forwards HTTP requests to the servers and forwards the replies to the client. In addition, the high-level proxy can maintain a cache of documents, potentially sharing this cache with other clients executing in the same cell. For medium-bandwidth environments, the high-level proxy filters the incoming in-line images to reduce the resolution. In a low-bandwidth environment, the high-level proxy filters in-line images to reduce both the resolution and the color. In this example, client and proxy communicate with the standard HTTP protocol. Some initial insights we gained with designing such a "transcoding" proxy are reported in El Shentenawy, Gaddah, Guo, Kunz, and Hafez (2000).

This first design follows the customary use of proxies to filter and compress the data stream, potentially making the proxy somewhat more adaptive based on feedback about the available bandwidth received from the monitor. A somewhat different design, emphasizing code mobility, is as follows. Based on information about the mobile device, routines to process and format the HTTP replies are assigned to either the portable device or the high-level proxy. The high-level proxy would send pixmaps representing the Web page to the client, who displays them and returns information about user actions. Full-color high-resolution pixmaps will increase the bandwidth requirement, but reduce the computational load on the client, saving energy. Grayscale and/or low-resolution pixmaps can help to reduce both energy and bandwidth consumption. In either design, the proxy communicates with the server following the HTTP protocol, hiding the mobile client and the current division of labor between client and proxy from the other servers.

Museum Guide

A different application is an interactive museum guide. A visitor wanders through a museum with a palmtop in his/her hands. Information about each exhibit is displayed as the visitor approaches an object. The application also provides the visitor with the option to inquire about a specific exhibit and to display the best path from his/her current location to that object.

To enable this application, the monitor must provide location information. This could be achieved either directly, with a system such as GPS, or indirectly, by deducing the current location from the base station with which the device communicates. Computing the shortest path is potentially rather complex and is therefore done at the high-level proxy. This proxy also provides a cache for previous information and the query routines to fetch information from the central database, based on the current location. The portable device executes the interface component. The available bandwidth will vary, depending on the number of people crowding in front of the more popular exhibits, and whether the object is indoors or outdoors. The application can adapt to these changes by offloading the graphical processing to the proxy, similar to the WWW browser example. In this case, the back end (the database that provides the information about exhibits) can serve other applications as well, for example, to generate dynamic Web pages.

Mail Reader

A mobile mail reader can use the monitor to inquire about locally available SMTP servers. It establishes connections to the closest SMTP server (potentially based on security and/or cost considerations) to send e-mail messages composed by the user. To read e-mail, the client must connect to the "home" message store. Typically, a user will have many different folders with many messages in each. Copies of these folders are downloaded to the high-level proxy server. Depending on the network conditions and the available space (memory, disk) at the mobile device, copies of the smaller folders can be downloaded to the mobile. The application will dynamically determine whether a mail folder exists locally or at the proxy server, processing requests for listing all messages or displaying certain messages at the appropriate location.

A partial version of such a mail reader is described in Kunz and Lo (1999). We experimented with different policies for placing the folders on either the mobile host or the proxy server. To evaluate the performance, we measured

Table 1.

Bandwidth	All folders on Mobile	All folders on Proxy	Adaptive scheme
10 Mbps	369	529	486
1 Mbps	1,346	577	532
100 kbps	2,018	637	669

the elapsed time to execute scripts representing user sessions for the various configurations over different bandwidths. Table 1 lists the results.

We found that the dynamic adaptation scheme, while not always resulting in the lowest possible response times, performs relatively well across all bandwidths. Furthermore, the two "static" designs, creating all folders at either the mobile device or the proxy independent of the current network condition, result in poor performance in some environments. For applications that encounter the whole range of bandwidths (and other characteristics of a dynamically changing environment), we need adaptive application designs. Otherwise we end up with applications that either result in extremely poor performance some of the time, or a user will need to install multiple binaries for the same task. As this example also demonstrates, the adaptation can be transparent to the user and application developer, assuming that a mobile code system with location-transparent method invocations is being used.

IMPLEMENTATION STATUS

We are working towards building a complete support infrastructure for adaptive mobile applications as outlined above, implementing appropriate applications, and considering the scalability of our approach to large-scale cellular networks. To date, the following progress has been achieved:

- **Monitoring**: As mentioned above, we already implemented a runtime system monitor (Kidston et al., 1998) and support for TCP data streams (Kidston, 1998; Lioy, 1997). This low-level monitor support was originally developed under Linux and we are currently in the process of porting the relevant parts to Windows CE and Palm OS. This exercise turned out to be more problematic than we originally envisioned, due to the constraints imposed on application programs, in particular on the Palm devices.

  We also developed a visualization tool to trace the migration of mobile objects (Y. Wang, 2000). This visualization is similar to the one commonly found in parallel and distributed debuggers and allows a user or

Table 2. Measured overhead of Voyager and our toolkit

	Voyager	**Our toolkit**
Memory footprint	2,620 KB	204 KB
Object migration	142 ms	80 ms
Method invocation	23 ms	110 ms

system administrator to monitor the life cycle of mobile objects. We expect this tool to be very useful when developing and deploying advanced mobile applications. The objects composing an application can execute either at the portable device or one of multiple proxy servers, which potentially may make it difficult to track down transient bugs and manage a cellular network. The visualizer provides a starting point for these tasks.

- **High-level proxy, mobile code**: Our work initially was based on Objectspace Voyager, a freely available mobile code technology. However, Objectspace supports Voyager on only a limited number of platforms (primarily Unix and Windows 98/NT). Also, Voyager has a larger footprint, supporting many features not directly relevant for our work. We therefore developed a more scaled-down version of a mobile code toolkit based on Java (Omar, 2000), which currently runs under Linux, Windows 98/NT, and Windows CE, and have started a port to PalmOS. Table 2 compares Voyager with our toolkit along a few selected dimensions and shows that while indeed our toolkit has a smaller footprint and a more efficient object migration mechanism, we need to optimize the remote method invocation overhead.

- **Proxy handoff**: As discussed above, a mobile device is not communicating with a single proxy server all the time. As users move, alternative proxy servers may provide better services, either because the current proxy, serving increasing numbers of users, is relatively overloaded or because bandwidth and latency to a "closer" server allow for faster interactions between client and proxy. Wang (2000) discusses the issues involved in the design of appropriate handoff algorithms and identification of relevant parameters.

- **Scalability**: All experiments conducted in our research group are by necessity limited in scope, involving only few portable devices and proxy servers in the same building. To evaluate the scalability of our ideas for regional and national networks with many users, we build performance prediction models, similar to the work described in Rolia and Sevcik and Woodside (1995) and Franks (1998). We trace user access to existing wireless data applications in a regional PCS network (Kunz, 2000), and build prediction models based on this data (Zhou, 2000). The model allows us to predict how many concurrent users can be maximally supported or how many proxy servers are needed, given the characteristics of a specific application. We are currently refining the model, identifying additional sources of information to improve the models and to validate the prediction accuracy. Early experience confirms that we can accurately predict the occurrence of performance bottlenecks for the currently available simple set of text-based applications. More work is needed to experiment with and validate our models for more resource-intense, multimedia applications that utilize the concepts of code mobility and proxy server support.

SUMMARY AND CONCLUSIONS

Mobile computing is a relatively new field. While the challenges arising from mobility and the limitations of the portable devices are relatively well understood, there is no consensus yet as to what should be done to address these challenges. A comprehensive solution has to address many different aspects, such as the issue of dynamically changing bandwidth; the power, computational, and other limitations of the portable devices; or the varying availability of services in different environments. This paper presents our architecture for such adaptive mobile applications. We motivated the architecture by classifying likely mobile applications and identified common properties. The architecture intends to be more general than previous work with respect to adaptability, flexibility, and user mobility. We developed various pieces of the overall architecture and collected some preliminary experience with adaptive mobile applications. The results so far are encouraging. Work is currently under way to implement the missing components of our architecture. Once completed, we will continue to explore the following questions: What are good indicators of relative resource scarcity and how do we collect them at runtime? What adaptation policies are appropriate for different resources (bandwidth, power, or memory)? Can we trade off one resource for another? How transparent can application adaptation be made to end users? How transparent can it be made to application developers? We are also cooperating with a Canadian cellular service provider to evaluate our ideas and explore the scalability of our architecture for regional cellular systems.

ACKNOWLEDGMENTS

This work was started at the University of Waterloo and continues in collaboration with the research group of Professor James P. Black. The research was supported financially by Motorola's Advanced Radiodata Research Centre, Bell Mobility Cellular, and NSERC.

REFERENCES

ACTS Mobility. (1997, December). *Evolving the UMTS Vision*. Retrieved from the World Wide Web: http://www.infowin.org/ACTS/IENM/ CONCERTATION/MOBILITY/.

Badrinath, B. R., Acharya, A. & Imielinski, T. (1994). Structuring Distributed Algorithms for Mobile Hosts, *Proc. of the 14th International Conference on Distributed Computing Systems*, 21-28.

Balakrishnan, H., Seshan, S., Amir, E., & Katz, R. H. (1995). Improving TCP/ IP Performance over Wireless Networks, *Proceedings of the First Annual International Conference on Mobile Computing and Communications*, 2-11.

Bolliger, J. & Gross, T. (1998). A framework-based approach to the development of network-aware applications. *IEEE Transactions on Software Engineering, 24*(5), 376-390.

Chang, H., Tait, C., Cohen, N., Shapiro, M., Mastrianni, S., Floyd, R., Housel, B. & Lindquist, D. (1997). Web Browsing in a Wireless Environment: Disconnected and Asynchronous Operation in ARTour Web Express, *Proceedings of the 3rd Annual ACM/IEEE Conference on Mobile Computing and Networking*, 260-269.

El Shentenawy, M., Gaddah, A., Guo, Q., Kunz, T. & Hafez, R. (2000). Image transcoding for proxy Internet wireless access, *Proceedings of the 12th Annual International Conference on Wireless Communications*, 542-552.

Franks, G. & Woodside, M. (1998). *Performance of multi-level client-server systems with parallel service operations*, Proceedings of the First International Workshop on Software and Performance, 120-130.

Gessler, S. & Kotulla, A. (1994). PDAs as mobile WWW browsers. *Proceedings of the Second World Wide Web Conference: Mosaic and the Web*, http://www.ncsa.uiuc.edu/SDG/IT94/Proceedings/DDay/gessler/ www_pda.html.

Han, R., Bhagwat, P., LaMaire, R., Mummert, T., Perret, V. & Rubas, J.

(1998). Dynamic adaptation in an image transcoding proxy for mobile Web browsing, *IEEE Personal Communications, 5*(6), 8-17.

Hodes, T. D., Katz, R. H., Servan-Schreiber, E. & Rowe, L. (1997). Composable ad-hoc mobile services for universal interaction, *Proceedings of the 3rd Annual ACM/IEEE Conference on Mobile Computing and Networking*, 1-12.

International Telecommunication Union (2000). *IMT-2000 Website*, http://www.itu.int/imt/.

Kavi, K., Browne, J. C. & Tripathi, A. (1999). Computer systems research: The pressure is on, *IEEE Computer*, 30-39.

Kidston, D., Black, J. P., Kunz, T., Nidd, M. E., Lioy, M., Elphick, B. & Ostrowski, M. (1998). Comma: A communication manager for mobile applications. *Proceedings of the 10th Annual International Conference on Wireless Communications*, 103-116.

Kidston, D. (1998). *Transparent communication management in wireless networks*, Master's Thesis, Dept. of Computer Science, University of Waterloo.

Kunz, T., & Lo, G. H.-Y. (1999). Adaptive mobile applications: A case study, *Proceedings of the 3rd European Personal Mobile Communications Conference*, 25-30.

Kunz, T., Barry, T., Zhou, X., Black, J. P. & Mahoney, H. (2000). WAP traffic: description and comparison to WWW traffic. *Proceedings of the 3rd ACM International Workshop on Modeling, Analysis and Simulation of Wireless and Mobile Systems*, 11-19.

Le, M. T., Seshan, S., Burghardt, F., et al. (1994). Software architecture of the InfoPad system, *Proceedings of the Mobidata Workshop on Mobile and Wireless Information Systems*.

Lin, F.G. (2000). An adaptive MPEG filter, Master's Thesis, Department of Computer Science, University of Waterloo, in progress.

Lioy, M. (1997). Providing TCP-level services to mobile computers in a wireless environment, Master's Thesis, Department of Computer Science, University of Waterloo.

Maass, H. (1997). Location-aware mobile applications based on directory services, *Proceedings of the 3rd Annual ACM/IEEE Conference on Mobile Computing and Networking*, 23-33.

Omar, S., & Kunz, T. (1999). Reducing power consumption and increasing application performance for PDAs through mobile code. *Proceedings of the 1999 International Conference on Parallel and Distributed Processing Techniques and Applications*, Vol. II, 1005-1011.

Omar, S. (2000). A mobile code toolkit for adaptive mobile applications,

Master's Thesis, School of Computer Science, Carleton University.

Othman, M. & Hailes, S. (1998). *Power conservation strategy for mobile computers using load sharing, Mobile Computing and Communications Review, 2*(1), 44-51.

Rolia, J. A. & Sevcik, K. C. (1995). The method of layers. *IEEE Transactions on Software Engineering, 21*(8), 689-700.

Rudenko, A., Reiher, P., Popek, G. J. & Kuenning, G. H. (1998). Saving portable computer battery power through remote process execution, *Mobile Computing and Communications Review, 2*(1), 19-26.

Wang, J. & Kunz, T. (2000). A proxy server infrastructure for adaptive mobile applications. *Proceedings of the 18ᵗʰ IASTED International Conference on Applied Informatics*, 561-567.

Wang, Y. (2000). Visualizing the execution of object-oriented applications with code mobility, Master's Thesis, Department of Systems and Computer Engineering, Carleton University.

Welling, G. & Badrinath, B. R. (1997). A framework for environment ware mobile applications, *Proceedings of the 17ᵗʰ International Conference on Distributed Computing Systems*, 384-391.

Whalen, T. J. (1997). Design issues for an adaptive mobile group editor, Master's Thesis, Department of Computer Science, University of Waterloo.

Zenel, B., & Duchamp, D. (1997). A general purpose proxy filtering mechanism applied to the mobile environment, *Proceedings of the 3ʳᵈ Annual ACM/IEEE Conference on Mobile Computing and Networking*, 238-259.

Zhou, X (2000). Cellular data traffic: analysis, modeling, and prediction, Master's Thesis, School of Computer Science, Carleton University.

Chapter IV

Space-Time Wireless Communications (a.k.a. Smart Antennas)

Arogyaswami J. Paulraj and Hemanth Sampath
Stanford University, USA
Iospan Wireless, Inc., USA

INTRODUCTION

The rapid progress in radio and electronics technology has triggered a communications revolution. Mobile wireless networks are being deployed throughout the world to meet increasing consumer demand. Wireless service revenues are currently growing at about 40% per year and these trends are likely to continue for several years.

A mobile wireless network (see Figure 1) has a cellular architecture. Each cell has a base station (BTS) that services multiple users. The BTS communicates with the users (forward link) and the users communicate to the BTS (reverse link). Typically, adjoining cells (cells 1, 2 and 3 in Figure 1) in a cluster are allotted distinct frequency blocks. These blocks are used once every *n* cells, where *n* is the cluster size or equivalently the frequency reuse factor. Radio links suffer from interference from cells that share the same frequency block. This interference is known as co-channel interference.

Successful deployment of wireless networks presents a number of challenges. These include limited availability of radio frequency spectrum, a complex, time-varying wireless environment, and user demand for higher data rates, better quality of service, fewer dropped calls, higher capacity and user coverage. A number of different radio technologies, using sophisticated

Figure 1. Mobile wireless network

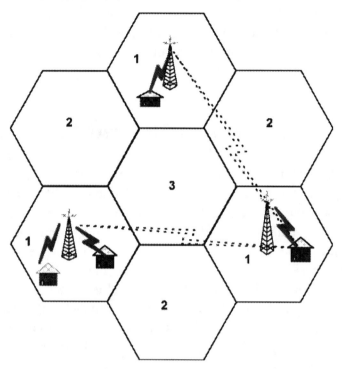

transmit and receive processing schemes, have been used to meet such diverse requirements.

Space-time processing technology is a powerful and recent tool to improve system performance. In this technology, multiple antennas and space-time processing are employed at the transmitter (Tx) and/or at the receiver (Rx). A space-time modem operates simultaneously on all antennas, processing signal samples both in space and time. Smart antennas provide four main leverages, namely *array gain, diversity gain, interference reduction*, and *multiplexing*. These leverages can be used to improve coverage, link quality, data rate and system capacity in a cellular network (see Table 1).

Table 1. Space-time processing leverages in a cellular network

	Coverage	Link Quality	Capacity	Data Rate
Array Gain	X	X		
Int Reduction		X	X	
Diversity		X	X	
Multiplexing			X	X

In this chapter, we briefly describe these four leverages of space-time processing. We first discuss wireless channel impairments, next we explain how space-time processing technology helps in combating such impairments and improves overall system performance, and finally, we conclude with a summary of current industry trends.

THE WIRELESS CHANNEL

A signal that is launched into the wireless environment, arrives at the receiver along a number of distinct paths, referred to as multipaths (see Figure 2). These paths arise from scattering and reflection of radiated energy from objects such as buildings, hills, trees, etc. Each of these paths has a distinct propagation loss, path delay, angle of arrival, and signal amplitude. As a result of multipath propagation, the transmitted signal undergoes spreading in different dimensions, namely, the time (delay spread), frequency (Doppler spread) and angle (angle spread). Delay spread is caused when multipaths arrive with different delays. Doppler spread is caused when the channel varies with time, either due to user mobility or a time-varying environment (wind, traffic, etc). Angle spread is caused when the multipaths arrive at different angles at the receiver.

The delay, Doppler and angle spreads cause the signal to fluctuate across frequency, time and space, respectively (see Figure 3). These fluctuations are

Figure 2. Multipath propagation in the wireless environment

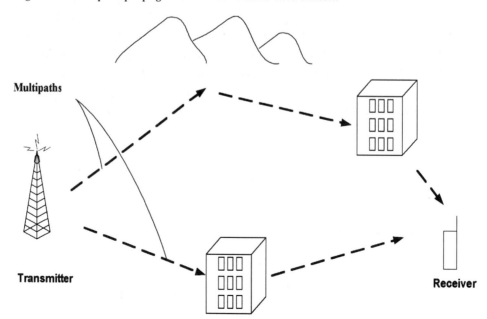

Multipaths

Transmitter

Receiver

Figure 3. Channel impairments in a wireless link-fading and co-channel interference

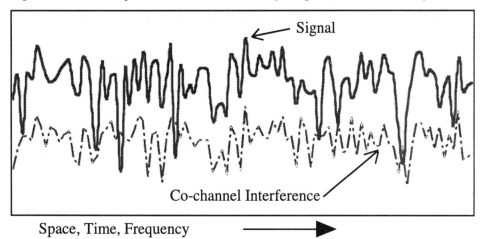

Signal

Co-channel Interference

Space, Time, Frequency ⟶

collectively referred to as *fading* and cause deterioration in link quality. There also exists another type of fading, which is caused by shadowing effects of buildings or natural features. In addition to fading, the signal strength drops with range due to *path loss*. Moreover, radio links suffer from co-channel interference from cells that share the same frequency block. Wireless systems must be designed to mitigate fading, ***co-channel interference*** and path loss.

CHANNEL ESTIMATION

Receive: In order to recover the transmitted information symbols, the receiver requires an estimate of the channel. Typically, training information is inserted in the transmitted signal, which the receiver can use to estimate the channel. In rapidly varying mobile channels, we may have to retrain the receiver frequently.

Transmit: There are two main approaches to estimating the channel at the transmitter. In a time division duplexing system, transmission and reception proceed in a ping-pong fashion. If the ping-pong time (time separating the transmit and receive signal) is small, the channel estimated on the receive mode can also be used in the transmit mode. In frequency division duplexing systems, forward and reverse link transmission occurs at different frequencies where the channels can potentially be very different. In this case, the receiver must estimate the transmit channel and feed it back to the transmitter.

SPACE-TIME PROCESSING TECHNIQUES

Space-time processing technology uses multiple antennas in the transmitter and/or the receiver with associated coding and modulation to enhance system performance. A detailed overview of space-time processing systems for use in cellular networks is available in (Smart Antenna Workshops, 1994-1999; Paulraj, 1997). As explained before, multiple antenna technology offers four key leverages which we now describe.

Array Gain: Consider a receiver with 2 antennas (see Figure 4). Signals (S_1 and S_2) received on the two antennas have different amplitudes and phases as dictated by the multipath propagation. These signals are appropriately combined by the receiver so that the resultant power of the output signal ($\hat{S}$) is enhanced. The output signal to noise ratio (SNR) is the sum of the signal to noise ratios (SNR_1 and SNR_2) on the receive antennas, leading to an improvement in signal quality. Array gain is proportional to the number of antennas used. This approach can also be implemented in the transmitter, where the transmit signals across the antennas can be phased so that the signal power at the receive antennas is increased. Array gain at the transmitter can be exploited only if the channel is known at the transmitter.

Diversity Gain: The multipath propagation in the wireless environment can cause the signal to fluctuate or fade as a function of time and spatial location. This causes a deterioration in link quality. Space-diversity is a technique that exploits (independently) fading signals on different antennas to mitigate fading and improve link quality. There are two forms of space diversity-receive and transmit diversity.

Figure 5 illustrates receive diversity for a receiver with 2 antennas. The received signals (S_1 and S_2) fade independently and are combined by the

Figure 4. Array gain

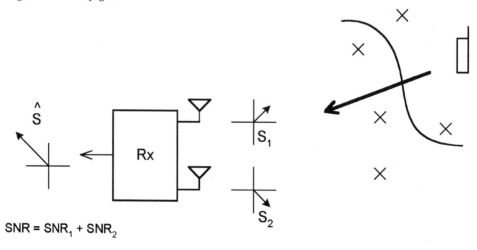

$$SNR = SNR_1 + SNR_2$$

Figure 5. Receive diversity

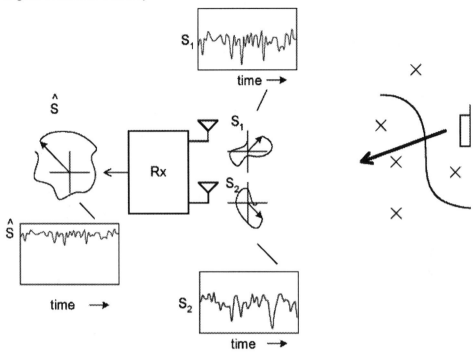

receiver so that the resultant signal exhibits much reduced fading. The received signal output, Ŝ, has reduced signal amplitude variability when compared to S_1 and S_2. Channel knowledge at the receiver is required to exploit receive diversity.

Figure 6 illustrates transmit diversity (Alamouti, 1998; Tarokh, Seshadri, & Calderbank, 1998) for a system with 2 transmit antennas and 1 receiver antenna. At the transmitter, two modified signals (S_1 and S_2) are created from the original signal (S) and transmitted on the two antennas. The received signals (S_{11} and S_{21}) are then combined by the receiver to reduce fading. The time waveform of the output signal, Ŝ, has reduced signal amplitude variability when compared to S_{11} and S_{21}. Transmit diversity can be exploited without requiring channel knowledge at the transmitter.

Interference Reduction: Co-channel interference adds to the overall noise of the system and deteriorates performance. Figure 7 illustrates interference reduction for a receiver with 2 antennas. Typically, the desired signal (S) and interference (I) arrive at the receive antennas with different spatial signatures (S_1, S_2 and I_1, I_2). Space-time signal processing can cancel or reduce the interference, and boost signal (Ŝ) power and reduce signal amplitude variability. The signal to interference ratio at the receiver output is enhanced.

Interference reduction can also be implemented in the transmitter, where

Figure 6. Transmit diversity

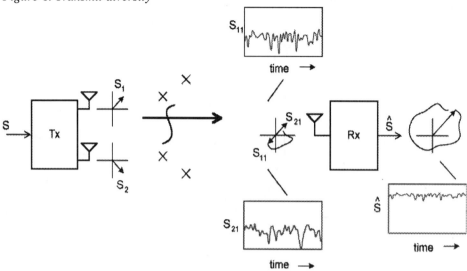

the goal is to enhance the signal power at the intended receiver and minimize the interference energy sent towards co-channel users (users that communicate over the same frequency block as the intended user). Interference reduction allows use of aggressive reuse factors and improves the system capacity.

Spatial Multiplexing: This is a technique used to improve data rates (Foschini, 1996) and increase system capacity. There are two types of multiplexing, namely, single-user spatial multiplexing (SU-SM) (Paulraj, 1994; Foschini, 1996) and multi-user spatial multiplexing (MU-SM) (Roy, 1997).

SU-SM (Paulraj, 1994; Foschini 1996) can increase bit rates in wireless radio links. SU-SM requires multiple antennas at both ends of the wireless link. Under favorable channel conditions (wireless environment with rich multipaths or well-separated antennas), multiple channels or data pipes can be created in the same frequency band to obtain an increase in data rates. SU-SM does not require channel knowledge at the transmitter, but, require channel knowledge at the receiver. Figure 8 illustrates a 2-transmit and 2-receive antenna SU-SM system. At the transmitter, the information symbol stream is split into 2 independent, lower rate sub-streams. These streams are modulated to form signals S_1 and S_2, which are transmitted on separate transmit antennas. If the spatial signatures of these signals (denoted by, S_{11}, S_{12},

Figure 7. Interference reduction

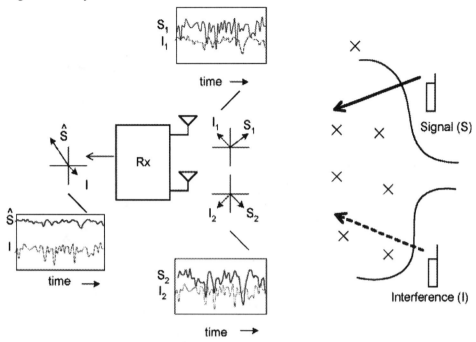

and S_{21}, S_{22}, respectively) induced at the receiver antennas are well separated, the receiver can separate the 2 transmitted signals to yield the sub-streams (1 and 2).

MU-SM, also referred to as spatial division multiple access (SDMA; Roy, 1997), is a technique in which several users may share the same frequency channel. Figure 9 illustrates the scheme with 2 users and a BTS with 2 antennas. In the forward link (see Figure 9a), the BTS processes the signals S_1 and S_2 intended for users 1 and 2 respectively, and transmits the corresponding phased signals (S_{11}, S_{12}) and (S_{21}, S_{22}) on the transmit antennas. Transmit processing is such that each user gets its own signal, $\hat{S}_1$ and $\hat{S}_2$, with low cross talk from the other user signal. This scheme requires a very accurate knowledge of the channel at the transmitter, which makes MU-SM hard to implement

Figure 8. Single-user spatial multiplexing (SU-SM)

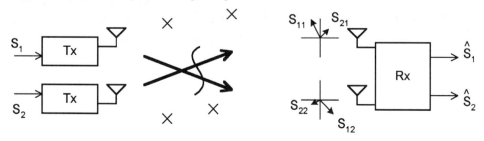

Figure 9. SDMA or multi-user spatial multiplexing (MU-SM)

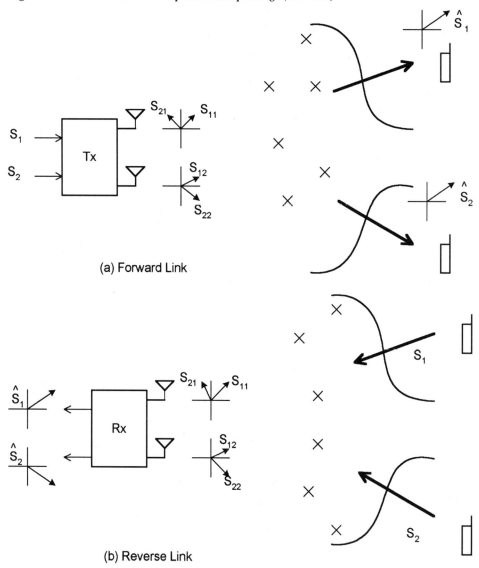

(a) Forward Link

(b) Reverse Link

in the forward link. In the reverse link (see Figure 9b), user signals S_1 and S_2 arrive at the receive antennas with different spatial signatures (S_{11}, S_{12}) and (S_{21}, S_{22}), respectively. The receiver exploits these different spatial signatures to separate the user signals. This technique is difficult to implement when the differences in received signal power from each user are large.

INDUSTRY TRENDS

There are a number of industry projects to commercialize space-time processing (or smart antenna) technology. We now discuss some important trends.

2G (Generation) Mobile Systems

These include the digital TDMA (IS-136 and GSM) and CDMA (IS-95) systems. Several vendors have implemented space-time processing in TDMA systems to reduce interference and improve signal quality. This is expected to achieve a two-fold increase in capacity. Ericsson and Nortel have expanded commercial/experimental deployments of this technology.

2.5G and 3G Mobile Systems

This includes the EDGE and UWC systems with a focus on TDMA technology, and the IMT-2000 system with a focus on wide-band CDMA technology. There is a major thrust within several companies to develop the architecture and algorithms to incorporate Tx diversity techniques in these networks.

Broadband Fixed Wireless Systems

Broadband fixed wireless is expected to be a major emerging market. Fixed systems need to offer very high quality and a high data rate that is approximately 50 times better than the mobile cellular systems. Space-time processing offers key leverages for successful performance of fixed wireless systems (Paulraj & Papadias, 1997; Sheikh, Gesbert, Gore, & Paulraj, 1999). The licensed frequencies for broadband wireless access lie in the 24-48 GHz band (e.g., LMDS) and below the 3 GHz (e.g., MDS, WCS and MMDS) bands. The high cost of millimeter electronics makes multiple antenna technology expensive in LMDS bands. However, in frequency bands below 3 GHz, multiple antenna technology is cost-effective. Iospan Wireless has developed a fixed wireless system with Tx-Rx diversity and SU-SM.

CONCLUSION

Wireless networks pose a significant challenge for high quality and high data rate communication. Space-time processing offers key leverages, such as array gain, interference reduction, diversity gain and multiplexing gain, to enhance performance.

REFERENCES

Alamouti, S. (1998, October). A simple transmitter diversity technique for wireless communications. *IEEE Journal on Selected Areas in Communications*. (Special Issue on Signal Processing for Wireless Communications). 16(8), 1451-8.

Foschini, G.J. (1996, Autumn). Layered space-time architecture for wireless communication in a fading environment when using multi-element antennas. *Bell Labs Technical Journal*, 41-59.

Foschini, G.J. & Gans, M. (1998, March). On the limits of wireless communications in a fading environment when using multiple antennas. Wireless Personal Communications. 6(3).

Paulraj, A., et al. (1994). Increasing capacity in wireless broadcast system using distributed transmission/directional reception. U.S. Patent, no. 5, 345, 599.

Paulraj, A. & Papadias, C. (1997, November). Space-time processing for wireless communications. *IEEE Signal Processing Magazine*, 49-83.

Proceedings of the First, Second, Third, Fourth, Fifth and Sixth Annual Workshops on Smart Antennas for Wireless Communications. (1994-1999). Stanford University, Stanford, CA.

Roy, R.H. (1997). Spatial division multiple access technology and its application to wireless communication systems. *IEEE 47th Vehicular Technology Conference*. 2, 730 -734.

Sheikh, K., Gesbert, D., Gore, D. & Paulraj, A. (1999, November). Smart Antennas for Broadband Wireless Access Networks. *IEEE Communications Magazine*.

Tarokh, V., Seshadri, N. & Calderbank, A. (1998, March). Space time codes for high data rates wireless communications - performance criterion and code construction. *IEEE Transactions on Information Theory*. 44, 744-65.

Chapter V

A New Business Dimension: SDMA and Intelligent Antennas

André L. Brandão
Nortel Networks, Canada

ABSTRACT

Space division multiple access (SDMA) is a promising technique useful for increasing capacity, reducing interference and improving overall wireless communication link quality. With a large-scale penetration expected for wireless Internet, the radio link will require significant reduction in cost and increase in capacity, benefits that the proper exploitation of the spatial dimension can offer. Market opportunities with SDMA are significant, as a number of companies have been recently formed to bring products based on this new concept to the wireless marketplace. The approach to SDMA is broad, ranging from "switched-beam techniques" to "adaptive-antennas." Basically the technique employs antenna arrays and digital signal processing to achieve the necessary increases in capacity and quality needed in the wireless world.

INTRODUCTION

Wireless communications has long been linked to businesses. More precisely, it became an important enterprise when the Marconi Company was founded in the early 1900s. Before that, the wireless subject was most confined inside academia. It started with Maxwell,[1] who formulated the theory of electromagnetic propagation and continued with Hertz,[2] who first demonstrated the phenomenon of radio waves in practice. However, neither Hertz nor early pioneers were able to start the radio revolution the way Marconi[3] did. Guglielmo Marconi was not only a scientist but also a businessman with a vision. He founded the Marconi Company that grew rapidly into a business embracing the globe, from Europe to South America (Marconi, 1931). Radio thrived initially with analogue amplitude modulation (AM) systems and subsequently with analogue frequency modulation (FM) stations.

Nowadays telecommunications has fused with computers and forged the modern information society. The association of computers with telecommunications, originally termed informatics, paved the way for businesses in such a scale that is comparable to the industrial revolution of the 19th century. Modern systems include the digital broadcast of radio and television channels, telemedicine, global positioning system (GPS), and the vast scenario of wireless Internet and wireless commerce (w-commerce), the latter being the equivalent of e-commerce in the wireless world ("Enabling a portable Web," 2000). For certain, since information was first conveyed by radio, the subject of wireless has become a driving force in the world economy.

This chapter addresses basic concepts of space division multiple access (SDMA) and intelligent antennas as the way to increase capacity and quality of service (higher transmission data rate and lower system delay) in wireless communications. We focus on the applications side of SDMA rather than on discussions about the technical challenges related to the technique. SDMA can be deployed as an alternative to cable TV and for point-to-point or point-to-multipoint high-speed data broadcast amongst many other possibilities. As for the technical difficulties, they range from the prediction of the radio frequency (RF) channel (i.e., RF channel varies randomly with time) to the problems associated with modern cellular mobile phone services (i.e., co-channel interference, fading and the Doppler phenomenon, to name a few; (Yacoub, 1993; Lee, 1993). Although the enterprise is new and far from being firmly established, it has already proved feasible (Mogensen et al., 1997) with a potential solid marketplace. Other aspects of intelligent antennas include diversity and spatial equalisation. But contrary to diversity and equalisation, which are well known and used in industry, SDMA represents new grounds yet to be developed. Moreover, SDMA can be implemented with already proven methods (such as diversity) in order to achieve the highest performances.

ACCESS TO THE NETWORK

Access refers to the method in which several users share the same communications medium (i.e., electromagnetic air space) in an orderly way so that users can be uniquely identified and attached to the network. When the network cannot provide access to all the users, the system is overloaded and said to have achieved its capacity limit. Wireless, in particular, came across a variety of modalities of access techniques during its evolution. For example, in early 1980s the analogue mobile cellular system known as Advanced Mobile Phone Service (AMPS) in the United States was deployed using frequency division multiple access (FDMA) technology (Proakis, 1995). In FDMA one radio channel is assigned entirely to one single user (i.e., a mobile phone in AMPS) during a phone call. Different users are assigned to different channels so that the number of phone calls matches with the number of frequencies allocated as shown in Figure 1.

Early wireless cellular systems using analogue FDMA technology gained widespread acceptance not only in the United States but also in Europe and Japan. However the cellular market grew to a point that analogue FDMA with constrained capacity had to be replaced. The greater the capacity the larger the number of users one can fit into a system given the same radio resources. Telecommunication companies were eager to increase the number of customers without having to commission more frequencies and so digital time division multiple access (TDMA) technology came naturally as the evolution in the portfolio of equipment manufacturers. Digital systems such as IS-136 in the United States and the Global System for Mobile Communications (GSM) in Europe were deployed during 1990s with TDMA access technique. In digital TDMA one frequency channel serves more than one user without degrading the service. This is possible because base band signals such as voice can be digitised, stored in small chunks of data, and transmitted in

Figure 1. Different users are assigned to different frequencies in FDMA

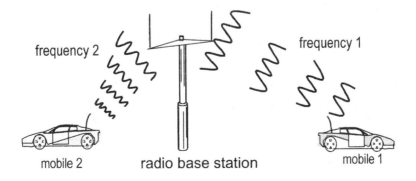

Figure 2. A TDMA burst is faster than the speed of signal sampling

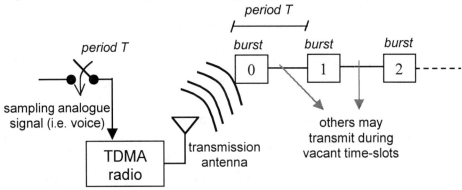

bursts. The transmission speed of the digital burst is higher than the rate of acquisition of the signal that is originally in analogue format. This creates an interval of time between the transmission of the burst and the acquisition of new data (i.e., samples of voice signal).

Other users take advantage of the existence of time windows between bursts in order to send their information inside vacant time slots (as shown in Figure 2). In this way it is possible to transmit signals from different users sharing the same frequency without conflict. This access technique is called time division multiple access precisely because different users access the air-interface but transmitting at different time slots.

Another popular access technique is the code division multiple access (CDMA; Liberti & Rappaport, 1999). The development of CDMA can be traced back to World War II when the military from several countries started searching for robust techniques to combat jamming of their radio links. The technique consists in the spreading of the energy of the signal carrying information over a large portion of the spectrum of frequencies. Note that in FDMA the signal bearing information is concentrated in a single tone so that the power of the carrier frequency is high (i.e., very much visible and prone to suffer jamming by enemy forces). In CDMA, however, the energy is ideally spread evenly in the spectrum so that no distinct pilot frequency exists.

In CDMA several users can transmit at the same time within the same spectrum of frequency. The channels (i.e., users) are distinguished by assigning different codes to different users. A fundamental result from communications theory states that mul-

Figure 3. CDMA has the information-bearing signal spread all over the spectrum

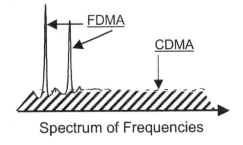

Spectrum of Frequencies

tiple users may share a common medium (frequency spectrum) as long as their signals are produced with distinct codes that are orthogonal. Orthogonal signals are cancelled when convoluted together. Convolution is a mathematical operation that can be programmed inside a CDMA radio receiver. Figure 4 illustrates the basic operation for multiuser detection in a CDMA receiver.

Note that in Figure 4 the receiver has a copy of the code of the wanted user (user A in this example). When the signal porting code-A from the transmitting source is convoluted with a copy of that code in the receiver, a resulting energy is produced at the output of the convoluting device. On the other hand code-B is orthogonal to code-A, and in this case the signal B convoluted with signal A will produce an output that is zero. In practice, however, different codes are not ideally orthogonal nor does the receiver have ideal convoluting devices. As a consequence the convolution operation between quasi-orthogonal codes is limited in its capability of cancelling interference. Unfortunately this limits the number of users that can share the same frequency spectrum at the same time, which constitutes a major limiting factor for the capacity of CDMA systems today.

The system capacity that bounds the maximum number of users sharing a radio link at the same time is therefore limited and is a function of the access technique:

1. FDMA: Capacity for multiple channels (users), each with frequency bandwidth f, is limited by the maximum number of frequencies that can be allocated at the same time for a given system spectrum with total bandwidth B.

Figure 4. CDMA distinguishes users by convoluting different orthogonal codes

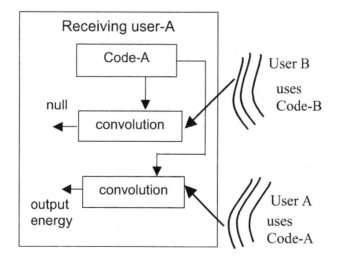

2. TDMA: Capacity for multiple channels (users), each with a time slot duration T, is limited by the maximum number of time slots that can fit into the system for a given spectrum with total bandwidth B.

3. CDMA: Capacity for multiple channels (users), each with a coding sequence C, is limited by the maximum number of coding sequences that can be de-convoluted in a system for a given spectrum with total bandwidth B.

All three methods of access listed above have their particularities, advantages and disadvantages. Most standards for digital wireless communications employ a mix of them (FDMA with CDMA or TDMA with FDMA).

SPATIAL DIMENSION FOR ACCESS

Access techniques such as FDMA, CDMA and TDMA are all related to time and/or frequency dimension. Communication service providers have used them in order to accommodate users sharing precious radio frequency resources. But system capacity is limited (as most things in nature) and when it reaches the boundaries it is like one trying to squeeze out juice from a dried orange. That is to say, the wireless business cannot grow in terms of number of customers beyond the capacity of a given system. This capacity issue has been a driving force pushing for solution and that includes the spatial division multiple access (Roy, 1997; Cooper & Goldburg, 1996).

During the 1990's SDMA consolidated its foundations (not as much in theoretical background as in practical terms) mostly due to advances in digital signal processor (DSP) technology. This has allowed the appearance of all-software radio system prototypes that are flexible, made with off-the-shelf components and in a cost-effective manner suitable for SDMA. It is notable the number of papers about the subject that appeared in technical journals and conferences all over the world throughout that decade. Contrary to early expectations, however, the new millennium has shown an industry in an anti-climax state concerning the deployment of this new technology. Perhaps, this is because the spatial access technique breaks radically with the legacy of hardware and software platforms already installed in industry. This is good news for start-up companies willing to invest in SDMA and intelligent antennas without the constraint of old platforms. Moreover, a boom in the commercial exploitation of intelligent antennas is expected soon, fuelled by the explosive growth of the wireless Internet.

In SDMA, several users may share a radio link with the same frequency, at the same time and with or without the same coding sequence. In other words, SDMA can be combined with CDMA, FDMA and TDMA because the spatial dimension is independent of time and frequency. Every user has a spatial identity that is unique. This forms a basic principle for SDMA and applies whenever different users present distinguishable spatial coordinates. Figure 5 shows an array of intelligent antennas implementing SDMA access for two different users.

In Figure 5 an array of antennas is used to create two distinct radiation patterns over user #1 and user #2. User #1 communicates with the base station through beam #1 while user #2 uses beam #2. The array is capable of creating multiple beams or multiple radiation patterns. A single omnidirectional antenna working alone cannot accomplish this. The reason an array is able to form multiple radiation beams is conceptually simple in the technique known as *array beamforming* (Haykin, Litva, & Shepherd, 1993). The geometric arrangement of the system and the proper phasing of the signal in each antenna determine the radiation pattern of the array. The "intelligent antennas" name refers to those arrays that are capable of adapting the radiation pattern dynamically according to specific situations and autonomously. Other names have been used such as "smart antennas" or "adaptive antennas." DSP processors normally control an intelligent antenna system. In order to understand the beamforming basic characteristic that is the null in the radiation pattern, consider for example a frequency (or more precisely a plane radio wave front) arriving to an array of two elements as in Figure 6. Each antenna element is represented in the figure by a small black circle. The antennas are spaced apart by a distance half of the size of the incoming radio wavelength (for instance, if the frequency is 1 GHz then half a wavelength is 15 cm).

Figure 5. In SDMA the access is based on the direction of arrival of the signal

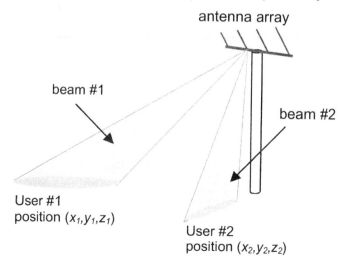

Figure 6. Determining the array beamforming response by arranging geometrically the antennas

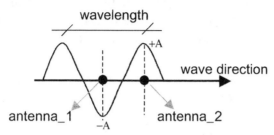

In Figure 6 the wave travels from left to right and hits antenna_1 first. Subsequently, the wave travels further and reaches antenna_2 with a phase delay of half-wavelength. The signal captured in antenna_2 has an exact opposite phase from that captured in antenna_1 (they have same amplitude but with different signs –A and +A). In this case, the antennas combined will produce a zero output as shown in Figure 7, where _/2 represents half wavelength distance. The radiation pattern of the array has a null point for the frequency arriving at an angle of +/- 90° from the array boresight (front of the array).

The array response is different when the wave hits the array at boresight. The boresight is the direction of the plane wave front hitting the antennas at the same time as in Figure 8.

Contrary to the case in Figure 7, at boresight the signals from antenna_1 and antenna_2 are in phase. Therefore the combination of the antennas will output twice as much energy than that produced by one antenna alone.

Selectivity is as a function of the direction of arrival of the radio wave. Figure 7 shows that signals arriving from the side of the array are cancelled whilst in Figure 9 the signals from boresight are enhanced. Essentially an array beamforming is a system where the wanted signal is combined in phase

Figure 7. Signal is cancelled (null in the radiation pattern)

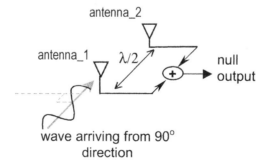

(enhanced) and interference signals are combined with opposite phases (cancelled). This can be achieved with more flexibility when phase shifters are added in the antenna branches of the array. Phase shifters are devices that impose a delay in the radio signal with great accuracy and thus are used to control the response of the array. The objective is to maximise the energy from the direction of arrival of the wanted signal and minimise the energy coming from the source of interference.

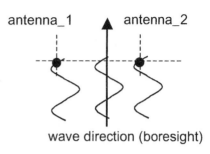

Figure 8. Radio wave arriving with same phase at the same time

Figure 10 shows an example of array radiation pattern, which is a graphical representation of the array amplitude response as a function of the direction of arrival of the signal. In the figure, the signal coming from the side of the array receives a small gain (represented by a small side lobe) whilst the larger gain (main lobe in the graphics) is for signals arriving by the front.

The phase shifters control the radiation pattern in such way that the main lobe (maximum gain direction) can be steered towards a preferred direction. Moreover, the phase shifters are programmable devices that are usually embedded in a system controlled by software. Normally the array is commanded to point a main lobe dynamically in SDMA. This dynamic control is reminiscent of radar, which was originally designed for tracking military targets. However, instead of missiles, the adaptive array in wireless communications is employed to a variety of commercial applications which includes: position location capability (used to locate a mobile terminal based on the direction of arrival of the signal); increase capacity; reduction of interference and increase coverage area for mobile systems.

Summarizing, in FDMA every user has a unique carrier frequency. In TDMA every user has a specific time slot to transmit/receive messages. In CDMA every user has a distinct code sequence. In SDMA every user has now a unique spatial location identification characterised by a set of phase shifters

Figure 9. Signal is enhanced at boresight

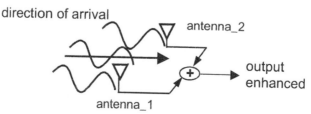

Figure 10. Array radiation pattern controlled by phase shifters

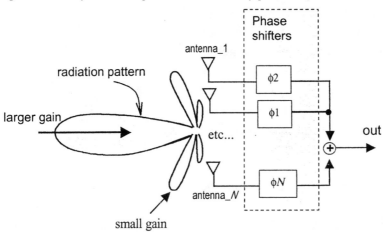

arranged for that particular user. In other words, in SDMA for every user a set of phase shifters is assigned. The phase shifters are also referred to as *array steering vectors*. The array steering vector is in fact a mathematical representation that models the functionality of the phase shifters and is used in the theoretical analysis of the array. It is also common to find that in SDMA every user is characterised by his/her own array steering vector. Every distinct user presents a steering vector that "steers" the main lobe towards that user. It is perfectly possible for a single array to serve many users, each one having an individual steering vector as shown in Figure 11.

Figure 11. Different users have distinct array steering vectors in SDMA

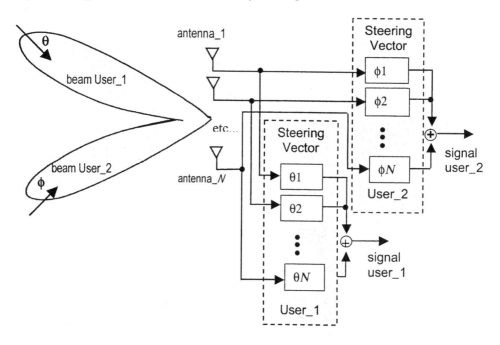

In Figure 11, the beam for user_1 captures the signal arriving from direction q. Similarly, the beam for user_2 selects the signal from direction f. The two radiation patterns with main lobes pointing to q and f coexist at the same time in the array. The SDMA access method works when each user has a set of steering vectors which identifies the angle of arrival of that particular user.

APPLICATIONS

Adaptive Antennas

In the adaptive antennas case, the steering vector for each user changes fast in order to track users with mobility (i.e., mobile cellular phones in cars, buses, etc.; Winters, 1993). The radiation pattern changes continuously, and the main lobe points always at the direction of the mobile. Radar systems have used this technology for a long time but only now has it been incorporated into the telecommunications industry (Haykin et al., 1993).

Multi-beam Systems

In this case, the system uses a number of fixed beams at a fixed antenna site. This system is preferred by broadcast operators distributing television channels, Internet access, telephony and multimedia in general for paying customers. This is a very attractive alternative to cable TV since the wireless

Figure 12. Adaptive antenna array has tracking capability

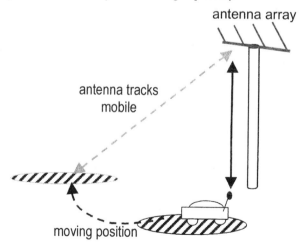

connection does not require cabling infrastructure in the customer's premises. For enterprises seeking fast deployment of networking access capabilities, the multi-beam access system is ideal (see Figure 13). In the multi-beam scheme the users are fixed and mobility is not allowed.

Commercial multi-beam systems include: local multipoint distribution service (LMDS) that operates in the 28 GHz to 31GHz band and the multichannel multipoint distribution service (MMDS) which has been designed mainly for broadcast of iterative TV services (Hart, 1998; Barber, Martin & Moore, 1998). Some other interesting projects on broadband radio access networks have also been developed by the European Telecommunications Standards Institute (ETSI), notably the Hiperaccess and Hiperlink programs (Haine, 1998; ETSI, 2000).

Switched-beam Systems

Mobile communications companies are now deploying switched-beam antennas in place of sectored cell systems. This new approach offers an increase in system capacity over traditional trisector cells. The switched-beam consists in radiating a cell with several narrow fixed beams. The transmission of information in the beams is turned on and off as the mobile passes under the coverage area of a particular beam (see Figure 14).

The transmission of data switches off in a particular beam as soon as the mobile leaves the radiation zone of that beam. An adjacent beam is activated when the mobile enters inside that beam's coverage boundary in the cell. The advantages of switched-beam technology is that it improves significantly interference problems and can be deployed over existing sectored systems

Figure 13. Multi-beam is an alternative to cable TV and multimedia

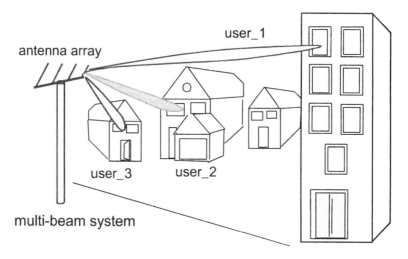

(i.e., traditional organization with three sectors per cell). It also allows reuse of old equipment in the base-band side of the system.

Spatial Diversity

This consists in the use of redundancy of two or more systems in order to transmit and/or receive a radio signal. When the redundancy is implemented in the transmitter, the method is called diversity transmission. Similarly, when the redundancy is in the receiver, the method is known as diversity receiving. The basic idea about spatial diversity is that the system replica and the original equipment work transmitting and/or receiving at the same time but they are placed by some distance apart. This distance should be enough so that each system perceives a different radio frequency channel. The radio link is a function of the physical surroundings, hence separate systems present distinct channels. The radio link also varies during the time and such variations cause fluctuations in the strength of the signal being transmitted and/or received (also known as fading). As a consequence the systems perceive fluctuations in their signal strength but at different moments in time since their channels are not equal. This means that when one system perceives signal degradation the other may be sensing an increase in the signal level. Instantaneous variations in one channel are not likely to occur simultaneously in the other channel; then two or more systems combined will produce a result that is better protected against fading than one single system alone.

Figure 14. Switched-beam used in sectored mobile cellular systems

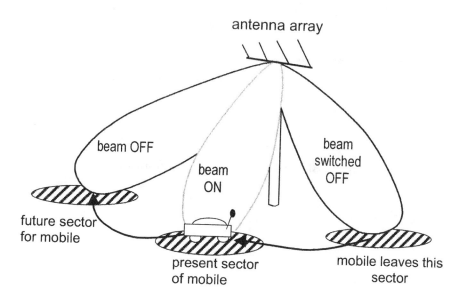

Spatial Equalisation

This is a generic term since diversity is also a form of channel equalisation. However, the word equalisation has been used throughout industry to designate systems built with the main purpose of combating multipath propagation (fast fading) and co-channel interference. The hardware implementation of an adaptive array for spatial equalisation is basically the same of that in SDMA. Note that SDMA refers to an access methodology while equalisation is a filtering process. In SDMA all users share the same frequency at the same time and the system provides the users an access to the network. In spatial equalisation the unwanted users (co-channel interference) and the multipath propagation are filtered out of the system and only a cleared desired signal remains (see Figure 15). A conclusion is that SDMA may be realised through the combination of several equalisers (i.e., multiuser detection where each equaliser filters its own user from others and delivers to the system) added with the capacity to provide connectivity to the network.

FINAL REMARKS AND
MARKET PERSPECTIVES

This chapter has presented some basic concepts of SDMA and intelligent antennas as the way to increase capacity and quality of service in wireless systems. We have focused on principles and applications rather than on discussions about the technical challenges related to the technique. We have shown that SDMA can be deployed as an alternative to cable TV, point-to-point or point-to-multipoint high-speed data transfer, amongst many other possibilities. Although the enterprise is new and far from being firmly

Figure 15. Spatial equalisation combats fast fading and co-channel interference

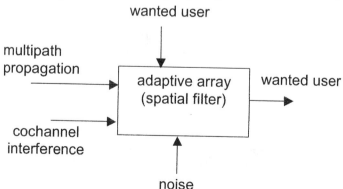

established, it has already proved feasible and is bound to be a key part in the broadband marketplace.

An area that is under revision by investors and deserves attention is the wireless local loop (WLL) targeting rural areas in developing countries. However WLL has not enjoyed the deployment levels that their functionality suggests, perhaps because the market has not yet enticed investors enough to boost this specific application. Also the economic instability in developing countries is a major contributor for the slow takeoff.

Position location using adaptive antennas is another area of interest for the wireless technology. However, position location using antenna arrays at the cellular base station finds a fierce competitor named GPS (global positioning systems). GPS, based on satellites, is becoming cheaper and seems to be the preferred method of position location service offered by telephone companies. NTT DoCoMo (Tokyo, Japan), for instance, has unveiled a mass-market high-performance GPS-based mobile personal location service, which has potential to become a trend to follow.

In general, market perspectives for wireless broadband access are optimistic, if not euphoric. In both hemispheres of the globe, the wireless broadband revenues are predicted to soar. Driven by the Internet and w-commerce (wireless electronic commerce), revenues are expected to grow at a 418% compound annual rate over the next five years. In the United States, technologies employing LMDS and MMDS are expected to reach revenues up to US$3.4 billion in 2003, compared with 1999 revenues of US$11.2 million, according to Strategis Group ("Enabling a portable Web," 2000). It is anticipated that at least 34% of the United States households and 45% of businesses will be using broadband wireless by 2003. Particularly LMDS is predicted to have phenomenal growth. LMDS is perceived as an inexpensive means to market entry for local services. The Strategis Group also points out that the telephone market reached US$110 billion in 1999, which is more than an incentive for market entry. Historically, narrowband services (i.e., voice and fax) have dominated the scenario, but today with the advent of multimedia, Internet and voice-over-IP (voice through an Internet connection), this is changing dramatically, pushing the demand for broadband. System capacity is at a premium, and the spatial dimension opens up many new businesses opportunities with SDMA and intelligent antennas.

REFERENCES

Barber, P. C., Martin, P. M. & Moore, T. A. (1998, October). Planning and operating a fixed access network. *Electronics & Communications Engi-*

neering Journal, 10(5), 221-228.

Cooper, M. & Goldburg, M. (1996). Intelligent antennas: Spatial division multiple access. *Annual Review of Communications.* pp. 999-1002. Chicago, USA: International Engineering Consortium.

Enabling a portable Web (2000, March). *Portable Design (supplement edition).* Tulsa, USA: PennWell Corporation. pp. 3-34.

ETSI technical report No. TR 101 177 (1998, May). Retrieved from the World Wide Web: *http://webapp.etsi.org/pda/home.asp?wki_id=5941.*

Haine, J. (1998). HiperAccess: an access system for the information age. *Electronics & Communications Engineering Journal,* 10(5), 229-235.

Hart, C. (1998, October). Fixed wireless access: A market and system overview. *Electronics & Communications Engineering Journal, vol. 10, No. 5.* pp. 213-220.

Haykin, S., Litva J. & Shepherd T. J. (1993). Radar array processing. Heidelberg: Springer-Verlag Berlim.

Lee, W. C. Y. (1993). Mobile communications design fundamentals (2nd ed.). New York, USA: Wiley.

Liberti, Jr. J. C. & Rappaport, T. S. (1999). Smart antennas for wireless communications – IS 95 and third generation CDMA applications. New Jersey, USA: Prentice-Hall, Inc.

Marconi, G. (1931, September/October). Phenomena accompanying radio transmission. *The Marconi Review,* No. 32. pp. 1-8.

Mogensen, P. E., Pedersen, K. I., Leth-Espensen, P., Fleury, B., Frederiksen, F., Olesen, K. & Larsen, S. L. (1997, May). Preliminary measurement results from an adaptive antenna array testbed for GSM/UMTS. *Proceedings of the 47th IEEE Vehicular Technology Conference,* 3, 1592-1596.

Proakis, J. G. (1995). Digital communications. New York, USA: McGraw-Hill.

Roy, R.H. (1997, May). Spatial division multiple access technology and its application to wireless communication systems. *Proceedings of the 47th IEEE Vehicular Technology Conference,* 2, 730-734.

Winters, J. H. (1993, November). Signal acquisition and tracking with adaptive arrays in digital mobile radio system IS-54 with flat fading. *IEEE Transactions on Vehicular Technology,* 42(4), 377-384.

Yacoub, M. D. (1993). Foundations of mobile radio engineering. Boca Raton, USA: CRC Press.

ENDNOTES

[1] Maxwell, James Clerk-Scottish physicist. He developed the theory of the electromagnetic field on a mathematical basis (1873).
[2] Hertz, Heinrich Rudolf-German physicist. He demonstrated the radio wave propagation phenomenon in practice.
[3] The Nobel prize winner Guglielmo Marconi made his first radio transmission in 1895 in Bologna, Italy. He is acclaimed one of the fathers of radio.

Chapter VI

Virtual Private Networks: Enhancing the Impact of the Internet

Lance Pickett and Kathy S. Lassila
University of Southern Colorado, USA

INTRODUCTION

Virtual private networks (VPNs) have recently emerged on the forefront of network and Internet development. They combine easy remote access and the low cost of the Internet with the management and security benefits of a private network. VPNs are replacing expensive cabling, leased lines, and proprietary equipment while extending the reach of traditional enterprise networks to individual workers, remote office locations, and business partners. VPNs are the first technology to provide full support, in a cost-effective and secure manner, for the connectivity needed to fulfill the promise of the "virtual organization."

Access to corporate resources from anywhere at any time has become a mission-critical requirement for today's organizations (Tuomenoksa, 1998). VPNs represent a new paradigm for remote access that is destined to replace current fixed wide area network (WAN) technologies within the next decade (LaBorde, 1999). The many advantages of VPNs over private networks make their eventual widespread adoption inevitable. VPNs require less equipment and fewer lines than private networks and are typically less of a management burden. VPNs also provide tremendous flexibility, with a single connection for corporate local area network (LAN) and Internet access. The VPN infrastructure is affordable, has worldwide reach, is easily maintained, and is highly scalable.

VPN development has been driven by the rapid growth of Internet access, the critical mass of companies with a Web presence or conducting some form of e-commerce over the Internet, and the great concern for saving money. The objectives of this chapter are to provide a brief background on the development and technology of VPNs, describe several current VPN implementations and their impacts, and discuss key management issues surrounding the adoption and implementation of VPNs.

VPN DEVELOPMENT AND TECHNOLOGY

A virtual private network, or VPN, refers to "any system that sends encrypted private traffic across public Internet connections" (Gaskin, 1999, p. 23). VPNs, which vary in scope and technology, were initially introduced in the mid-1990s. Their popularity upon introduction was little to none. Organizations could not take full advantage of the Internet due to technical restrictions (i.e., modem speeds of 2400-9600 bps). Speed and efficiency on the VPN platform could not be realized. Eventually, as telephone monopolies vanished, government regulatory policies changed and technology-advanced Internet connections on regular phone lines at speeds as high as 56,600 BPS became possible. This innovation insured high speed and great efficiency for data transmission and, in turn, made VPN technology more attractive. Virtual private networks began to rise in popularity in early 1997. Worldwide expenditures for VPN services could hit $10 billion in 2001 and may be more than $29 billion in 2003 (LaBarba, 1999).

The key word in VPN is "virtual"–meaning the individual packets traversing the network can take any route to get from point A to point B. A packet is a group of fixed-length binary digits that include data and control information (Gaskin, 1999). The encrypted secure channel over which the packet travels is not a fixed pipe, but a dynamic, constantly shifting encrypted communications path that may take various routes to move data from a remote laptop to company headquarters (Schwartau, 1998). The Internet-based VPN consists of five key elements: IP security, tunneling protocols, Network Address Translation, authentication, and firewalls (LaBorde, 1998). These items are illustrated in Figure 1 and described below.

The Internet Engineering Task Force (IETF) created standards for IP (Internet protocol) security, named IPSec, to describe how Internet-based VPNs carry IP traffic securely (LaBorde, 1999). IPSec establishes essential services for protection of network resources, proof of identity, and privacy of information. IPSec provisions are robust and easy to use, offering authentic-

Figure 1. Key elements of a virtual private network

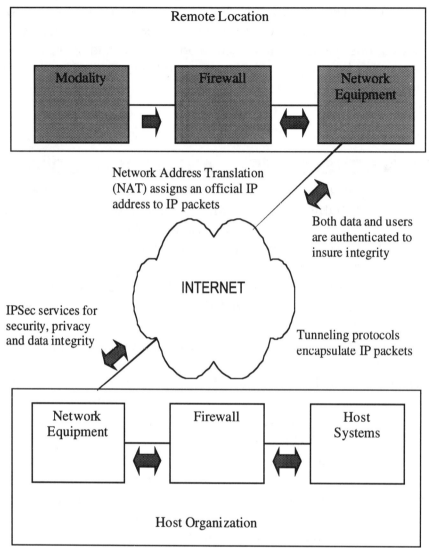

ity, integrity and confidentiality for all information that is either transmitted over or accessible from a VPN.

Tunneling protocols are another important element of a VPN. Tunnels are special "envelopes" that encapsulate packets (LaBorde, 1998). The encapsulated packets or envelopes are new IP packet headers that contain source and destination addresses. Tunneling provides a way to transmit private IP and non-IP applications, such as IPX, over the Internet. Security for tunneled packets is implemented using IPSec with a mode of encryption (LaBorde, 1998).

Network Address Translation (NAT) is a third element of a VPN. When a user wants access to the Internet or an Internet-based VPN, NAT temporarily assigns an official IP address in place of a user's private IP address. NAT only works on IP packets, while tunneling can support virtually any protocol, including IP. NAT alone does not provide a secure VPN, so organizations need to incorporate network access equipment that supports both NAT and IPSec. The use of IPSec, tunneling and NAT can eliminate conflicts and security holes that may lead to operating problems and security exposures.

Authentication of all users, clients, servers, and the data transmitted is necessary to achieve integrity for a VPN (LaBorde, 1998). Authentication uses digital signatures based on public-key cryptography to validate the "authenticity" of machines and ensures that the correct clients and servers are communicating in the Internet environment (Tittel, Madden & Smith, 1996). Relatively simple technologies exist for authenticating users, such as the Password Authentication Protocol or the Challenge-Handshake Authentication Protocol. Data authentication is more complicated since it simultaneously authenticates users. Both user and data authentication may be used together in a scenario where users are authenticated at log-on and all data transmissions are authenticated. Sophisticated authentication schemes may involve distributed client/server architectures where databases of VPN profiles act as servers and network access equipment are clients.

Firewalls provide a cost-effective VPN security control since every Internet interface typically has a firewall. A firewall is software that runs on the computer between a LAN and the outside world. Firewalls are designed to keep unwanted outside users from accessing a local area network (Tittel, Madden & Smith, 1996). The firewall's presence and its ability to monitor all traffic make it a logical focal point for the administration of security provisions (LaBorde, 1998). Firewalls can create a balance between protection and performance by using resource-intensive encryption schemes only when needed. Some firewalls can be configured remotely from a central site, thereby easing the maintenance and support burden.

Initially VPN components were offered by a wide variety of vendors and compatibility between technological components was a key issue for network managers during implementation decision-making. Advances by many vendor companies now combine different elements in a single VPN component, such as network routers that combine encryption, firewalls, and IP security in a single product. This integration will enhance the ongoing development and acceptance of VPNs.

CURRENT VPN IMPLEMENTATIONS

VPNs are being used extensively by major corporations that are realizing their cost benefits over dedicated connectivity and proprietary systems for their users, external suppliers, customers, and telecommuters. VPNs support one of three general configurations (Kovac, 1999): intranet links, remote access links, or extranet links. Each of these configurations is presented in Table 1 and described below. An example of each configuration is illustrated by a discussion of an actual VPN implementation.

Intranet VPNs link the main office network of an organization with remote or branch office networks. The organization typically maintains each end (source and destination) of the network. Kansas Bureau of Investigation (KBI) became the first state law enforcement agency in the United States to launch a VPN to exchange highly sensitive files with the state's police departments over the Internet. The VPN initially served 250 Kansas law enforcement offices with 4,000 employees; by the beginning of 2000, it was expected to reach 750 offices with 12,000 law enforcement officials. For the KBI, security features of a network were the most critical factor in deciding

Table 1. Three general VPN configurations

Configuration	Description	Example
Intranet	Links the main office network of an organization with remote or branch office networks.	Kansas Bureau of Investigation (KBI) exchanges highly sensitive files with 250-750 Kansas law enforcement offices via a VPN.
Remote Access	Links remote employees, travelers, or telecommuters to the corporate network.	East Coast college implements a VPN that allows up to 5,000 faculty and students simultaneous access to the campus network.
Extranet	Links organizational partners, suppliers, customers, and investors to share information.	Financial services firm uses VPN to allow brokers access to trading, portfolio management applications, and proprietary market research.

which network to develop. Additionally, the KBI determined that a private network to meet their needs would have cost $2.5 million more than the VPN (Korzeniowski, 1999).

Remote access VPNs have become increasingly important since they link remote employees, travelers or telecommuters with the corporate network. Forecasters predict that nearly 50% of the workforce will shift to part- or full-time telecommuting (Kovac, 1999). VPNs provide reliable connections to the corporate network for these employees. An example of a remote access VPN is found within an academic institution. An East Coast college developed a VPN to open its network resources to satellite campuses, telecommuters and local public schools (Greene, 1999). Until the VPN was set up late in 1998, the school's remote access system consisted of 32 modems used mainly for accessing e-mail and supporting terminal emulation. Thousands of remote users can be authenticated and granted restricted rights to the campus network with the VPN. The VPN technology will enable up to 5,000 simultaneous sessions with the help of an Altiga concentrator, which cost approximately $10,000 and took about an hour to install. At implementation, no single driving application acted as the catalyst for the VPN. The VPN was implemented with maximum flexibility in mind. Primary motivations included: allowing middle school kids to post academic questions to college professors with the development of a Web site for homework support; allowing faculty to work more at home; offering courses and degrees to students in remote locations that have no four-year colleges. At implementation, only a dozen staff members were using the VPN while other remote users were going through an existing firewall for access (Greene, 1999). The VPN is currently being evaluated to support a wider variety of applications, including filing electronic admissions applications, remote registration for classes and printing unofficial transcripts.

Another example of a remote access VPN is found in a medical software company. A company that develops and distributes medical records software and knowledge-based modules turned to a VPN as a remote access solution to support its sales force and remote employees by providing quick, easy access to the data-intensive corporate intranet. Security was among the top concern, and the VPN provided encryption to guarantee data safety during transit and authentication to avoid intrusion of unauthorized users. Other important criteria the company used in selecting a VPN included ease of use, high reliability, utilization of open standards, transparency at the application level, and straightforward installation and use (Aventail, 1999).

Extranet VPNs link organizational partners, suppliers, customers, and investors together to share and distribute information. These VPNs provide seamless connectivity across time zones and continents without investment in expensive dedicated communication networks. An example of an extranet VPN is found in the financial services industry. A financial services firm focused on transaction-based trade clearing replaced its manual trading process with an extranet VPN in an effort to keep clients satisfied while increasing transactions and improving trading quality. Brokers now have access to trading applications, portfolio management applications, proprietary market research, and other services over the highly secure, transparent, cost-effective connection.

IMPACT OF VPNS

By extending remote access to enterprise computing systems, VPN technologies have had, and are projected to have, numerous impacts on individual workers, work groups, organizations, and society. This section synthesizes information about the current impacts realized by VPN implementation and identifies the opportunities for enhancing these impacts in future implementations.

It is predicted that VPNs will experience explosive growth in the coming years for the simple reason that they save money (Hilton, 1999). VPNs are displacing direct-dial remote access in many corporate environments as modem pools fall out of favor (Greene, 1999). Network executives are tired of tending to hundreds or thousands of modems, dealing with the snarls of phone wires and troubleshooting remote user problems. With Internet-based VPNs, remote users no longer dial headquarters directly using an 800 or long-distance number. Instead, they dial a local ISP and use the Internet as a long-haul connection, thereby eliminating phone tolls. Corporate headquarters now manages only a single, fast Internet connection such as T-1, DSL, or ISDN line. By eliminating dial-up costs, VPNs save as much as 60% of line costs in many companies (Edwards, 1999). Cutting the staffs that maintain equipment and provide support for remote users generates further savings (Greene, 1999).

In addition to reducing the operating costs of corporate IT infrastructure, VPNs have the potential to significantly impact individuals. An East Coast hospital uses a VPN to provide physicians with access to patient records and test results (Duffy, 1998). Timely access to patient information is tied to improvements in the quality of patient care and increased levels of physician satisfaction.

By leveraging Internet economies of scale, VPNs offer the promise of reducing the cost of operating the critical corporate IT infrastructure. Combined with improved flexibility, security, and global reach facilitated by VPNs, additional benefits can be realized (Hilton, 1999). Examples of VPN implementations supporting access to organization resources from remote locations include a major window and door manufacturer, a financial services firm, and an Internet pharmacy (Wallace, 1999; Duffy, 1998; Aventail, 1999). In addition to cost savings, the VPN infrastructure can support revenue increases and customer goodwill. The positive results of providing employees and business partners in remote locations access to corporate resources are: higher levels of customer satisfaction, an increase in customer retention, an increase in employee retention, an increase in business transactions, reduction in data errors, and easy deployment of new applications and services.

KEY MANAGEMENT ISSUES OF VPN IMPLEMENTATION

A VPN is purported to make businesses more competitive, more secure and easier to access. It should not be applied as technology for technology's sake or be perceived as a "silver bullet" to resolve WAN issues. To determine a starting point for VPN development, each organization should review its strategic business plan. The key business processes, both current and proposed, that support the business plan should be identified. The information flows that feed these processes should be clearly specified, including the source and destinations of the information flows. This information should be used to determine the organization's present and projected secure communication requirements (Schwartau, 1998). If indicated by the systematic identification and analysis of the organization's communications needs, the development of the VPN should be pursued. The adoption of VPNs, as any technology, should be driven by business needs that support the organizational strategy and mission.

If it is determined that a VPN is appropriate to support business needs, one of the key issues confronting organizations and network managers is the classic "make or buy" decision–whether to invest in a corporate VPN or outsource the VPN to a network service provider. A third option, the shared control or hybrid model, combines in-house development with outsourcing. In 1998, approximately $126 million was spent on VPNs, with around 60% of expenditures made by companies implementing their own VPN. In the year 2002, it is predicted that $1.32 billion will be invested in VPNs, with approximately 79% of expenditures going to network service providers

(Source: Frost & Sullivan reported by Gaskin, 1999). A 1999 survey of WAN managers found that of companies with VPNs, only 20% had outsourced the service totally. Over 43% had implemented managed firewall or security solutions as a supplement to Internet access, while more than 26% were using VPN hardware and/or software (Edwards, 1999).

Network managers migrating to VPNs and public data networks need to know what systems to acquire and implement. Existing systems must be examined to determine how they can be used with remote access VPNs. Requirements for new routers, network access switches, and other network equipment must be defined. The exact equipment needs will depend on whether the VPN is implemented in-house, is outsourced, or is a hybrid of the two (LaBorde, 1998).

In-house VPN architecture places most of the responsibility with the organization; ISPs become mere "carriers" of ISP traffic. With an in-house VPN, the clients, servers, and/or their edge devices should be capable of providing all necessary network elements including the Internet interface, IP routing, tunneling, NAT, firewall, IPSec and other desired forms of security. A large number of vendors produce VPN products that add onto an existing network to VPN-enable it (Kovac, 1999). Using the same technologies, and in many cases the same infrastructure that companies have already established for Web and Internet access, VPNs create a "virtual," dynamic network that operates as reliably and securely as private data networks using low-cost and ubiquitous shared public data facilities (Kagan, 1997). Available products range from the simple to the complex and include VPN software, VPN hardware, and VPN-enabled software firewalls. No single vendor has all the solutions, and mixing and matching vendors and equipment is crucial to building an effective VPN (Snyder, 1999). To successfully build a VPN from an existing network, the organization needs an experienced network manager knowledgeable with firewalls, network design, and TCP/IP. While in-house architecture requires more effort, it also provides substantially greater control–a highly desirable factor with something as new as VPNs.

A second option and alternative to the design, installation and maintenance of an in-house VPN is outsourcing the VPN to a service provider (Kovac, 1999). Service providers offer all the characteristics of a VPN bundled into a service, including reliability, security, connectivity, value-added service and service level agreements. VPN service providers are typically either Internet service providers or network service providers. For outsourced VPNs, ISPs or carriers handle all details. These VPNs normally utilize the gateway mode of tunneling, which only requires that the edge device provide IP routing and firewall protection. Because no other special features are required, most existing systems can be used in a fully outsourced VPN.

If the outsourcing decision is made, selecting the right service provider becomes a key issue. The ideal approach for selecting a service provider should involve comparing the various offerings and a criterion of a VPN with the organization's unique needs. The main components of the VPN package must focus on: guaranteed security levels, dial-access availability for remote and itinerate users, ease of use, support, redundancy measures, network monitoring, and reporting capabilities. Most service level agreements (SLAs) or contracts consider these items as well as guaranteed accessibility, latency, and response time (Kovac, 1999). In addition, three levels of security–encryption, authentication, and protocol-should be included in the total VPN package. Ease of installation of on-site software and software implemented for remote users is also important. Remote users should gain access to the network in a simple and straightforward manner and should also be provided with 24-hour customer support. Throughput of information, service delay estimates, and a contingency plan in case of failure should also be clearly addressed by the vendor. If the VPN selected for outsourcing involves international locations, the problem of selecting a service provider becomes more complex. Most ISPs or network service providers do not have the capability of providing true end-to-end management.

Given the challenge of integrating required hardware and software from multiple vendors, outsourcing some or all of the VPN to a service provider is an attractive option. Outsourcing requires that less equipment be purchased and maintained, and the service provider takes responsibility for implementation and end-to-end management. Even so, most organizations still prefer to keep at least part of the VPN implementation in-house, if only to retain control of security and such functions as user authentication (Edwards, 1999). When VPN services use this shared control model, customers are able to perform certain network and configuration tasks. A shared control model allows customers to outsource VPN management to have similar types of control over their VPNs as they would with a self-managed approach (Yuan, 1999). The shared control or "hybrid" model combines in-house and outsourcing, made possible by the tunnel origination and termination in different places depending on the fundamental architecture of the VPN.

Scalability is another key factor in VPN decisions (Yuan, 1999). Most companies start out cautiously with VPNs, but should plan for rapid growth. The VPN may become the primary means of communication internally, as well as externally between buyers and suppliers. Only those systems that can scale to meet the growth in users and applications that migrate to the VPN should be selected.

Network managers must chose from among several protocols that specify how VPNs should be built. Network executives must determine which protocol best suits the need of their organizations. The Point-to-Point Tunneling Protocol (PPTP) and Internet Protocol Security (IPSec) protocols enable private sessions over the Internet and securely link remote users and organizational networks. PPTP was initially developed for dial-up VPNs and was meant to facilitate remote access usage by allowing users to dial in to local ISPs and tunnel into their organizational networks. The PPTP client is typically the Microsoft desktop and the encryption protocol is Microsoft Point-to-Point Encryption (MPPE), which supports 40-bit and 12-bit encryption. It is generally regarded as less secure than some encryption algorithms offered by IPSec, particularly 168-bit Triple-Data Encryption Standard (DES; Marcotte, 1999). On the other hand, IPSec was primarily intended for LAN-

Table 2. VPN Protocols

Protocol	Best For	Description	Strengths	Weaknesses
PPTP	Dial-Up VPN	Developed to use functionality of PPP to tunnel data across the Internet to the destination receiver in a secure fashion. One of the first protocols deployed for VPNs.	Can handle protocols other than IP. Works well with Windows NT.	Might become obsolete soon. Weak encryption and authentication technology. Not able to encrypt data in its own specifications.
IPSec	LAN-To-LAN VPN	Establishes essential services for protection of network resources, security, and authentication.	Provides various security services for IP protocols. Can support IPv4 and IPv6. Robust and easy to use. Standard for future VPN technology growth.	Gateways must have similar security policies. Performance issues.
Layer-2 Forwarding (L2F)	Dial-Up VPN	Like PPTP, developed to use functionality of PPP in order to tunnel data across the Internet to the destination receiver in a secure fashion.	Can work directly with other media, like frame-relay or ATM. Tunnels can support more than one connection.	Not able to encrypt data in its own specifications. Security issues.
Layer-2 Tunneling Protocol (L2TP)	Dial-Up VPN	L2TP is designed apparently to address the shortcomings of past protocols and become a standard for present and future VPN solutions.	Can handle protocols other than IP. Uses IPSec's encryption technology. Supports many authentication methods.	Not able to encrypt data in its own specifications. Security issues.

to-LAN secure tunneling between organizations. Its focus was providing secure connectivity with a remote office, another LAN or corporate supplier. It also supports connections between remote users and corporate networks. IPSec is generally regarded as superior to PPTP in strong encryption and data integrity.

Layer-2 Forwarding (L2F) and Layer-2 Tunneling Protocol (L2TP) are two more recently developed protocols (Nortel Networks, 2000). Similar to PPTP, L2F uses the functionality of PPP to tunnel the data across the Internet. L2F can work directly with other media, such as frame-relay or ATM, and tunnels can support more than one connection. L2TP was designed to address the shortcomings of past protocols and become the standard for present and future VPN development. Attributes of each of the four protocols are presented in Table 2.

A variety of other issues are involved in developing a successful VPN. First, interoperability continues to be a problem with VPN products (Snyder, 1999). No vendor has a single good solution for all environments and multivendor interoperability is a key to successful deployment. Second, the additional overhead of a VPN increases the size of IP packets. Adding encryption to the mix utilizes extra bandwidth, and if VPN capabilities are added to an existing firewall or server, performance becomes a major concern. Maintaining throughput will likely increase network costs. VPN performance varies greatly depending on the tunneling protocols and encryption schemes used between two points (Salmone, 1998).

FUTURE TRENDS

VPN is an emerging technology with huge growth potential. Current trends are toward standards-based solutions with IPSec as the core security technology (Yuan, 1999). Trends that should be considered when choosing and securing a VPN are:

- Firewalls and/or VPN devices: VPN gateways and firewalls have traditionally been separate devices. There is a growing trend to combine the two functions into a single appliance.
- Self-management vs. ISP-shared management: There is a growing trend for corporations to outsource their network services to service providers; the same is true for VPNs since ISPs have the infrastructure and expertise to manage complex VPNs. In the extranet scenario, ISPs are uniquely positioned to serve as a third party communications bridge for different corporations to connect for business transactions.
- Quality of service: Since different applications have different size and

delay sensitivities, corporations transferring mission-critical applications onto a VPN need a guaranteed QoS in terms of measurable metrics, specifically committed throughput or fixed maximum delay.

Network executives must consider a standards-based, scalable architecture with high performance when selecting a VPN solution. Comprehensive and proactive service level guarantees, excellent management and monitoring capabilities and strong consulting and integration services are needed in an ISP-managed service (Yuan, 1999).

As the evolution continues, the next generation of VPNs will become a collection of interwoven networks linking mobile workers, trading partners and suppliers to IP-enabled mission-critical applications (Gasparro, 1999). VPNs are destined to provide a platform for new business processes and services that will speed time to market, streamline manufacturing and production, and make it far easier to meet customer needs. Experts predict the first major component of the future VPN will be a directory server. This repository of end user profiles and network configuration data will allow a corporate network to be easily extended across the public infrastructure, further blurring the traditional lines between public and private networks in the process. This component will make it easier for end users to set up ad hoc VPN connections and integrate a variety of multimedia applications for transmission cross-country.

A significant trend in VPN hardware is the integration of VPN features such as quality-of-service and encryption features to enhance security. Routers that integrate high-speed routing with VPN tunneling, data encryption, security, firewall, advanced bandwidth management, and quality-of-service features by putting information about routing priorities on a tag outside of the encrypted packet are beginning to emerge. These routers have a very reasonable price tag starting at $12,000 and offer high performance for up to 250,000 connections. These integrated features are important to some organizations, such as hospitals, that want to provide doctors at remote locations with secure access to delay-sensitive, moving images such as sonograms (Thyfault, 1999).

Industry leaders identify the trends driving the recent interest in VPNs as performance guarantees and application hosting (Taylor & Taylor, 1999). Since the IPSec standard has addressed many security concerns, quality has become the main VPN issue for most organizations. Companies expect fault-tolerant, reliable, and robust performance and tools that allow them to measure the performance. Such quality-of-service guarantees offer a sound mechanism for the delivery of mission-critical applications. As one industry expert stated, "New standards are emerging to ensure that quality-of-service keeps improving, but the applications really put the value into VPN" (Taylor & Taylor, 1999, p. 94).

With the growth of services such as Internet telephony and video over IP, enterprise VPNs could become the vehicle for integrating all forms of traffic onto a single, scalable IP network that maximizes bandwidth efficiency and simplifies policy-based management (Edwards, 1999).

CONCLUSION

Virtual private networks are a fast and reliable network infrastructure solution to almost any organization. VPNs offer a full array of benefits for any organization–great cost savings, scalability, extranet capabilities, more manageable network infrastructure, strategic flexibility, and interconnectivity to branch offices and mobile associates. Technological advancement and a favorable regulatory environment have fueled the growth of VPNs. VPNs are clearly here to stay and will continue to support the ever-evolving virtual organization.

REFERENCES

Aventail Corporation. (1999). Financial services industry, Retrieved March 27, 1999, from the World Wide Web: http://www.aventail.com/index.phtml/ solutions/case_studies/financial.phtml.

Aventail Corporation. (1999). Health Care/MedicaLogic. Retrieved March 27, 1999, from the World Wide Web: http://www.aventail.com.

Duffy, T. (1998, May 18). Saving with VPNs. *Network World*, 52.

Edwards, M. (1999, August). It's a VPN thing. *Communications News*, 94-95.

Gaskin, J. (1999, May 3). Demand for VPNs creates new opportunities for ISPs. Internet World, 23.

Gasparro, D. (1999, September). Next-gen VPNs: The design challenge. Data Communications, 83-95.

Greene, T. (1999, November 8). The days of dial-up are numbered. Network World, 28.

Greene, T. (1999, March 1). Massachusetts college takes a class in VPNs. Network World, 15, 18.

Hilton, S. (1999, February). Adding the 'N' to virtual private networking. Telecommunications (Americas Edition), 43-44.

Kagan, R. (1997, May). The business case for virtual private networks.

Computer Technology Review, 12, 16.

Korzeniowski, P. (1999, March). A virtual private network lets Kansas law enforcement agents swap secure case files. VPNs, Retrieved March 27, 1999 from the World Wide Web: http://www.civic.com/march/civ-casestudy-3-1-99.html.

Kovac, R. (1999, April). VPN basics. Communications News, 14-17.

LaBarba, L. (1999, April 26). Learning to spell VPN. Telephony, 68.

LaBorde, D. (1998, February). Understanding and implementing effective VPN's. Computer Technology Review, 13-15.

Marcotte, G. (1999, May 31). Protocols serve up VPN security. Network World, 41.

Nortel Networks. (2000, June 8). Virtual Private Networks (VPNs) Tutorial. Web ProForums. Retrieved August 1, 2000 from the World Wide Web: http://www.webproforum.com/vpn/topic05.html.

Salmone, S. (1998, January 5). VPNs poised for takeoff: management issues still remain. Technology Information, 9.

Schwartau, W. (1998, April 6). What they never told you about VPNs. Network World, 35.

Snyder, J. (1999, May 24). Interoperability and standards are keys to VPN success. Network World, 41.

Taylor, B., Taylor D. (1999, September). IP VPNs: Ready to move up the value chain? Communications News, 94.

Thyfault, M. (1999, May 10). Safe, trustworthy VPNs. Informationweek, 20.

Tittel, E., Madden, M. & Smith, D. B. (1996). *Building WindowsNT web servers*. Foster City, CA: IDG Books Worldwide.

Tuomenoksa, M. (1998, November). Virtual private networks: The big payoff. Telecommunications (Americas Edition), 55-57.

Wallace, Bob. (1999, November 22). Andersen turns to VPNs to cut costs. Informationweek, 91.

Yuan, R. (1999, August). Securing your VPN. Telecommunications (Americas Edition), 47-50.

Part Two:

International Experiences in Telecommunications and Networking Infrastructure Development

Chapter VII

Global Competition and Cooperation in Standardization of Wireless Communications

Zixiang (Alex) Tan
Syracuse University, USA

INTRODUCTION

Since the first installation of cellular-based wireless public telephone systems back in the early 1980s, the number of wireless communication subscribers has seen dramatic and continuous growth across the world. The total global mobile subscribers grew from 11 million in 1990 to 472 million in 1999, according to ITU's (International Telecommunications Union) statistics. It is forecasted that global mobile subscribers will surpass global main line users (fixed phone lines) in the first decade of 21st century as shown in Figure 1 (ITU, 1999).

At the same time, the global Internet has emerged as a new and powerful communication medium with a combined function of communicating, broadcasting and publishing. Until recently, the Internet has been accessed mainly through the wireline telecommunications infrastructure. With the third generation (3G) of wireless communication systems focusing on their integration with the Internet, future wireless systems are projected as channels to offer

Figure 1.

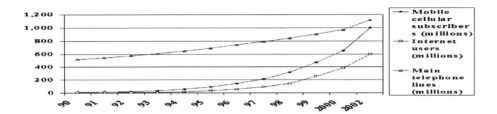

anytime and anywhere access to sophisticated information. This possibility serves to satisfy users' perceived economic and social needs for constant interaction with information. Wireless communication has been positioned as one of the strategic driving forces for the global telecommunications industry in the 21st century.

One of the challenges as well as opportunities for the success of wireless communication in the 21st century is the standardization that, in a simplified term, defines how specific technologies are used in a particular wireless communication system. Standardization goes beyond a technical decision made by engineers. This chapter first examines the history and the status of standardization in wireless communications in the world. Global cooperation and competition among different standards are then examined. Finally, the chapter analyzes ITU's efforts on the 3G standardization that aim to bring harmony among the world's wireless communication developers and providers.

BACKGROUND

Standards govern many aspects of human society, including economic activities, technology development and applications, psychological behavior, politics, and social life. According to the most prestigious standard organization, ISO (International Standards Organization), "Standards are documented agreements containing technical specifications or other precise criteria to be used consistently as rules, guidelines, or definitions of characteristics, to ensure that materials, products, processes and services are fit for their purpose" (ISO, 1995). Standardization, defined by ISO (1995), is the process of formulating and applying agreements reached among all concerned. The goal of standardization is to facilitate trade, exchange and technology transfer.

Applications and diffusion of wireless communications in the world are determined by many factors. Among them, standard setting is seen to "assume a pivotal role in determining the future evolutionary course of wireless systems" (Paetsch, 1993). Standard setting influences the market structure, technology evolution, and realization of economies of scale. More importantly, standard setting determines if a compatible and universal wireless communications system can be developed.

Standardization per se is an activity involving cooperation among various players. However, standardization has long been recognized as an important component in competition that reaches beyond a technical agreement. Both firms and nations have used it to realize their economic and political goals. The literature has concentrated more on the economic side of the strategic significance of standardization for firms (Berg, 1987; Besen & Saloner, 1989; Farrell & Saloner, 1985, 1986; Gabel, 1987; Greenstein, 1993; Sherif & Sparrell, 1992). Companies compete to have their technologies set the standard and to get the "bandwagon" rolling by engaging in strategic activities (Farrell & Saloner, 1985). Greenstein (1993) argues that a standard may not be adopted widely if most potential users are lukewarm about it due to technical uncertainty and other reasons. However, bandwagons may grow remarkably and quickly once the adoption base for the standard reaches a certain level to justify investments by potential adopters who have delayed making commitments in the early stage.

Several researchers have studied political influences on standardization by national governments (Crane, 1979; Lecraw, 1987; Pelkmans & Beuter, 1987). In her study on the French color TV standard, Crane (1979) concluded that the political ambitions of maintaining France's global market share and cultural influence were the driving forces for developing the French TV standard. Today, national or regional involvement in standardization has been even more pervasive in telecommunications, which combines economic interests closely with nations' or regions' industrial policies and other political goals (Hawkins, 1992; Sung, 1993). Sung (1993) argues that "the foremost obstacle to the international standard, FPLMTS (i.e., renamed as 3G standards, IMT-2000), is a political one: nations and regions have imposed industrial policy toward mobile communications, which is now deemed a strategic component of the general telecommunications policy."

Competition as well as cooperation among firms and nations has had significant implications on the standardization in wireless communications across the world. Although many standards have been developed and used in wireless communication systems, standardization activities have been mainly centered on three regions-US/North America, Europe, Japan/Asia. The ITU is now involved in the standard development of the 3G after having failed to participate in the first- and second-generation standardization. There has been cooperation in the processes of developing standards such as the case of promoting the GSM as a Pan-European standard and extending its coverage to the rest of the world. Another example is the current cooperative effort among major global players to work out a feasible IMT-2000 standard coordinated by the ITU. However, different standards are still competing with each other for the global market share and for the leadership position in the technology.

THREE GENERATIONS OF STANDARDIZATION IN GLOBAL WIRELESS COMMUNICATIONS

Up until now, wireless standardization activities can be divided into three generations. The first-generation (1G) standards were developed and installed in the early 1980s. All of the 1G standards used analog technology. Frequency division multiple access (FDMA) technology was adopted to create multiple radio channels within a certain frequency spectrum. American Mobile Phone System (AMPS), Nordic Mobile Telephone 900 (NMT900), and Total Access Communication System (TACS) were among the first-generation standards.

The second-generation (2G) standards, developed and installed in the early 1990s, shifted to digital technology from analog technology. Time division multiple access (TDMA) and code division multiple access (CDMA) technologies were utilized to replace the previous FDMA technology, together with other technology improvements. This technology advance represented a significant improvement in system capacity, service quality, and information security among other things. Global System for Mobile (GSM), US TDMA, and US CDMA are among the 2G standards.

The third-generation standards are currently in the process of development. One of the most significant standards is the International Mobile Telephone 2000 (IMT-2000) by the International Telecommunications Union (ITU). The major improvements targeted by the 3G standards include better compatibility among different access technologies and a larger bandwidth for high-speed data/Internet communication. Almost all the standards are based on CDMA technology. The three generations of standards are summarized in Table 1.

Table 1. The three generations of standards

	1G	2G	3G
The US	AMPS	IS-54 (TDMA), IS-95 (CDMA)	ITU's IMT-2000, co-existing with many other standards in the world.
European Union	NMT 450, NMT 900, TACS, C450, Radiocom 2000, and RTMS.	GSM	
Japan	NTT standard, JTACS/NTACS	JDC, PHS	

The First-Generation Standardization

The 1G standardization activities are nation oriented. They were developed by the United States, several European countries, and Japan.

1G Standards in the US

In the United States, the "cellular" concept and the frequency reuse in small cells were originated from AT&T's Bell Laboratory in 1947 (McDonald, 1979), which has provided a fundamental basis for all the wireless systems in the world. AT&T then developed a new public mobile phone system called AMPS (American Mobile Phone Systems), which fulfilled the following objectives.

i)   Large subscriber capacity
ii)   Efficient use of spectrum
iii)   Nationwide compatibility
iv)   Widespread availability
v)   Adaptability to traffic density
vi)   Service to vehicles and to portables
vii)   Regular telephone service and special services, including "dispatch"
viii) "Telephone" quality of service
ix)   Affordability

AMPS was technically ready to roll out to the market in the early 1970s. The commercialization process was delayed by frequency allocation, regulatory policy, and industry politics. The first developmental system trial was granted in 1977 and actually was conducted by Illinois Bell in Chicago in 1978. Subsequently, the Chicago cellular system began the first AMPS commercial operation by AT&T on October 13, 1983.

Despite the delay of the service introduction, AMPS was the only standard for the first-generation US public mobile system. Two major factors made it possible. First, only AT&T had conducted serious standards setting activities until the early 1980s. The AMPS was thus the only standard commercially available. No competing standards existed. This was a perfect result of AT&T's monopoly in standards setting. Secondly, the FCC's licensing process specified AMPS as the unified, nationwide standard.

1G Standards in Europe

The first-generation public mobile systems in Europe were developed and widely installed in the early 1980s. The first European analog system, NMT450 (Nordic Mobile Phone 450), was developed in Sweden. The four continental Nordic countries (Denmark, Finland, Norway and Sweden) first introduced a common 450 MHz cellular system in 1981-2. Other European countries followed suit rapidly. By 1985, all European countries except Greece and Portugal had cellular phone services in operation.

Europe's analog cellular systems enjoyed a rapid growth rate. By 1990, there were already 3 million subscribers in total. However, incompatible technical standards were utilized. There were in total six major incompatible standards in Europe-NMT 450, NMT 900, TACS, C450, Radiocom 2000 and RTMS.

NMT450 and NMT900 were developed and first used in the Nordic countries. They were the most widely adopted standards in Europe by 1990. In addition to Finland, Norway and Sweden, Denmark, Netherlands, Belgium and Luxenburg also adopted NMT system. An international roaming agreement was reached among them to allow subscribers to use their phone sets in the other countries.

However, other major European telecommunications markets adopted their own standards. TACS (Total Access Communication System) is a British standard, which was a modified version of the US AMPS system. It was the only official standard in the UK. By 1990 TACS had gained a substantial market share outside Britain, including Ireland, Greece, and Spain. TACS systems had also been adopted in many countries outside Europe, including Hong Kong, Singapore, and China. Germany developed its own C450 standard. C450 was exported to Austria and Portugal. However, its subscriber pool was relatively small in 1990, compared with the TACS and NMT systems. Radiocom 2000 was designed in France. It was used only in France. RTMS is an Italian standard. RTMS's significance was diminished when Italy bought a TACS system from Britain in 1990.

The European market was fragmented by incompatible standards. Service stopped at a nation's borders because of this incompatibility. With the incompatible standards in use, the roaming function could only be engaged in a few limited geographical areas where the same standards were adopted, such as above mentioned Nordic-Benelux countries, and the possible roaming between the UK and Ireland. In addition, European manufacturers had not realized a Europe-wide economy of scale, which hindered a rapid decrease in equipment prices. Efforts in marketing, maintenance services, and research and development could not be coordinated in a European level. Europeans viewed their fragmented home market as a serious obstacle in competing with US and Japanese firms efficiently and effectively in the global market.

1G Standards in Japan

Japan's first analog public mobile standard was designed and developed by NTT in the late 1970s. The NTT system was put into service by the then monopoly, NTT Mobile Communications Network, in 1979. This made Japan the pioneer in applying cellular technologies for public mobile services.

After the introduction of Japan's new telecommunications laws in April 1985, the MPT licensed two new public mobile service providers, IDO and DDI, in 1987. DDI introduced the JTACS/NTACS standard adopted from the British TACS standard. While having initially deployed the NTT high capacity system, IDO also shifted to the NTACS standard. DDI and IDO interconnected with each other to form a national roaming network based on the JTACS/NTACS standard, which directly competed with the NTT's national network (Nishuilleabhain & Carrel, 1994).

The coexistence of two incompatible standards had not hindered national roaming for either of the two systems in Japan. However, it was blamed for diminishing the economies of scale of domestic equipment vendors (USITC, 1993). In addition, none of the Japanese analog standards was adopted by other operators outside Japan. This had seriously handicapped the export efforts by Japanese equipment manufacturers. The reasons for this failure included the closed Japanese (actually it was the NTT's standard-setting in this case) standardization process and the Japanese government's weak efforts in promoting the standards in overseas markets.

The Second-Generation Standardization

The second generation of standardization continued to concentrate in the United States, the European nations, and Japan. However, new models emerged to replace the old ones of the first generation. The important contributing factors during the second-generation standardization included the global trend toward telecommunications liberalization and deregulation, changing national policy on standards, and the changing economic and political environment as well as advances in technology.

2G Standards in the US

In the United States, several changes occurred in the new standardization era. After its 1984 divestiture, AT&T was literally dismantled from its monopoly both in telecom services and in standards setting (Besen & Saloner, 1989; Wallenstein, 1990). The FCC gradually withdrew from its involvement in most standards setting activities in the early 1980s. The FCC decided not to specify any mandatory standard for the second-generation public mobile phone systems. This was in recognition of the technological dynamics and the FCC's limited resources and expertise. At the same time, standards setting fell into the hands of industry associations such as TIA (Telecommunications Industry Association) and CTIA (Cellular Telephone Industry Association), which produced consensus-based, but often multiple, voluntary standards.

Starting from 1985, CTIA launched a systematic evaluation of various technological alternatives. This was endorsed by cellular operators and major equipment manufacturers including Motorola, AT&T, Nortel, Ericsson, and IMM. TDMA, CDMA, N-AMPS, and E-TDMA were among the candidates. In 1989, CTIA members voted TDMA as the standard for the 2G mobile systems mainly based on its commercial availability. CTIA then requested the EIA/TIA to set up the detailed technical specifications for the TDMA standard.

In April 1992, EIA/TIA published the TDMA standard as IS-54 and validation tests were undertaken in 1991. However, the deployment of TDMA proceeded slowly. CDMA, which was considered too far from commercial deployment in the early 1990s, has rapidly and successfully caught up. Since its initial discussion with PacTel in February 1989, Qualcomm successfully persuaded CTIA to bring the CDMA technology to EIA/TIA. In July 1993, EIA/TIA published its CDMA standard as IS-95. Standardization in the US wireless industry shifted from its 1G of a single standard approach to its 2G of multiple, competitive standards.

2G Standards in Europe

In Europe, standardization moved to an integrated and converged approach in the second generation from the fragmented approach of the first generation. A scenario of a Pan-European mobile telephone system was first proposed by five PTT Administrations from the Netherlands, Denmark, Finland, Norway and Sweden in 1982 (Cattaneo, 1994). The proposal was accepted. The study group GSM (Group Special Mobile) was formed to study the specifications of a possible Pan-European standard in the same year. Because of the conflicts and vested interests among European nations and major corporations, there was not much progress until 1987.

A GSM meeting in February 1987 succeeded in an agreement on the outline of a basic GSM standard. This resulted in a balanced standard that could be acceptable to all concerned interest groups. It was achieved through intensive consultation and coordination with German and French PTTs. They finally agreed to make the compromise: adopting a digital instead of an analog technology as the pan-European standard. However, it was a new digital standard but not Alcatel-SEL's proprietary one which was favorable to the German and French PTTs.

On the political side, in May 1987 ministries from the four largest markets-France, Germany, Italy, and the UK-agreed to accept the basic GSM standard proposed by the GSM working group. The four countries actually drafted a memorandum of understanding (MoU) to commit themselves to the elaboration and deployment of the GSM standard. The MoU laid down a series of milestones for the remaining technical and regulatory issues. It also planned to start commercial GSM services in June 1991. By September 1987, 13 other countries joined the effort, increasing the signatory countries of the MoU to 17. Meanwhile, the EC used its political influence on its member countries to guarantee GSM's success. On June 25, 1987, EC's Council of Ministers adopted a recommendation and a directive that played a crucial role for Europe to achieve consensus agreement about public mobile communication.

GSM began its implementation stage in 1988 after the above-mentioned key events in 1987. The detailed technical specifications were developed by the GSM working group. The GSM system finally hit the market in 1992. By 1995, there were already 50 networks in operation in the world. This achievement puts an end to the incompatible standards in Europe. The European public mobile market has evolved to a single and unified standard.

2G Standards in Japan

In Japan, the development of a 2G standard was used by the Japanese government as an opportunity to support its equipment manufacturers to compete in the overseas markets. The MPT decided to apply an open standardization process when initiating the development of a single Japanese digital standard in 1989. Foreign manufacturers such as Ericsson, Motorola, and AT&T were permitted to take part in the standard setting process. The new digital standard, the Japanese Digital Cellular (JDC), was approved by the MPT in 1991 (Padgett et al., 1995). Strategies were carried out to promote the JDC standard. Foreign manufacturers including Ericsson and Motorola were invited to market the JDC systems in Japan's neighboring Asian countries, together with Japanese partners. The JDC was renamed Pacific

Digital Cellular (PDC) in 1993, which strongly suggested Japan's ambition to promote its domestic standard as a regional standard among Pacific countries.

In 1989, the MPT issued a report to address the standard for the new portable telephone systems. It has developed into today's Personal Handyphone System (PHS). PHS is basically a digital cordless phone standard. Like the Digital European Cordless Telephone (DECT) system, PHS is designed for low cost and flexible environments. The PHS standard also uses TDMA access method and time division duplexing (TDD) technology. Unlike the traditional cordless phone systems, the PHS system is projected to be both for home and office uses and for public operations. The trial tests for the PHS standard were conducted in several sites in 1995. The services were launched in 1996 (Okinaka, 1996).

The Third-Generation Standardization

3G History

While the first two generations of standardization were dominated by the US, the European Union, and Japan, ITU has taken a leadership role in the third-generation standardization. ITU started to develop the 3G global standard, Future Public Land Mobile Telecommunication Systems (FPLMTS), with the establishment of its Interim Working Party 8/13 (IWP 8/13) by Decision 69 in 1985. The activities were intensified after the 2 GHz spectrum was identified for 3G global wireless communications at the 1992 World Administrative Radio Conference (WARC-92). FPLMTS are aimed at serving as a global standard. A new name, International Mobile Telecommunications-2000 (IMT-2000), has been adopted because of the difficulty in pronouncing the acronym FPLMTS. The IMT-2000 will begin to be deployed around the world in year 2000.

Compared with the first two generations of wireless standards, the IMT-2000 has two major features (a more detailed list of IMT-2000's key features is available at http://www.itu.int/imt/7_faqs/index.htm#Howdoes). IMT-2000 systems will shift away from the voice-dominated application and provide high-speed wireless access to data communications and Internet applications. Most IMT-2000 systems will also adopt CDMA technology. More significantly, IMT-2000 will create a globally compatible environment. The first two generations of standardization left the world with multiple competitive standards that are often incompatible. ITU's IMT-2000 is aimed at unifying the diverse systems we have today into a wireless infrastructure that will be able to provide a wide range of wireless services. It is built to

Figure 2. Potential standards covered by the IMT-2000

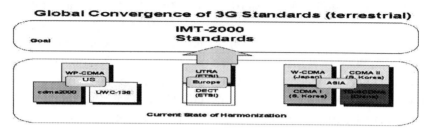

Source: AT&T

Table 2. Identified spectrum by WARC-92 and WARC-2000

Bands identified at WARC-92	Spectrum at 2 GHz: • 1,885 - 2,025 MHz • 2,110 - 2,200 MHz
Bands identified at WARC-2000	Spectrum below 1 GHz: 806-960 MHz Spectrum above 1 GHz: • 1.7 GHz (1,710–1,885 MHz) • 2.5 GHz (2,500–2,690 MHz)
Implementation principles agreed at WARC-2000	"The (WARC-2000) decision provides for a number of bands, available on a global basis for countries wishing to implement IMT-2000. Making use of existing mobile and mobile-satellite frequency allocations, the agreement also provides for a high degree of flexibility to allow operators to migrate towards IMT-2000 according to market and other national considerations. At the same time it does not preclude the use of these bands for other types of mobile applications or by other services to which these bands are allocated-a key factor that enabled the consensus to be reached. While the decision of the Conference globally provides for the licensing and manufacturing of IMT-2000 in the identified bands on a globally harmonized basis, each country will decide on the timing of availability at the national level according to need." (ITU, 2000)

accommodate multiple standards developed around the world.

3G Recent Developments

Currently, ITU is working with equipment manufacturers and service providers from different countries on the implementation of the IMT-2000 standard. IMT-2000 will select its standards from a group of candidates shown in Figure 2. All the standards will conform to the IMT radio interfaces standards (RSPC, which is available at http://www.itu.int/imt/2_rad_devt/rspc/final_approval/index.html) approved by the ITU's Radio Assembly (RA–2000) in May 2000.

Spectrum assignment for the IMT-2000 was first decided by WARC-92, when two bands in the 2 GHz neighborhood (1,885 – 2,025 MHz and 2,110 – 2,200 MHz) were identified for IMT-2000 globally. In May 2000, WARC-2000 further identified three extra bands for the implementation of IMT-2000 globally and agreed on implementation principles. See Table 2.

With the approval of IMT radio interface standards and the assignment of extra spectrum bands for IMT-2000, IMT-2000 has positioned itself as a solid foundation for global 3G standards.

COMPARISONS, IMPLICATIONS, AND TRENDS

The Dominance and Difference of Institutional Standards Setting

While general market, institution, and government standard setting mechanisms are all deployed to develop standards, the global wireless communications industry has been dominated by institutional standard setting. The US, Europe, Japan, and the ITU all rely on institutions/committees to set standards for their public mobile communication systems. In the US, the Telecommunications Industry Association (TIA) has the sole responsibility for its 2G standards. Current standard development for the 3G systems is carried out by the Joint Technical Committee (JTC) between TIA and Committee T1. European Telecommunications Standard Institute (ETSI) has been conducting standard setting both for the 2G Pan-European GSM standard and for the 3G Universal Mobile Telecommunications System (UMTS) standard. The Japanese standard setting is organized by two committees, the Telecommunications Technology Committee (TTC) and the Research and Development Center for Radio System (RCR). ITU has special working groups to develop its IMT-2000 standards for the global 3G wireless systems.

Standard setting activities, therefore, have some common attributes among the US, Europe, Japan, and the ITU. Like other institutional standardization processes, they all facilitate better communication among market participants in the relevant regions. They have adopted the principle of a "consensus" decision-making process. However, they are different in many aspects mainly because of the different government or institutional policies toward standardization, which leads to rather different solutions.

The situation in the US could be best described as a market-oriented institutional process. The standard committees solicit proposals from the industry. They then work out the detailed specifications. After reaching a certain level of consensus among the participants, standards are published for voluntary adoption. However, standard committees do not recommend which is the right or wrong standard and which is technically superior or inferior. It is a forum for participants to exchange information and work out the detailed specifications. This has been proved to be an efficient process to work out standards quickly when several factors are extremely dynamic, such as the rapidly changing technologies and the vested interest groups. Meanwhile, this often leads to several standards that compete among each other. This is evident in the past and current US wireless standards setting.

The actual standardization activities in Europe could be described as a government-intervened institutional process. The focal point of all the European wireless standard setting activities is the European Telecommunications Standard Institute (ETSI), created in 1988 specifically to integrate the standard efforts of EU member nations. ETSI has successfully functioned as an information exchange forum in Europe. It has drawn broad memberships including government agencies, operators, manufacturers, and user groups of all member nations and some non-EU member nations. Most importantly, ETSI's technical output, standards, are often supported by the European Union's political and economic policies when there is a threat to challenge a Pan-European standard. The success of the GSM is a perfect example in which the EU facilitated and promoted the signature of the memorandum of understanding (MoU) as well as passing relevant recommendations and directives. The involvement of EU's coordination among member governments and individual players has certainly prevented the long waiting time and possible multiple standard solution of ETSI's standard setting efforts.

The case in Japan could be described as a government-guided institutional process. Standardization activities for Japan's public mobile systems are conducted by two institutions, TTC and RCR. They also rely on voting to decide the final standards. However, the Japanese government plays a profound role in the standard setting process. The request for standards may come from operators and manufacturers; however, the official initiation of starting the standard setting is often launched by the Japanese MPT (Ministry of Posts and Telecommunications). More importantly, the final standards adopted by operators have to be approved by the MPT. What the TTC and RCR have done are only the detailed technical specifications of relevant standards. The institutions are not in a position to make decisions on those strategic issues such as single or multiple standard solution and compatibility with international standards.

The ITU's standardization could be summarized as a globally compromised institutional process. ITU missed its opportunity to develop any 1G and 2G wireless standards. Its 3G standard, IMT-2000, has been one of its priority activities in recent years. In 1985, the Interim Working Party 8/13 (IWP 8/13) was established to be in charge of the 3G standardization. Realizing the keen competition among standards developed by different nations and the difficulty, if not impossibility, of agreeing on a single global standard, ITU has dropped its traditional approach of trying to specify a single global standard. Instead, ITU's IMT-2000 would create a globally compatible environment aimed at unifying the diverse and competing systems into a wireless infrastructure that would be able to provide a wide range of wireless services. It is built to accommodate multiple standards developed around the world. This is obviously a compromise on the competitive 3G standards that are supported and promoted by different nations and interest groups.

Impacts on Service Provision

The outcome of different standardizations in the US, Europe, and Japan has had very different implications on the service provisions in the world (Kano, 2000). In the United States, wireless communication is filled with the chaos, confusion, and delay. It is moving slowly toward the 2G systems. Many of US subscribers are 1G, AMPS, users. The ratio of 2G system users is relatively low, compared with Europe and Japan.

Many factors contributed to the delay, including the unavailability of dual-mode handsets and the high penetration rate of the analog mobile infrastructure. However, the delay has been widely blamed on the result of TDMA vs CDMA standard competition (USITC, 1993; OTA, 1995). TDMA technology is mature, but technically inferior. CDMA is still in the trial stage, but has many technical improvements such as higher capacity and advanced services. Operators and users are not certain which standard will win in the market. Operators are worried about choosing a losing standard, which would cost them a large sum of investment and a potential loss of market share. Manufacturers are not certain to which standard they should commit given the unclear business plans of service operators. Their general strategies are to position themselves as ready to produce both CDMA and TDMA equipment. This situation is even more confusing to ordinary customers, given their relatively poor technical understanding of the competition between TDMA and CDMA standards.

In Europe we have seen a rapid expansion of the 2G wireless systems pushed by the unified single European standard, GSM. GSM systems were installed in most European countries starting from 1992. Great progress was achieved within only three to four years. According to a survey by Financial Times (1995), the number of digital GSM system networks caught up with that of 1G analog networks in Western Europe by the middle of 1995.

A single unified Pan-European standard, GSM, is the most significant factor to the service expansion, although the lower penetration rate in countries other than the UK and the Scandinavian countries does provide a window of opportunity. Service operators, equipment manufacturers, and users are all certain that everyone is going to use the same standard, GSM. Their business plans for GSM applications are not hampered, to any extent, by the concerns on the future of the standard because there is no rival 2G standard in Europe.

In Japan, the single standard created moderate growth. Japan has developed his own digital standard, PDC (Pacific Digital Cellular), which is independent of European and US standards. PDC is the single approved 2G standard in the Japanese market although another 2.5G standard, Personal Handyphone system, joined the market later. Three operators were licensed by the Japanese MPT to offer PDC services in early 1992. Two more licensees were added later. The five operators served 250,000 users by the end of 1994. PDC services are "gaining popularity due to high quality, high security, and a longer handset battery life" (Padgett, et al., 1995). Apparently, a single standard is promoting, instead of postponing, the expansion of 2G wireless services in Japan.

Impacts on Global Competition

As Funk (1998) argues, the outcome of standardization in different regions is closely related to the success and failure of such standards in the global market. Equipment export is a complicated process, which is determined by many factors including economic, political, and cultural ties as well as the product standards. The precondition of successful equipment exportation is to export the standards first. Standard-adopting countries have their own considerations when choosing a national standard or standards. Theoretical work has illustrated that "bandwagon" is one of the most profound phenomena in standard adoption (Greenstein, 1993). Once a standard reaches a certain installation base, latecomers tend to join the bandwagon. Research has also revealed the role of political, cultural, and even geographic ties in exporting standards (USITC, 1993).

A solid installed base is the first step to start the bandwagon. The base is a test bed for the technology and for the scale of production. This often happens in the domestic market. The US has successfully established the

AMPS standard, based on the US market. Europe has set up the momentum for its GSM standard by coordinately introducing the GSM services across Europe. Such efforts often lead to a successful standard export to other nations.

Except for the United States, Japan, and many European nations, other countries in the world have adopted the standards from the three regions. This is true both for the 1G analog systems and for the 2G digital systems. For the 1G systems, the US AMPS standard has fully occupied the Latin American/Caribbean markets and European standards have controlled the Eastern European/NIS (Newly Independent States) countries. The Africa/Middle East area is dominated by the European standards with a few countries using the US AMPS standard. The Asia-Pacific is a fully mixed area where the AMPS standard has been adopted in almost all the countries. Meanwhile, European standards have also been deployed in many countries. Japanese standards have not been adopted by any country except Japan itself. This process has reflected the influence of political, economic, cultural, and geographic factors in shaping standard adoption and global marketing competition.

As the services moved from 1G to 2G systems in the world, the results of domestic approaches and government policies in the US, Europe, and Japan have influenced the evolution of the technology in other countries. The GSM standard has enjoyed success in standard adoption. Almost all the previous European standards users have chosen GSM as their 2G standard. More importantly, many previous AMPS users such as Australia and New Zealand have shifted to choosing GSM as their 2G standard. Other countries such as India, which did not have analog services, have directly jumped to GSM standard.

On the other hand, only a few previous AMPS users have decided to continue their support of US standards, meaning using the US TDMA or CDMA standards. Many other AMPS users, especially in Latin America, have also committed to the GSM standard. There is no previous European standards user who has switched to US 2G standards. The Japanese 2G standard has failed to be adopted outside Japan.

Apparently, the EU's single standard policy has fulfilled one of its goals, to compete successfully with the US and Japan in the global market. As the first available 2G standard in the world and with a solid installed base in EU member nations, the GSM standard has successfully created the bandwagon as a mature and tested commercial technology and with a solid installed base.

The US digital standards suffer from their domestic competition. The confusion and delayed installation in the market have demonstrated that US operators themselves are not certain which one is the better standard between the TDMA and CDMA standards. The significant installed bases for the US standards have not been established. This situation has made it difficult to persuade other countries to adopt US digital standards although the CDMA standard promises some technical advantages over the European GSM standard.

IMT-2000: The Global Hope

While the first two generations of global standardization of wireless systems left us with a fragmented wireless world, several incompatible standards still compete in the global market. ITU's IMT-2000 is expected to unify the incompatible global wireless communication systems. IMT-2000 has actually adopted a compromised approach that is aimed at creating a wireless infrastructure. Many competitive standards developed by nations and multinational corporations will coexist under the umbrella of IMT-2000. Given this structure, the competition for global standardization will certainly continue. What IMT-2000 could bring to the world is a competition within a compatible environment.

CONCLUSIONS

Europe, the US, and Japan have adopted different standardization policies toward their public mobile systems. With the completion of standards for 2G systems and the move to 3G standards, the gains and losses of the different approaches have become visible.

The European Union has successfully aided Europe's standard body, ETSI, in converging six incompatible 1G standards into a single European 2G standard. The immediate implication is a unified European market-a single standard is adopted and roaming is possible throughout Europe. European manufacturers have gained the advantages of economy of scale. Users have access to a pan-European service by using a single mobile terminal. In addition, many developing countries outside Europe have also adopted the European standard. This is consistent with what is explained by the theory of "bandwagon" effects. Europe has certainly obtained the leading global position by developing a pan-European standard. However, the European standard suffers the danger of choosing an inferior technology, compared with the US's CDMA technology. European firms have been improving their standard by adding more features. In addition, its large installation base in the world might protect its market share from being taken over by other standards.

The US market has seen at least two competitive 2G standards. More standards are possible for the 3G systems. The emergence of competing standards is obviously an inevitable result of the government's laissez-faire policy and the existence of competing interest groups. It usually takes some time for the competition to run its course. The market will then choose its winner. Therefore, the delay of service introduction, the confusion, and the chaos in the domestic market are all not surprising to policy makers. However, the laissez-faire policy has a direct impact on US firms' competitive capability in the global market. Most developing countries can not afford to wait for the results of market competition in the US. With the delayed system installation and without a national champion, US 2G standards lost their popularity in the world market. Most developing countries have joined the bandwagon to adopt the European 2G standard. However, the competition in the US has created an opportunity for its CDMA standard to emerge and grow. The world has shifted to CDMA technology for almost all 3G standards. It is unclear whether the US CDMA standards will take over the global market since other nations have also developed their own CDMA standards.

Japan has continued its tradition of close government intervention in standardization. Japan's Ministry of Posts and Telecommunications (MPT) has, in fact, controlled the standardization process through the involvement of its Telecommunication Technology Committee (TTC). Japanese 1G and 2G standards have not been adopted by any nation other than Japan itself. However, the Japanese government changed its policy after realizing that a global single standard is not a near future reality. A task force has been established to promote Japan's new standard, the Personal Handyphone System (PHS). An important part of Japan's future standardization policy is the claim to promote Japan's standards to developing countries and to promote ITU's standards.

For developing countries, the wait-and-see attitude has served as an interim policy at various stages in each country. Most of them have joined the bandwagon by adopting the European 2G standard when they could no longer wait. Another interesting approach is to adopt multiple standards from Europe and the US in order to take advantage of their relevant benefits.

The future will continue to see global competition and cooperation in standardization for global wireless communication systems. The involvement of the ITU through its IMT-2000 will possibly create a unifying global wireless infrastructure. This could be a base for global cooperation. But the US, Europe, Japan, and other countries all have their political and economic rationales for continuing their competition in standardization.

Perhaps the most significant issue for the future of wireless standardization is closely related to the general debate of standardization versus de-standardization (or multiple standards). There is a strong belief, especially among the community of engineers, that a single, uniform global standard is a prerequisite for the expansion of public mobile services. The former president of AT&T's Bell Labs has argued that "as we contemplate options for this next generation of technology (digital cellular), we have the lesson of the current generation and how it has grown and developed. The major growing pain, of course, has been the proliferation and divergence of standards. We now have the opportunity to avoid this problem and to provide future generations of customers with universal connectivity-all by working together to agree on worldwide uniform cellular standards" (Ross, 1986). This argument has called for an extreme standardization of worldwide public mobile systems.

On the opposite side is the argument for de-standardization. This school of thought has argued that a single global standard is the manufacturers' idea to reduce the product costs, but with many other drawbacks. It is an out-of-date concept that could not be applied to today's environment. The success of the computer industry is often cited to support this argument. De-standardization is believed to have contributed to the rapid price reduction and technology advancement in the computer industry. Custom tailoring rather than standardized mass production is seen as the trend of modern society. An extreme voice of this school is that of Mr. Hiroshi Kojima, the former director of the Telecommunications Systems Division of the Japanese MPT. Mr. Kojima (1987) argues that, "Standardization was initially a concept of the 19th century age of mass production. However, we are now entering an era of custom-oriented standards. To put it in a nutshell, as long as networks can be linked up, they can be utilized according to how individuals wish to use them. This may sound strange, but I think that standards may have to become de-standardized standards, that is to say, standardization will be based on user needs and shifted from single standard to sophisticated standards."

In reality, global wireless communications have moved into the "de-standardization" era. ITU's IMT-2000, will definitely accommodate the coexistence of multiple standards that compete in the global market.

REFERENCES:

Berg, (1987). "AM versus FM stereo systems" in Gabel's *Product standardization and competitive strategy*. Armesterdam, Netherland: Elsevier Science Publishers B.V.

Besen, S. & Saloner, G. (1989). The economics of telecommunications standards. In Crandall, R. & Flamm, K. (Eds.) *Changing the rules*.

Washington, D.C.: The Brookings Institute.

Cattaneo, G. (1994). "The making of a Pan-European network as a path-dependency process: the case of GSM versus IBC (Integrated Broadband Communication) Network". in Pogorel, G (eds). *Global Telecommunications Strategies and Technological Changes*. The Netherlands: Elsevier Science B.V.

Crane, R.J. (1979). *The politics of international standards: France and the color TV war*. Norwood, NJ: Ablex.

Farrell, J. & Saloner, G. (1985, Spring). Standardization, compatibility and innovation. *Rand Journal of Economics*.

Farrell, J. & Saloner, G. (1986). Installed base and compatibility: Innovation, product preannouncements, and predation. *American Economic Review, 76*, 940-955.

Financial Times (1995, November). Survey on Mobile Communications. *Financial Times*, London, UK.

Funk, J.L. (1998). Competition between regional standards and the success and failure of firms in the world-wide mobile communication market. *Telecommunications Policy, 22*(4-5), 419 - 441.

Gabel, H.L. (1987). Open standards in the European computer industry: the case of X/OPEN. In Gabel's *Product Standardization and Competitive Strategy*. Armesterdam, Netherland: Elsevier Science Publishers B.V.

Greenstein, S. (1993, January). Invisible hands versus invisible advisers: coordination mechanism in economic networks. University of Illinois, Urbana-Champaign.

Hawkins, R. (1992, May/June). The doctrine of regionalism. *Telecommunications Policy*. 339-353.

ISO. (1995). Introduction to International Organization for Standardization (ISO). It's available at http://www.iso.ch.

ITU. (2000, May). Thumps up for IMT-2000, ITU press release. (Available at http://www.itu.int/newsroom/press/releases/2000/12.html).

ITU. (1999). ITU 1999 Telecommunications Indicators at http://www.itu.int/ti/industryoverview/at_glance/KeyTelecom99.htm.

Kano, S. (2000, May). Technical Innovations, Standardization and Regional Comparison: A case study in mobile telecommunications, *Telecommunications Policy, 24*(4).

Kojima, H. (1987, August). De-Standardization proposed for 21st century. *The Telecom Tribune*, 2.

Lecraw, D.J. (1987). Japanese Standards: A barrier to trade? in Gabel's *Product standardization and competitive strategy*. Armesterdam, Netherland: Elsevier Science Publishers B.V.

McDonald, V.H. (1979). The Cellular Concept. *Bell System Technology Journal*, 58(1), 15-41.

Nishuilleabhain, A. & Carrel, H. (1994). *Asian Cellular Operators*. Northern Business Information of McGraw-Hill, Inc.

Okinaka, H. (1996, January). PHS: A new advanced infrastructure for mobile communications and wireless local loop applications. *Pacific Telecommunications Conference (PTC'96) Proceedings*, Hawaii.

OTA, (1995). *Wireless Technologies and the National Information Infrastructure*. Washington D.C.

Padgett, J., Gunther, C. & Hattori, T. (1995, January). Overview of wireless personal Communications, *IEEE Communcations Magazine*, 28-41.

Paetsch, M. (1993). *Mobile communications in the US and Europe: Regulation, technology, and market*. Boston, MA: Artech House.

Pelkmans, J. & Beuter, R. (1987). Strategies in the EC color TV industry. In Gabel's *Product standardization and competitive strategy*. Armesterdam, Netherland: Elsevier Science Publishers B.V.

Ross, I. (1986, May). Uniform standards are required to ensure global cellular growth. *Mobile Radio Technology*, 26-30.

Sherif, M.H. & Sparrell, D.K. (1992). Standards and innovation in telecommunications. *IEEE Communications Magazine. 30*(7), 22.

Sung, L. (1993). The political economy of international standardization: the case of the third generation mobile communications system, unpublished paper.

USITC. (1993). *Global Competitiveness of U.S. Advanced-Technology Industries: Cellular Communications*. Investigation No. 332-329, 1995, Washington, D.C.

Wallenstein, G. (1990). *Setting global telecommunications standards: the stakes, the players and the process*. Boston, MA: Artech House.

Chapter VIII

Telecommunications in Transition: The Chinese Experience in the International Context

Ping Gao and Kalle Lyytinen
University of Jyväskylä, Finland

INTRODUCTION

For about one century, since the telephone was invented and telecommunications services were launched, the telecommunications industry has been operated primarily as a state monopoly.[1] This situation has changed drastically in recent decades. Countries have adopted various reform strategies. Among them, China provides one of the most interesting cases for study, being the largest potential market for telecommunications services and because of its unique economic and political environment. Telecommunications reform in China has been without doubt a success. The reform has made China's telecommunications sector one of the fastest developing in the world.

A large number of publications have addressed telecommunications reforms in Europe and the US (Baliga & Santalainen, 1999; Finland Ministry, 1996; Noam & Kramer, 1994). Some scholars have also analyzed other countries' experiences. For example, Petrazzini (1995) and his coauthor (1998) focused on the developing world. By analyzing reforms in India and nine other countries, he delineates the factors that can lead to success of telecommunications reform in the developing world. Chinese telecommunications reform has been discussed in several studies. Most scholars have focused on specific aspects of the reform, like Internet regulation and diffusion (Tan, Foster & Goodman, 1999). Mueller & Tan (1997) examined telecommunications reform in China in its early stages. International comparisons, which are useful in understanding the special characteristics of Chinese telecommunications reform, have not been carried out. Ure (1997) is an exception in that it compares telecommunications reforms in China's mainland and in the "four dragons."[2] These articles have not included some important changes in the Chinese telecommunications sector, especially those that have taken place since 1998. A systematic analysis on Chinese telecommunications reform is still missing.

In this article, we seek to provide a deep insight into telecommunications reform strategies by studying the Chinese experience in the international context. We argue that, while the telecommunications sector generally has been moving towards full liberalization and deregulation on the global scale, there is great variation in how this has been achieved in individual countries. Countries have adopted a variety of transitional mechanisms in their telecommunications reform process. We suggest that an efficient reform program should be formulated by correctly analyzing the context, including the development stage of the telecommunications sector, and the economic and political environment. China presents one such experience.

Our analysis is organized as follows. We first survey experiences of international telecommunications reform. Thereafter we investigate the Chinese program of telecommunications reform. Then we carry out a comparative analysis to provide an understanding of the characteristics of China's reform strategy in the international context. Finally, we draw some conclusions from varying international telecommunications reform experiences and discuss the prospects for telecommunications development in China.

INTERNATIONAL OVERVIEW

Obviously, it is too ambitious to address every country's reform program in one article like this. Therefore, we want to provide a description of the essential properties of various telecommunications reforms, by dividing all countries into three groups according to their different times of starting telecommunications reform. The countries leading telecommunications reform are classified into the first group. Here, the US and UK will be chosen as study objects, because of their important "position" within international telecommunications reforms. The second group covers the general EU model. The third group consists of the developing countries. Considering the vast number of developing countries and a large variance in their telecommunications reform strategies, only some representative cases will be examined.

With regard to the mechanisms of promoting competition, we can divide reforms into gradual and radical reforms. A gradual reform strategy aims at liberalizing the market step by step and seeks to introduce competition gradually in terms of environmental evolution. In contrast, a radical reform strategy intends to reach full competition directly without a need of a transition period. It also leaves out considerations of having necessary support within the economic and political environment.

THE US AND UK: LEADING COUNTRIES IN TELECOMMUNICATIONS REFORM

The US

Traditional monopoly structure in telecommunications has undergone a major change in the recent decades, with the US playing a leading role. In the US AT&T had been the de facto monopoly, not only in services and infrastructure, but also in equipment and research. However, AT&T had never been granted a monopoly franchise by the law. Therefore, the challenge to AT&T's position in the market had been a constant, and the market was opened systematically. As early as in 1956, a consent decree, which confined AT&T's business activity to providing regulated public communications facilities and services, began the purposeful introduction of competition into the telecommunications sector. Based on the 1956 Consent Decree, the Federal Communications Commission (FCC) began to adopt competitive policies. In 1962, when MCI was awarded permission to provide private microwave service, the dedicated telecommunications market was liberalized. In 1971, the FCC's First Computer Inquiry ruled that new data communications should not be regulated, thereby opening them to competition. In 1977 the FCC's Execunet Decision granted MCI the right to offer toll service. In 1979 the Second Computer Inquiry liberalized all customer premises equipment (Snow, 1995).

In 1982, as a revision to the 1956 Consent Decree, modification of final judgement (MFJ) was issued by the Department of Justice, which commenced important changes in the basic telecommunications market. With January 1, 1984, as the deadline, the MFJ had AT&T divest itself of its local service sector, which was regrouped under seven regional holding companies (RBOCs). Hence, regional monopolies substituted the monopoly in local services, with a prohibition on providing long-distance services and information services, and involvement in equipment manufacturing. Meanwhile AT&T was allowed to enter into information services and other markets outside the regulated telecommunications as stipulated by the 1956 Consent Decree. Furthermore, in 1994 the mobile market was liberalized, by replacing its regional duopoly structure. At the same time AT&T entered into the mobile operations by acquiring McCaw Cellular (Snow, 1995).

In 1996, a new Telecommunications Act marked the introduction of a full-competition phase. The 1996 Telecommunications Act attempts to remove all the restrictions on the service scope of an operator. Particularly, it released the restriction that had hitherto prevented firms in telecommunications, CATV and broadcasting from actively competing in each other's arenas and ended the separation of local and toll service operation. Consequently, the American market was fully liberalized, and a tide of enterprise mergers crossing national boundaries and spanning industries like telecommunications, computing and media has emerged (Baliga & Santalainen, 1999).

The UK

The UK is a pacesetter in challenging the traditional idea of a natural telecommunications monopoly in the world. Initialized in 1981 by a new Telecommunications Act, the telecommunications reform in the UK was originally a part of government's policy of improving state-owned industries (Spiller & Vogelsang, 1996). The 1981 Telecommunications Act broke apart the PTT (Post, Telegraph and Telephone). It established British Telecom (BT) as a public corporation being responsible for telecommunications services. At the same time, it transferred the regulatory responsibility to the Department of Industry. The 1981 Telecommunications Act also introduced competition. In 1982, Mercury began operating a dedicated digital network. In mobile services, a duopoly structure was adopted. In mobile services a duopoly structure has been adopted, in TACS, GSM, and DCS-1800 systems respectively (Thatcher, 1999).

In 1984, a new Telecommunications Act resulted in competition being greatly accelerated and extended. The 1984 act abolished BT's exclusive right in public telecommunications services. Mercury's license was widened enabling it to become a long-distance carrier competing with BT. The act also led to the privatization of BT. In three rounds in 1984, 1991 and 1993 the government sold all its interest in BT, and BT became a publicly quoted company. At the same, the Office of Telecommunications (Oftel) was formed as a regulatory body. By adopting a competitive policy, Oftel actively extended competition and influenced the speed of reform. Impelled by Oftel, the government began to issue VAS licenses and authorize the sales of all types of customer premises equipment. Furthermore, in 1991 the government announced a white paper on future telecommunications policy. Since then, the CATV companies have been permitted to provide telecommunications services, becoming the main competitors to BT in the local loop. By granting new licenses, the government ended the duopoly structure in the long-distance market. Mobile operators were now allowed to enter fixed services, and the limit on the number of licenses was lifted by allowing other telecommunications carriers to enter the market. Consequently, the telecommunications market was fully liberalized (Thatcher, 1999).

In both the US and the UK, during the transitional period towards a full liberalization, sustainable and fair competition was guaranteed by asymmetric regulation. The asymmetric regulation supported new competitors by securing compensation from incumbents with advantages in economies of scale and customer base and placing more restrictions on the incumbents (Finland Ministry, 1996; Thatcher, 1999).

While liberalization is the main trend, deregulation is necessary to lower the entry barriers to the market. Nevertheless, even after a full liberalization has been declared, some regulations still play a crucial role, especially concerning foreign capital entry. For example, in the US, foreign stakes can now exceed the previous 25% limit. But the prerequisite is that effective competitive opportunities (ECO) are available to the US entities in the concerned countries (Finland Ministry, 1996).

EU COUNTRIES: A CAUTIOUS MODEL

With exception of the UK and a few smaller countries like Finland, most EU members have been cautious in opening their markets. They have followed the schedules that have been planned on the community level as issued by EC directives (Noam & Kramer, 1994). Competition measures have been introduced in a piecemeal fashion, starting with market segments of low importance and gradually establishing EC's power to open the core markets, which include equipment, services and networks. In the beginning of 1989, the terminal market was first opened to competition. The deadline set by EC for opening VAS and dedicated networks was the end of 1990. 1992 was the designated final year for data communications liberalization. With regard to mobile communications, the liberalization deadline was set to February 1996. The January 1, of 1998, was the deadline of full liberalization.[3] In practice there are variances in different EU countries in their reform progress (European Commission, 1997).

Within EU countries, partial privatization has been used to reorganize the incumbent national operators. With regard to market liberalization, now the tide of domestic and international operators' entry in large numbers has receded. Instead, market combination has become a new trend. For example, in Germany, the forming of alliances as well as consortia of alliances has made the number of competitors tend to reduce (Finland Ministry, 1996).

THE DEVELOPING WORLD: BIG DIVERSITY IN THE PROGRAMS OF DIFFERENT COUNTRIES

According to Pisciotta (1997), in most developing countries the telecommunications sector is still organized under the traditional state monopoly or the process of corporatization on PTTs has just been initiated. Whilst in other developing countries, a clear trend towards liberalization has emerged over the last few years.

As described above, gradual reform has been the strategy followed by the developed world. However, within those developing countries that have initiated their telecommunications reform, both a gradual and a radical change have been employed. India and Brazil are examples of developing countries that have executed a gradual reform program. In India, limited competition was introduced in basic telecommunications in 1986. A new company, Mahanagar Nigam Telephone Limited (MNTL), was established to compete in some metropolitan areas with the state-owned Department of Telecommunications (DoT) in local services. MNTL has a 67/33 mixed state/private ownership. Another recently established company, Videsh Sanchar Nigam Limited (VSNL), with 85/15 mixture of state/private ownership, monopolized international services. In 1994, the government enacted a National Telecommunications Policy, which allowed foreign competition and introduced more private competition into the market. Under the new policy, foreign firms could hold up to 49% of the shares. A regional competition structure has been adopted in local and mobile services so as to achieve a well-balanced development. In each cellular or wireline circle, one or two private companies (with no more than 49% foreign participation) might be licensed respectively. DoT and VSNL were allowed to maintain a monopoly over intra-circle long-distance and international services respectively for at least five years. In addition, the Telecom Regulatory Authority of India (TRAI) was formed as the regulatory agency. As of now, India is still in the transitional period towards full competition (Petrazzini & Krishnaswamy, 1998).

In Brazil, it was as late as in 1995 when the constitutional amendment proposed to extinguish the state monopoly over public services. The structural reform was carried out in two stages: by means of the Specific Law and the General Law. In 1996, the Specific Law was issued with provisions for opening some segments of the telecommunications market. These include cellular services, VAS and services via satellite and corporate networks. In 1997, the General Law deeply changed the Brazilian telecommunications model. The General Law authorized the government to promote the restructuring of national monopoly while the state kept the control. It established ANATEL (Agencia Nacional de Telecom) as an independent regulatory body. As in India, Brazil adopted a regional competition structure to achieve balanced development. The next step, which will start from 2002, is towards full-competition. The regional operators will be allowed to engage in nationwide operations, as well as provide a wide range of services (Sant'Andre, 1998).

Contrasting with the general case represented by Brazil and India where competition has been introduced step by step, some countries in Latin America and Asia have adopted a radical reform strategy. To obtain a strong financial basis of fast telecommunications development, some Latin American countries allowed foreign carriers and private investors to get directly involved in the market liberalization. In these situations, the investors have had superior bargaining power because of the poor state of the local political and economic situation. These investors preferred to purchase the national operators, while maintaining a monopoly franchise. For example, in Argentina, in 1990 the privatization plan broke the national monopoly into two parts. While 40% of share was floated, the other remaining shares were purchased mainly by foreign companies with a condition of a 10-year guarantee of exclusivity in basic services. Hence, private duopoly substituted state monopoly, and Argentina's plan in the early 1990s of liberalizing basic services and VAS network failed. Jamaica followed the same pattern in basic telecommunications and Mexico, in toll services. A few Asian countries have also implemented a radical reform strategy. For example, in Malaysia four new licenses of basic service were issued in the mid-1990s to launch competition with the incumbent monopoly. In the Philippines 10 licenses, some being regional, have been added. Yet, countrywide competition has not materialized as expected. Instead, the competitors have concentrated their investments on lucrative urban areas (Petrazzini, 1995).

Efficient reform in regulation is necessary to guarantee a successful market change, as indicated by Brazil's and India's experiences. We can observe the same result from the Mexican experience. In Mexico, local services were opened to competition from December 1990 onward. Yet, TELMEX as the national monopoly of long-distance services and the integrated national network was not obliged to interconnect new entrants to the market by law. What is more, restricted by the Mexican political system, the regulatory body did not obtain autonomy in operations and finance. Thereby, TELMEX could use its advantage of being a dominant national carrier to lobby government and high officials for support. Hence, the regulator could not efficiently regulate TELMEX for network accesses. Consequently, the potential competitors could not survive, and the liberalization on local services failed (Petrazzini, 1995).

In sum, though different reform programs have been adopted in different countries due to varying macro environments and motivations, the general trend is toward full liberalization and deregulation. While most countries prefer a stepwise change, a few developing countries have employed a radical reform strategy.

CHINESE TELECOMMUNICATIONS TRANSFORMATION

In China the macro administrative system had been organized under a planned economy. It had the following characteristic: Different state-owned industries were under the central control of specific ministries. These ministries had two functions: taking charge of specific industries as governmental branches and acting as the headquarters of their affiliated companies. On top of these ministries was the State Council that supervised and coordinated different ministries.

Just like most other countries, historically China followed a monopoly structure in public telecommunications. The Ministry of Posts and Telecommunications (MPT), being the Chinese PTT, monopolized the public telecommunications. As a department of MPT, the Directorate General of Telecommunications (DGT) was responsible for network operations. Influenced by the macro administrative system of the planned economy, a vertically centralized, horizontally fragmented system was employed in telecommunications regulation. Horizontally, several bodies carried out the regulation. The MPT did not have an exclusive power to regulate the whole telecommunications industry. The State Planning Commission was involved in drafting development plans for telecommunications industry and setting up tariff regulations. The State Economic and Trade Commission administrated large-scale state-owned enterprises, like the DGT. The State Radio Regulatory Committee was in charge of radio administration. Ministry of Broadcast, Film and TV had a monopoly over CATV operations. Ministry of Electronic Industry had the authority over electronic manufacturing. Vertically, the State Council was involved in telecommunications regulations on the highest administrative level, and it coordinated different authorities when necessary.

The Chinese telecommunications sector began to undergo major changes in the early 1980s, as China entered the era called "macro system reform and market opening." Accordingly, China organized its telecommunications reform into three stages by following the progress of national reforms in the macro economic and political system.

Up to 1994: Primary Attempts at Liberalization

The first stage of telecommunications reform began in 1982 in the equipment market. Because of the backwardness of Chinese manufacturing industry, China's telecommunications equipment market was fully liberalized to domestic and foreign competition so that the telecommunications network could develop with advanced technologies. Now there are more than 2,000 manufacturers in China (MII, 1999).

Some services without high network dependence, e.g., VAS, paging service, etc., were opened to non-private enterprises gradually from the late 1980s. In fact, this had been illegal according to decree No. 216 issued by the MPT in 1989. It was as late as 1993 when the State Council issued decree No. 55 to legalize the opening of these markets to domestic non-private institutions (MPT, 1992 & 1995). It reflected the Chinese characteristic that, during the transitional period, there are no complete and timely rules to regulate new service markets. Unable to meet the huge market demand and counter the social desires of opening markets supported by some governmental branches, the MPT showed a willingness to ignore, or a political inability to obstruct, these changes. Currently these are highly competitive markets with thousands of operators (MII, 1999).

The basic telecommunications market was a state monopoly, which enabled the state to concentrate on constructing an advanced, complete national network by granting preferential policies to the telecommunications sector. The central government permitted the MPT to charge an installation fee for each subscriber that corresponded to the construction cost for one line. Before 1995, the MPT also enjoyed the privilege in advancing equipment depreciation, using foreign currency and taxation. According to MII (1999), by 1995 the money attained from preferential policies was more than half of the total investment.

From 1994 to 1998: Limited Liberalization in Basic Telecommunications

From the middle 1990s, China's national telecommunications policies have changed because of the fast development of the telecommunications industry. According to Yang's (1997) calculation, from the middle 1990s the telecommunications development level has been equivalent to the general growth level of the macro economy in China. The telecommunications market has shifted from a buyer's pull to a seller's push. Therefore, unlike before when the development speed was the overriding objective, service quality improvements and tariff reductions currently have become the focus of both government and society. Using experiences from developed countries, competition has been advocated as an efficient mechanism to promote efficiency and improve service quality. Consequently, the second phase of the telecommunications market opening began from the middle 1990s, which led to a duopoly market (MII, 1999).

In 1994, the Ministry of Electronic Industry, together with another two ministries and some state-owned enterprises, formed Unicom. At the same time, the regulatory regime organized in line with the traditional monopoly structure was changed. This was a part of a statewide governmental reform initiated by the central government, that aimed at separating enterprise management functions from governmental branches. Consequently, a company registered as China Telecom (CT), the DGT was changed from a functional department of the MPT to an enterprise responsible for operating and managing the MPT's fixed and mobile networks. At that time, state-owned CT and Unicom were the only two comprehensive public operators. Unicom started competition with CT in mobile services. Local competition was launched in Tianjin City in 1997 and was gradually extended to other cities (MII, 1999).

At that time, CT was still under the control of the MPT in terms of finance, investment, and personnel. Hence CT was not a "real" enterprise, and the MPT was not a "pure" regulatory authority either. The situation was just like the progress in macroeconomic reform. It was only superficial, in that overall relationships between enterprises and their backers did not change. The MPT without neutrality could not function as expected. Therefore, a de facto asymmetric regulation with a twisted direction had been created. The incumbent CT was in a favored position in market regulation. Consequently, though Unicom could survive with the regular intervention of central government, its development was restricted. For example, after five years of development, Unicom shared only about 5% of the market in mobile communications in

1998. The situation is even worse in local competition (MII, 1999). This market situation corresponded to the original purpose of the government for forming Unicom. Because of the slow advances in the macroeconomic reform, the government confined the forming of Unicom to test for further market openings in the future (MPT, 1996).

Following the establishment of Unicom, other competitive elements have also emerged in the market. In 1994, state-owned Jitong Communications Co. Ltd. was established with a license to build and operate the second public data network. Formed from some provincial GSM networks, China Telecom Hong Kong (CTHK) was formed in 1997. CT holds a 51% share, while the other remaining shares are floated on the Hong Kong stock market (MII, 1999).

From 1998: Changes Towards Full-Competition

In the late 1990s China's telecommunications development entered a new phase, marked by the forming of advanced, complete, cross-country national networks. It was hence believed that the national telecommunications industry had become capable of standing private and foreign competition (MII, 1999). In 1998, a new round of macro reforms started which resulted in thorough changes in the governmental structure and a clear separation of enterprise management from governmental bodies. Therefore, a fundamental change in the regulatory regime is now possible. In brief, an appropriate economic and political environment has been provided for carrying out deeper telecommunications reform.

Consequently, China's telecommunications sector entered the third phase of reforms in 1998. As part of the macro reform, the telecommunications regulatory regime underwent a thorough change. By taking over the regulatory responsibilities shared by the MPT and other administrations and giving up CT's affiliation, the Ministry of Information Industry (MII) substituted MPT as an exclusive, neutral regulator. The central government set principles of supporting Unicom and protecting fair competition (MII, 1999). As a result a properly designed regulatory regime, that can protect competition, has been formed.

In market change, the basic strategy is market restructuring in order to form a fair structure. This was accomplished by breaking up CT, and at the same time strengthening Unicom. Consequently, CT now only keeps its fixed network and operations. Its mobile sector, including CT's share in CTHK, has been split to form an independent body: China Mobile Group. The paging sector of CT, whose turnover was five times of Unicom, has been appropriated to Unicom.

The satellite communications market has been dominated by some state-owned enterprises since 1994. Affiliated to the MPT, ChinaSat is the leading player formed in 1985. The Sino Satellite Communications, a non-MPT consortium, was formed by some state institutions in 1994. China Orient is the third player, with the MPT as the dominant shareholder. During this round the three operators will be merged to a group called China Satellite Group (MII, 1999). This has resulted in strengthening of the competitive capability of national operators through the formation of a "national fleet" composed by four "carriers", i.e. the CT, Unicom, China Mobile Group and China Satellite Group. Thus, a market structure capable of meeting the upcoming international competition has been formed (MII, 1999).

In the meantime, as the market was being restructured, more competition was introduced. In fixed telephone services, after Unicom, Jitong has also joined the competition with CT by providing Internet phone service. All three received such licenses in April 1999 (MII, 1999). In August 1999, four state institutions formed China Net Communications to compete with CT, Unicom, and Jitong on wide-band networks and services. From May 2000 Unicom

Table 1. Chinese telecommunications reform progress

Time period	Telecom development situation	Macro reform progress	Telecom reform program
First stage: Before 1994	User-pull market.	Early stage of macro reform on planned economy.	MPT as PTT. Monopoly in basic services and network. Fully open in facility. Limited open in VAS.
Second stage: 1994 till 1998	Most attractive market of the world. Market demands met, operator-push market.	Superficial reform.	Limited separation of administrative and enterprise functions within MPT. Duopoly in basic services and networks as a transitional step.
Third stage: From 1998	Advanced, nationwide network formed.	Deeper reform, separation of enterprise functions from governmental bodies.	MII as the independent, unique regulator. Restructuring CT. A market adapting to full competition formed.

began to provide domestic toll services. Now Unicom is preparing to operate international services (People's Daily, 2000, 05 January, 16 May).

To summarize, China has been cautious in its telecommunications reform. Its gradual reform strategy has been designed according to the stage of telecommunications development and the macroeconomic reform (Table 1). Now an overall competition structure has taken its shape. With the exception of CTHK, the telecommunications competition has been confined to state-owned enterprises. At present, the reform is still not in its last step, in that only a market favoring full competition has been provided, while more competitive elements need to be introduced later.

COMPARATIVE ANALYSIS
Market Changes

We can observe great variations in the starting times of telecommunications reforms in different countries. In contrast to the US and UK, most EU countries initialized reforms late and followed a cautious model. In developing countries, while most of them still retain the traditional monopoly structure, some fit into the middle. By and large, Chinese reform presents a cautious characteristic. Concerning the mechanisms for introducing competition, while a few developing countries adopted a radical reform strategy, the developed world in general and most developing countries have carried out a gradual reform. Like the general case, China has preferred a gradual reform.

Generally, VAS services have been "the frontier" in terms of opening to competition. The dedicated networks were usually the "early birds" of entering into public telecommunications competition, like the cases of MCI in the US and Mercury in the UK (Snow, 1995; Thatcher, 1999). In China, the market opening of VAS services occurred in the first round of liberalization. However, the dedicated networks were excluded from market competition.

In most countries, the segments without incumbent monopoly like cellular services have been successfully opened to competition from the beginning. In China, the competition has been delayed. Cellular services were launched in China in the middle 1980s under the monopoly of the MPT. A duopoly was introduced as late as 1994, when the second phase of market liberalization began. Competition was slow to take off as the new company faced a number of hurdles presented by the incumbent operator, such as advantages in economies of scale and regulation. Therefore, the new entrant, Unicom, has only obtained a very small percentage of the market.

The provision of basic telecommunication services, entrenched as a monopoly, has been the last field opening to competition. Different countries chose various ways of transition to full competition. In the UK, it went from a monopoly through duopoly to a plural market. In the US, a full competition was reached after a phased market restructuring. India's and Brazil's transitional markets were characterized by regional competition in both local and mobile services. China adopted an unbalanced duopoly during the transition. Usually the toll service went ahead to competition in the basic sector. Like India and Brazil, China is exceptional in that the basic competition began from local services.

The Chinese equipment market has been fully deregulated to domestic and international competition since the early 1980s. By comparison, China opened the equipment market earlier and more intensively than most countries. For example, it was only from 1988 onward that EU members opened equipment sales, then only within the Community and to countries which had agreements of equal market access with them (European Commission, 1997).

Now many developed countries have entered the full competition phase. Yet, in China the focus of current reform is still on restructuring incumbent elements. China Net Communications is the only new element introduced in the market. By international comparison, the current stage of China's telecommunications reform corresponds to that of the US in 1984 and the UK in 1982. However, Chinese market restructuring is not the mechanistic replication of AT&T divestiture in that in China the market change is more of a consolidation than devolution. In addition to Unicom's restructuring and China Satellite Group's founding, the forming of China Mobile Group by splitting it from CT also serves the purpose of reinforcing the national telecommunications sector. As an independent operator of mobile services, China Mobile Group may obtain more flexible mechanisms for growth without tight control of the state, when compared with CT, that owns the national networks.

Regulatory Regime Transformation

Generally, regulatory reforms in telecommunications should be carried out simultaneously with market changes, if not beforehand. But China presents a different case. In China, the regulatory reforms in the telecommunications sector have been carried out by following the national macroeconomic reform program. Because of the slow progress of macroeconomic reforms, the regulatory reforms in telecommunications have lagged behind, and thereby hindered market development.

From international experiences, we find that necessary laws and directives, which direct market regulations, have governed the reform. For instance in the US, the 1956 Consent Decree, 1982 MFJ and 1996 Telecommunications Acts have been the basis of reforms (Baliga & Santalainen, 1999;

Snow, 1995). In the UK, the 1981 and 1984 Telecommunications Act have promoted the reforms (Thatcher, 1999). In Brazil and India, there were the 1996 Specific Law and 1997 General Law, and the 1994 National Telecommunications Policy respectively (Petrazzini & Krishnaswamy, 1998; Sant'Andre, 1998). In China the market change has been carried out without the supervision of the necessary laws. Until now, the Telecommunication Law has not been published. The regulation has been executed by administrative interventions, referring to governmental directives, and by applying administrative measures. This has been restricted by the slow progress of China's macroeconomic reforms on its planned economy.

Concerning regulatory institutions, the formation of an independent regulatory body is necessary when a market is liberalized. For example, in the UK, the regulatory power was transferred to the Department of Industry when the market reform began in 1981. Furthermore, the independent regulatory body Oftel was formed in 1994, as market liberalization went deeper (Spiller & Vogelsang, 1996). In Brazil and India, there are the similar examples of creating of ANATEL and TRAI respectively (Petrazzini & Krishnaswamy, 1998; Sant'Andre, 1998). In China, the forming of a neutral regulatory body was brought about in 1998 by deeper reform at the macro level. Before, in its already opened market, China had adopted a centralized regulatory system, which allowed the central government to coordinate and monitor different regulatory institutions. Therefore, unlike Mexico, where an inefficient reform in the regulatory institution led to the failure of market liberalization, China's telecommunications competition could survive, though the development is seriously restricted.

An appropriate regulatory approach is necessary. For example, in the UK sustainable and fair competition has been delivered by asymmetric regulation (Collins & Murroni, 1997). In the United States, an asymmetric regulation was executed up until 1995 when the FCC stopped the classification of dominant carriers (Finland Ministry, 1996). In China, restricted by the advance in macroeconomic reform, a proper asymmetric regulation became a reality only after 1998. Before, a convoluted asymmetric regulatory regime existed.

Participation of Private and Foreign Capital

Whilst allowing private investment, many countries have placed restrictions on participation in the telecommunications sector. In most countries the public telecommunications operators are still state-owned or controlled by states like MNTL and VSNL in India. Allowing a limited public ownership of shares is one of the more popular measures in restructuring state-owned monopoly and attracting private investment. For example, in Germany and France, a partial floatation of shares of Deutsche Telekom and French Telecom has been made (Pisciotta, 1997). In Brazil, the government has emphasized that, since telecommunications are public services, it will not lose the monopoly over the rights but will temporarily grant private entrepreneurs the exploitation rights in exchange for financial compensation. After partial privatization of state-owned monopoly, the state still controls 50.04% of voting capital and 21.45% of total capital (Sant'Andre, 1998).

The involvement of foreign capital in competition, especially in basic services, has been postponed to the last step in most countries. Even for the US as a leading country of market liberalization, there are also regulatory restrictions, e.g., the ECO criterion, on foreign entrance (Finland Ministry, 1996). While allowing foreign participation in the market competition, most countries set an upper limit for the percentage of foreign capital in a firm. For example, in India, there is an upper limit of 49% for foreign shares in a consortium (Petrazzini & Krishnaswamy, 1998).

Different from general cases that take the introduction of foreign and private investment as a major aim of reform, China has been highly discreet in introducing private and foreign capital to telecommunications industry. With CTHK as the only exception, the competition has been between state-owned operators, even in the VAS sector, where an open policy has been adopted by other countries. China strictly adhered to a socialist regime, which preferred a state-controlled public ownership. Though the reform has been carried out continuously and most state-owned industries have been opened to private and foreign investment, the telecommunications sector being seen as a part of national infrastructure has been deemed necessary to retain in the strict state control.

Motivations of Reform

Various choices with regard to telecommunications reforms in different countries can be explained by their varying motivations shaped by specific environments. In the US, the unofficial status of AT&T as a monopoly made it a target of attacks by antitrust laws. Accordingly, the market structure has changed continuously. Because of the superior capacity of its domestic telecommunications operators, the US has encouraged international competition to a certain degree so as to get reciprocal rights to enter into other countries' markets. In the UK the market liberalization was initiated by the government's policy of improving state-owned enterprises. Being weary of large foreign operators entering their markets before domestic operators were ready, and being satisfied with their universal service level, most EU countries have preferred cautious reforms (Collins & Murroni, 1997; Finland Ministry, 1996). Some developing countries have adopted radical changes so that economy can be promoted by the fast development of telecommunications. In China, in the early 1980s when the Chinese government began to change its focus from social ideology to economic development, telecommunications industry formed a major bottleneck. Hence Chinese telecommunications reform has been intensified gradually so as to promote development in telecommunications, and furthermore the whole economy (MII, 1999). A deep reform has been conducted from 1998 onward, so that China can get ready for the forthcoming international competition while it enters the World Trade Organization (WTO).

Economic Implications

Positive results have been obtained for countries where gradual programs have been adopted. According to the Council of Economic Advisers (1999), competition has enabled fast development of telecommunications in the US. In the UK, the performance of telecommunications industry has improved markedly (Collins & Murroni, 1997). For other countries that have executed a gradual reform, including most EU countries, as well as India and Brazil, etc., we can observe the same result (OECD, 1995; Petrazzini & Krishnaswamy, 1998; Sant'Andre, 1998). Yet, a limited number of countries have adopted radical changes, offering cases that present mediocre results. In the Argentine, Jamaica and Mexico, the intentions of liberalization could not be met. The privatization became a feasible solution to attract investment, and the consortia that bought state-owned operators comprised one of those groups that have been most favored by the reform. In Malaysia and the Philippines, the target of forming cross-country networks was not achieved, by allowing the entry of too many operators. Meanwhile the "over-competition" structure made some operators face financial problems (Petrazzini, 1995).

China has adopted a gradual reform. According to the conspicuous development of Chinese telecommunications, we can conclude that Chinese reform has been successful.[4] Chinese telecommunications has achieved one of the greatest developments in the global scale, which can be possible only through proper reforms in the market structure and regulatory regime. Consider the following examples. In China the total capacity of telephone exchanges exceeded 115 million lines in 1997, which was about 260 times higher than the level of the year 1980, when the reform was initialized. Now China owns the second largest fixed network, the third largest mobile network, and the largest GSM network in the world (MII, 1999).

CONCLUSIONS AND PROSPECTS

The general trend in telecommunications reforms is towards full competition and deregulation. With regard to the strategies of achieving full competition, countries have made alternative choices to follow a gradual or a radical reform. Like most other countries, China has accepted a gradual reform strategy.

In addition to technological innovation, the development situation in telecommunications industry, the macroeconomic change, and the political system should be the main considerations in forming a telecommunications reform program. There is no universal solution for telecommunications deregulation. Instead of mechanically following the experiences of other countries, each country should draw up its reform program by correctly analyzing its situation and specific environment. The Chinese experience provides one demonstration and can be used as a reference by developing countries in planning their reform programs. Like China, these countries have a poor economic basis and a bad political background.

Unlike fully liberalized developed countries, where a tide of market consolidations and enterprise mergers has begun to form, China is still in the transition towards full competition. While a fully competitive environment is being formed, the next stage of market change will be characterized by the introduction of additional competitive elements, for which China will hold on a stepwise change strategy. It is most likely that state-owned dedicated networks will be first to benefit from further liberalization. This also applies to the state-owned CATV sector as the most powerful prospective competitor of incumbent telecommunications operators. The Chinese telecommunications market will be further opened to foreign capital. As a condition for joining WTO, China has promised to open its telecommunications sector to foreign investment with an upper limit in shares (People's Daily, March 16, 1999). Non-basic services like VAS may be opened to foreign capital at first. Morever, the market may be first opened to private capital before foreign competition is allowed. For a long time in the future, most likely the state will still control the main part of networks by totally owning CT. For other components of the "national fleet," the public ownership of stock will be the preferential policy. For example, the more provincial networks of China Mobile Group may be allowed to go to stock by joining in CTHK. A clearer framework of regulatory regime and market structure will be laid out by the Telecommunications Law, which is in the process of legislative approval (MII, 1999).

REFERENCES

Baliga, R. & Santalainen, T. (1999). *Telecommunications in transition: The US experience.* Helsinki: HeSE Print.

Collins, R. & Murroni, C. (1997). Future Directions in Telecom Regulation: The Case of the United Kingdom. In W.H. Melody, *Telecom reform: Principles, policies & regulatory practices.* Lyngby: Technical University of Denmark.

Council of Economic Advisers. (1999). *Progress report: Growth and competition in U.S. telecommunications 1993-1998.* Washington, 8 February.

European Commission. (1997, May). *Status report on EU telecommunications policy.* DGXIII/A/1.

Finland Ministry of Transport & Communications. (1996). *Study on the development of legal structure and ownership of telecommunications companies.* Helsinki: Author.

MII. (1999). *China telecommunications over 50 years.* Beijing: MII.

MPT. (1996, 1995, 1992). *Collection of China P&T laws & regulations.* Beijing: China Legality Press.

Mueller, M. & Tan, Z. (1997). *China in the information age: Telecommunications and the dilemmas of reform.* Westport CT: CSIS/Praeger.

Noam, E., Kramer, R. (1994). Telecommunications Strategies in the Developed World: A Hundred Flowers Blooming or Old Wine in New Bottles. In C. Steinfield, J. Bauer, and L. Caby, *Telecommunications in transition: policies, services and technologies in the European community.* Sage.

OECD (1995). *Telecommunications Infrastructure: the Benefits of Competition.* Paris: OECD

People's Daily (2000, 1999). Beijing: Central Committee of China Communist Party.

Petrazzini, B., Krishnaswamy, G. (1998). Socioeconomic Implications of Telecommunications Liberalization: India in the International Context. *The Information Society,* 14, 3-18.

Petrazzini, B. (1995). *The Political economy of telecommunications reform in developing countries: Privatization and liberalization in comparative perspective.* Westport CT: Praeger Publishers.

Pisciotta, A. (1997). Global Trends in Privatization and Liberalization. In W.H. Melody, *Telecom reform: Principles, policies & regulatory practices.* Lyngby: Technical University of Denmark.

Sant'Andre, R. (1998). *Brazilian telecommunications sector development, restructuring, privatization and emerging competition.* Presentation in the 12th Biennial Conference of ITS. Stockholm.

Snow, M. (1995). The AT&T Divestiture: A 10-year Retrospective. In D. Lamberton, *Beyond competition: The future of telecommunications*. B.V.: Elseiver Science.

Spiller, P., Vogelsang, I. (1996). The United Kingdom: A Pacesetter in Regulatory Incentives. In B. Levy & P. Spiller, *Regulation, institutions, and commitment*. New York: Cambridge University Press.

Tan, Z., Foster, W., Goodman, S. (1999). China's State-coordinated Internet Infrastructure. *Communications of the ACM*. 42(6), 44-52.

Thatcher, M. (1999). Liberalization in Britain: from Monopoly to Regulation of Competition. In K. Eliassen & M. Sjovaag, *European telecommunications liberalization*. London: Routledge.

Ure, J. (1997). Telecommunications in China and the Four Dragons. In J. Ure, *Telecommunications in Asia: Policy, planning and development*. Hong Kong: Hong Kong University Press.

Yang, P. (1997). A Calculation of China Telecommunications Development Situation. *P & T soft science research*, 39, 3-7.

ENDNOTES

1. There are few exceptions, e.g., in Finland there is no history of a monopoly in local services. Instead Finland has adopted a regional monopoly. As to state monopoly, the US is exceptional in that the monopoly AT&T is a publicly quoted corporation.
2. Hong Kong, Singapore, Korea, and Taiwan.
3. Not including Greece, Ireland, Portugal and Spain under derogation permission.
4. Obviously there are certain elements affecting telecommunications development. But undoubtedly a proper reform strategy is the most important one of them. In other words, a significant development can not be realized without an appropriate telecommunications reform.

Chapter IX

The Impact of Deregulation on the Quality of IDD Services: The Case of Hong Kong

Xu Yan
Hong Kong University of Science and Technology, China
International Telecommunication Union (ITU), Switzerland

James Y.L. Thong
Hong Kong University of Science and Technology, China

ABSTRACT

The introduction of deregulation in IDD service with effect from January 1999 triggered a round of extremely fierce competition in Hong Kong's IDD market. In response, both the incumbent operator and the new entrants had to adopt aggressive strategies to defend or gain market share. This chapter reports on an intensive experiment of the quality of IDD services provided by the major IDD operators in Hong Kong. An innovative research methodology was designed and 240 members of the public participated in the controlled experiment. Based on 1,790 successful IDD calls to the 10 most popular destinations from Hong Kong, the IDD quality of the major operators was benchmarked. To the best of our knowledge, this was the first large-scale experiment of its kind that had ever been conducted. The experiment revealed some interesting findings. First, the monopoly control of the international gateway by the incumbent operator puts pressure on the other IDD operators to devise an appropriate strategy balancing tariffs against the quality of the IDD line. Second, when competition becomes mature, all IDD operators must place more emphasis on quality. Finally, the full benefits of quality improvement in telecommunications service in a specific region are also subject to the level of development of telecommunications infrastructure in its counterpart economies.

INTRODUCTION

Telecommunications services have historically been operated as a monopoly industry in most countries until recently. In an environment that lacks competition, operators tend to take a conservative and bureaucratic approach in managing their telecommunications systems. Consequently, for decades subscribers have to contend with poor-quality service, lack of choice, and successive large price increase (Redwood, 1988).

However, in recent years, incumbent operators are facing an increasingly competitive market due to the growing trend of deregulation. At the same time, new technologies have provided effective means for new entrants to penetrate the market. Consequently, telecommunications has become one of the most competitive industries around the world. Telecommunications management in the 21st century is no longer an issue of technical operation, but of strategic planning that is challenged by the increasingly intensified competition. In this case, a profound knowledge of the potential impact of deregulation is critical for telecommunications management.

This chapter, based on an intensive experiment of international direct dialing (IDD) service quality in Hong Kong and interviews with individual operators, attempts to provide a panorama review of the competitive strategies of the incumbent operator and the new entrants in a resale-based competitive telecommunications market. It examines the significance of IDD quality in forming an effective competitive strategy within a market transitioning from a monopoly to full liberalization. Finally, the implications of deregulation on telecommunications management are highlighted.

BACKGROUND

In a highly competitive telecommunications market, various operators will adopt different strategies at their own pace (Carney, 1986; Shaw, 2000). Correspondingly, approaches adopted by the operators may have different effects on the quality of service. For example, the application of Internet Protocol in the IDD service can significantly improve circuit efficiency, allowing the operators to offer extremely attractive tariffs to subscribers. However, there is a tradeoff as this type of IDD service is susceptible to voice distortion and time delay due to the high rate of data compression and the limited bandwidth (ITU, 2000). As such, setting the proper level of service quality to meet a specific marketing objective is probably one of the key factors in formulating a competitive strategy.

At the same time, the quality of service in the telecommunications industry is a major issue of concern to regulators (Brewer, 1989). To ensure that customers can enjoy the full benefits of competition, including choice of operators, quality of line, and lower tariffs, regulators have to adopt an effective regulatory approach. However, there does not appear to be a unified approach. According to a survey of regulatory authorities in the host markets of the top 50 carriers in the world, except the US, the approaches taken by individual regulators in regulating service quality have evidently been different (Banfield, 1999). In Europe, regulators from Finland, Sweden, Norway, and the UK are vociferous champions of the free market as a guarantor of service quality. Meanwhile, Australia's ACA (Australian Communications Authority) has adopted a rigorous monitoring technique even though its market is fully competitive. In order to evaluate the effectiveness of individual regulatory approaches, a comprehensive study of the impact of deregulation on telecommunications service quality is critical.

There have been some prior studies that investigated issues relating to telecommunications quality. Godfrey and Endres (1994) conducted a comprehensive review of the evolution of quality management within telecommunications over more than 100 years and concluded that competition has led to the realization in the telecommunications industry that quality had become a strategic issue in telecommunications management. Xu (1999) provided an evolutionary review of British Telecom's billing system and highlighted that deregulation has led to the transition of British Telecom from an operation-orientated behavior to a customer-orientated one, and quality has become a key part of its competitive strategy. By making comparisons between the telecommunications service quality of Australian operators with that of other OECD countries, Xavier (1996) concluded that there has been considerable improvement in network reliability since the introduction of competition. In general, most studies suggest that deregulation is one of the most powerful drivers of quality improvement in telecommunications.

However, most of the prior studies on quality focus on the viewpoints of telecommunications operators, mainly on the technical operation of the telecommunications network (e.g., Oodan, Ward, & Mullee, 1997; Xavier, 1996). The customers' perspectives of IDD quality have not been well measured or studied. Quality has also been studied in an isolated manner (Berg & Lynch, 1992; Xu, 1999), while in the current competitive market-place firms usually offer price-quality combinations and potential customers can choose the bundles that maximize their net benefits. A study following a quality-only approach is certainly incomplete. Additionally, the conclusions of previous studies are based on traditional telecommunications systems (Elbert, 1990; Lynch, Buzas, & Berg, 1994; Mullee & Oodan, 1994) while the appearances of new technologies such as Internet Protocol have provided operators with additional choices to formulate their competitive strategies. Lastly, most of the previous literature studied telecommunications markets where competition has mature (Godfrey & Endres 1994; Xavier, 1996). In the case of a telecommunications market that is undergoing a turbulent transition from monopoly operation to full competition, the determinants of a successful competitive strategy may be significantly different. Findings drawn from studies of a general stable market may not be applicable to the evolving telecommunications sector.

Shaw (1997) argued that there is a necessity for further research on determinants of competitive strategy formulation and provided some theoretical guidelines. However, to the best of our knowledge, there is no such empirical study in the literature. One possible reason is that such studies will involve extremely labor-intensive work. Another possible reason is that only a limited number of markets are fully deregulated, which means that such an empirical study is restricted to scholars in a small number of countries and regions.

This study is different from prior studies in several aspects. The first difference lies in the context. Instead of studying the operational strategy in a mature competitive market or a monopolized market, this study focuses on competitive strategies in a telecommunications market transitioning from monopoly to full competition. The second difference lies in the scope of study. Instead of studying service quality solely, this study also investigates the significance of other determinants in formulating competitive strategy, including tariffs and new technologies such as Internet Protocol. Finally, this study is based on empirical research to complement the theoretical analysis, and the quality of the IDD service is measured from the customers' perspective in a controlled experimental environment.

THE CASE OF IDD SERVICES IN HONG KONG

In Hong Kong, international telephone service in the form of IDD service was monopolized by the incumbent operator under its franchise that was due to expire in the year 2006. On 20 January 1998, the Hong Kong Government concluded an agreement with the incumbent operator for the early termination of its exclusive franchise over IDD service. Key elements of this agreement include the surrender of the franchised license in March 1998, the introduction of resale-based competition in IDD service with effect from January 1999, and the introduction of facility-based competition from 1 January 2000 (Hong Kong Telecom, 1998). This means new entrants could provide IDD service via leased international circuits from the incumbent operator from 1 January 1999 and could either lease circuits from other facility owners or construct their own facilities after 1 January 2000.

The removal of regulatory entry barriers to providing IDD service triggered a round of extremely fierce competition in Hong Kong's IDD market. By the end of 1999, the regulator had issued 148 external telecommunications service licenses (OFTA, 2000). Although not all of these licensees have formally launched their services, the fact that Hong Kong is a city with a population of only 6.8 million implies that the entry of any single new entrant will significantly affect the market share of the others. To meet this competitive challenge, both the incumbent and the new entrants will have to formulate their strategies in an innovative and aggressive way.

However, these strategies are subject to certain constraints for the year 1999 due to the fact that the new entrants can only provide IDD service on a resale basis. This means that they have to lease circuits from the incumbent operator and the traffic has to go through the incumbent's international gateway. As a result, the rental prices for leased lines are high due to the absence of competition in international facility provision. This has imposed high economic constraints on the new entrants in formulating their competitive strategies.

The existence of multiparty players in the market suggests that there is a diversity of competitive strategies. Consequently, these different strategies have various effects on the quality of telecommunications services. An in-depth study of the differences in quality can reveal each individual operator's strategic objectives and hence the impact of telecommunications deregulation on the service quality can be highlighted.

THE EXPERIMENT

An experiment was conducted to benchmark the IDD quality of all the major operators in Hong Kong. The use of an experiment is justified as it allows us to control for different situations which may have unintended effects on the variable of interest. For example, in using other methodologies such as surveys and interviews, there is the problem of how well the participants can recall their perceptions of the various dimensions of IDD quality of a line. Further, participants may have preconceived attitudes toward certain IDD operators due to factors such as word of mouth, pricing, and advertisement. By subjecting all participants to the same experimental control, we can reduce the effect of confounding variables and increase the validity of our findings (Cook & Campbell, 1979; Martin, 2000).

Timeline

The experiment was conducted over a period of four weeks in the middle of 1999, six months after the start of competition in the provision of IDD services. Six months as deemed to be more than sufficient time for all the operators to stabilize their quality of IDD services. We conducted the experiment over four weeks to reduce fluctuations in daily and weekly usage of IDD services. Further, the experiment took place every day of the week including weekends. The experiment started at 9 am in the morning and ran till 11 pm at night. This allowed us to take into account the fluctuation in IDD usage between peak time and off-peak time.

Questionnaires

Three questionnaires were designed specifically for the experiment. The purpose of the first questionnaire (questionnaire A) was to collect demographic data and general IDD usage of each participant. It was completed by the participants before the start of the experiment. The purpose of the second questionnaire (questionnaire B) was to measure the participants' perception of the voice quality of the five different IDD lines. We adapted the measures from the ITU-T Recommendation P.82 on Telephone Transmission Quality (Subjective Opinion Tests) for evaluation of telephone transmission quality of international calls (ITU, 1993). The ITU-T (Telecommunication Standardization Sector) is a permanent organ of the International Telecommunication Union (ITU), the United Nations specialized agency in the field of telecommunications, which produces recommendations on telecommunication topics with a view to standardizing them on a worldwide basis. We used seven items to measure the dimensions of voice quality, including echo of sender's voice, noise on the line, cross talk, time delay in hearing the receiver's voice, distortion in the receiver's voice, volume of the receiver's voice, and the overall quality. All items were measured on a 5-point Likert scale. According to the ITU-T Recommendation P.82, where a written presentation of the choices is used, five classes of choice are appropriate and have been shown to yield reliable responses. The participants completed this questionnaire immediately after making each IDD call during the experiment. Two versions of the questionnaire (English and Chinese) were developed for this experiment. The English version was developed first. Next, the English version was translated into Chinese. Another person then translated the Chinese version into English. Through this procedure, we confirmed that both versions of the questionnaires were equivalent.

The purpose of the third questionnaire (questionnaire C) was to measure the call setup time and the completion rate for the five IDD lines. According to the ITU-T recommendations, the call setup time and the completion rate are also important criteria of international line quality (ITU, 1992; 1996). The call setup time assesses how quickly end-to-end connections are implemented while the completion rate helps to assess the quality of service obtained by the calling subscriber. The experimenter completed this questionnaire during the experiment.

Procedure

The experiment was conducted in an experiment room at a local Hong Kong university. In the experiment room, two tables were arranged to allow the experimenter and the participant to work separately. Two sub-phone sets, belonging to the same telephone number and connected with five IDD lines, were installed and placed on both tables. An opaque screen was installed between the experimenter and the participant to ensure that the participant could not see the dialed number.

When the participants arrived, they were shown to a waiting room. In the waiting room, the participants completed questionnaire A. They provided the phone number of a friend or relative that they wanted to call in one of the 10 designated countries. These countries were Australia, Canada, Japan, North China (all provinces except Guangdong), Philippines, Singapore, South China (Guangdong province), Taiwan, the United Kingdom, and the United States. These ten places represented the most popular destinations of IDD calls from Hong Kong (Cable and Wireless HKT, 1999). It also implies that competition is greater for services to these ten destinations than to other destinations. China was divided into North and South China, as it was the usual practice in Hong Kong for the purposes of IDD destinations with separate tariffs applied. Hence, there was external validity to the results of the experiment.

Each participant made five telephone calls to the same number, each lasting two minutes. These five telephone calls were dialed using the five different IDD services. The experimenter dialed the number for the participant, so that the participant did not know which IDD service he or she was using when making the telephone calls. The experimenter also measured the call setup time with a stopwatch that was accurate up to one-hundredth of a second. Call setup time was defined as the time lag between dialing the last digit of the phone number and hearing the first dial tone. If the line did not connect, there would be different types of abnormal signals. In such cases, the experimenter noted down whether there was an announcement from the operator, silence, congestion tone, or busy tone. On completion of each telephone call, the participant answered the seven questions regarding the quality of the IDD line. The order of IDD services that the experimenter used was randomized for each participant to avoid systematic bias toward any one operator.

Only when all five telephone calls to the same number were successful did we consider the data to be valid. Otherwise, the data were discarded due to incomplete information on the quality of any one of the IDD lines. Further, all the IDD operators were not aware of this experiment. Prior to the start of the actual experiment, the experimental procedure and questionnaires were pilot-tested with 10 participants drawn from the general public. The purpose of the pilot-test stage was to confirm that the experimental procedure was clear and the questionnaires were understandable and unambiguous.

Due to the scale of the experiment, we used five full-time experimenters to reduce experimenter fatigue. The experimenters were given two days training to familiarize themselves with the experimental procedure and the different signal tones. Statistical analysis shows that there is no significant interviewer bias on the results of the experiment.

Participants

The experiment was advertised to the general public in a residential area of Hong Kong. Two methods of promotion were used. First, we posted advertisements around the university including on the university's electronic notice board. Second, advertisements were posted at major entrances to apartment buildings, residential homes' post boxes, as well as bus stops in the suburb where the university was located. All participants were given a monetary incentive of HK$50 to take part in the experiment. This incentive allowed us to secure enough participants to make a total of 1,790 successful calls altogether with an average of 35.8 participants calling each of the 10 most popular destinations.

THE GAME OF TARIFF AND QUALITY

The IDD operators that were included in the experiment are the incumbent operator and three other fixed telecommunications network licensees. While there were 148 external telecommunications service licensees, only four operators were issued fixed network licenses. Except for the incumbent, the other three licensees have provided IDD service through callback since they obtained their fixed local network licenses in 1995. Using callback, they forwarded their Hong Kong-located customer's number and other information to one of their foreign partner operators when the customer wanted to call a foreign destination. Then, their partner operator dialed back to Hong Kong from abroad using the caller's number and connected the other end of the circuit to its local subscriber being called. In this way, the call is defined as originating from abroad so that it does not infringe the incumbent operator's franchise over IDD service. Interestingly, in response to this, the incumbent has also begun to provide a low-tariff service on the basis of callback arrangement since 1995. Hence, a certain degree of competition in IDD services had actually existed even before the incumbent surrendered its franchise at the beginning of 1999.

From January 1999, all new operators began to provide IDD service on the basis of International Simple Resale (ISR) due to economic consideration. By leasing an international circuit for fixed rent from the incumbent, a new operator can easily enjoy economies of scale if it can expand its subscriber base. Reduction in tariff has been used as an effective strategy to attract subscriptions. Figure 1 shows the dramatic IDD tariff reduction to some major destinations during the period from July 1998 to July 1999, which was offered by one of the new operators. Due to their early establishment in the market, the four main operators controlled the major share of the IDD market. For this reason, this study focused on these four operators only. For confidentiality sake, we refer to the incumbent operator as operator A, while B, C, and D are used to represent the other three licensees. Additionally, A1 and A2 represent the incumbent operator's two IDD services (high-tariff and low-tariff respectively).

The Privileged Incumbent

For the incumbent operator, the objective of its competitive strategy is to defend its dominance in the market and to enhance existing customers' loyalty. To achieve this objective, the incumbent takes two approaches. The first is to provide a higher quality IDD service for customers, especially business customers, who are more concerned with quality than with tariff rates. The second approach is to provide a certain degree of discount on tariff rates for a relatively lower quality IDD service. The regular peak-time tariffs of the four licensees to the 10 most popular destinations are listed in Table 1. For the purpose of clarity, these tariffs are unified by defining A1's tariff to be 1.00. On average, the tariff rates for the lower quality IDD service (i.e., A2) are almost 23 percent cheaper than that of the higher quality IDD service (i.e., A1).

The results of the experiment show that IDD service A1 has consistently superior quality on almost all indicators including lesser degrees of echo, noise, cross talk, time delay, distortion, and volume. Figure 2 presents the results of the participants' assessment of the overall voice quality of each individual IDD operator. The responses ranged from 1, which signifies very dissatisfied with the IDD service, to 5, which signifies very satisfied with the IDD service.

The results indicate that the IDD quality of the incumbent operator, including both IDD service A1 and IDD service A2, is much higher than that of the other three licensees. This is partly due to its decades-long operation and maintenance experience, but mainly due to its ownership of the international gateway and its huge capacity of international circuits, which enable it to provide circuit switching-based, high quality services. Also, as 1999 was the first year for resale-based service provision after the end of the incumbent's

Figure 1. IDD tariff reduction of Operator E (Source: Operator B's promotion leaflet)

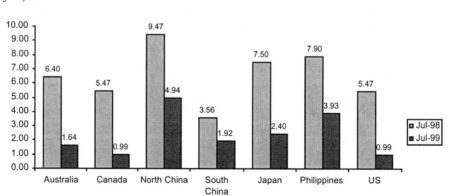

Table 1. Unified regular tariff of the licensees (peak time rate as on 21/07/1999)

| Country | IDD Service | | | | | |
	A1	A2	B	C	D	Average
Australia	1.00	0.69	0.22	0.68	0.23	0.56
Canada	1.00	0.44	0.15	0.43	0.15	0.43
Japan	1.00	0.73	0.30	0.70	0.30	0.61
North China	1.00	1.00	0.52	0.93	0.52	0.79
Philippines	1.00	1.00	0.50	0.99	0.49	0.80
Singapore	1.00	0.67	0.30	0.67	0.30	0.60
South China	1.00	1.00	0.80	0.96	0.79	0.91
Taiwan	1.00	0.73	0.26	0.72	0.26	0.59
UK	1.00	0.61	0.19	0.61	0.19	0.52
USA	1.00	0.44	0.15	0.42	0.14	0.43
Average	1.00	0.73	0.34	0.71	0.34	0.62

century-long monopoly operation, there existed cost cross-subsidization due to the difficulty in implementing accounting separation because of the absence of historical cost data. This privilege enabled the incumbent to provide a higher quality service without being constrained by the cost. As for the new entrants, they have to pay high rentals to lease international circuits from the incumbent operator and use technologies such as Internet Protocol to improve the efficiency of their circuits. This leads to a deterioration of their IDD service quality. Hence, the new entrants have to offer significantly lower tariff rates than the incumbent operator in order to attract subscribers. This puts them in

Figure 2. Overall voice quality

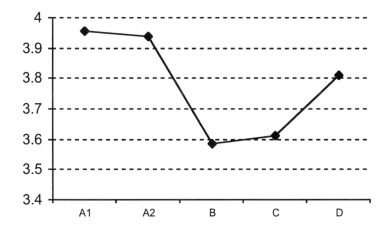

a very vulnerable position. For example, IDD service C has similar tariff levels as IDD service A2, but its quality is much lower than that of A2; hence, it is very difficult for operator C to compete with the incumbent without reducing its tariff further.

Another disadvantage faced by the new entrants is the relatively longer time needed to set up a call due to their inability to directly access the international gateway. This is due to the technologies used by the new entrants and the relatively complicated process of accessing the incumbent's international gateway. For example, if the new entrants use Internet Protocol, the regular telephone signal has to be converted into packets before transmission and these packets will then be converted back to regular signals again at the destination. This process will inevitably lead to a delay in establishing the appropriate route. Figure 3 presents the average time needed to set up an IDD call by each individual operator.

The implication of the above analysis is that resale-based competition with a monopolized international gateway is probably not the best solution for telecommunications deregulation. The high rental for leased lines charged by the incumbent operator will put pressure on the new entrants to devise an appropriate balance between tariff rates and IDD quality. As a result, subscribers cannot enjoy both improved quality and decreased tariff rates simultaneously. In the meantime, the incumbent still enjoys certain privileges. Figure 4 shows that the incumbent still dominated the IDD market in the middle of 1999 when this experiment was conducted.

The following events that happened in Hong Kong's telecommunications market soon after facility-based competition became available provided further evidence to support the conclusions drawn above. In February 2000, one of the new entrants began to provide International Private Leased Circuit

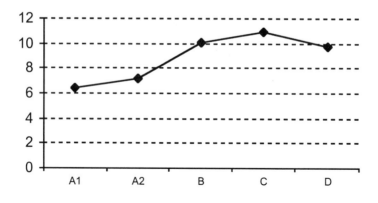

Figure 3. Call Set-Up Time (Unit: Second)

(IPLC) service in competition with the incumbent. Its rental charge during the promotion phase was almost 65 percent cheaper than that of the incumbent (Telecom News, 2000). The cost savings from either owning their own facilities or leasing circuits from alternative suppliers provided more opportunities for the new entrants to reduce their tariffs and improve their quality. Figure 5 shows that operator B had further reduced its tariff in May 2000 with the installation of its self-owned facility. The reduced cost constraints would undoubtedly provide more impetus for further quality improvement, as the new entrants can reduce the rate of data compression or use more bandwidth.

Quality: The Final Decisive Determinant

Due to Hong Kong's specific geographic location, business relationships, and historical links with certain countries, there are specific high-traffic

Figure 4. IDD market share

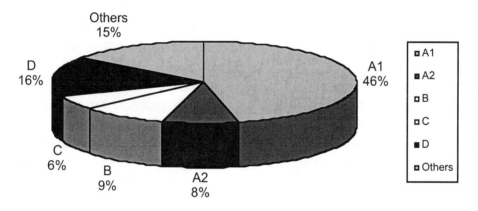

Figure 5. Operator B's IDD tariff reduction in May 2000 (HK$) (Source: Corporate promotion leaflets)

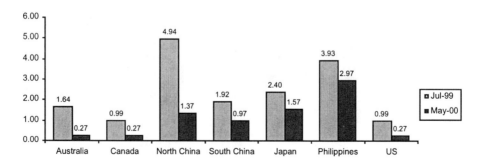

destinations for IDD services. Figure 6 shows the frequency of calls to the 10 most popular destinations. China, the US, and Canada were the most popular destinations for IDD calls from Hong Kong. This is similar to the statistical pattern provided by the operator of the international gateway (Cable and Wireless HKT, 1999). Consequently, these destinations become battlegrounds for fierce competition. However, due to the different degrees of market liberalization in different destinations, competitive strategies are evidently different.

The introduction of callback service by one company in 1995 posed a strong challenge to the incumbent operator. While Hong Kong's regulator did not consider the callback service to be an infringement of the franchise as the traffic originated from a foreign destination, it might be considered illegal in some other regions and countries. For example, callback service is banned in China for both outgoing and incoming calls. As a result, although callback-based competition for IDD service started in 1995, it was mainly limited to a few destinations where the market has been liberalized, e.g., the US. The tariff rates to the US and Canada had dropped from HK\$9.80 in 1995 (Wong, 1997) to about HK\$1.00 at the beginning of 1999 (Xu & Pitt, 1999). There is not much room left for further tariff reduction. To increase their market share, the strategy adopted by all operators is to improve their IDD quality. Figure 7 and Figure 8 show that for IDD services to the US and Canada, there is no significant difference in IDD quality among the individual operators.

Interestingly, the incumbent operator increased the quality of its lower rate IDD service, A2. The incumbent operator probably realized that reducing tariff rate by itself is no longer the sole selling point to keep customers loyal

Figure 6. Frequency of IDD calls to top 10 destinations

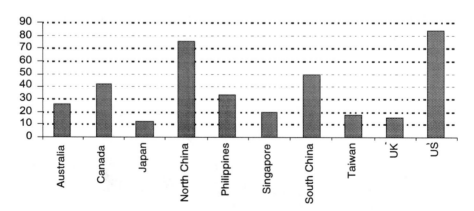

in a highly competitive IDD market. A combination of low tariff and high quality is the only way to succeed in a market where the competition has matured.

In contrast to the case of IDD services to the US and Canada, the real competition for IDD service to China started in the year 1999. Previously, Hong Kong's incumbent operator faced no competition for IDD calls to China due to the Chinese government's restriction on callback service. The tariff rate to North China was about HK$9.00 at the end of 1998. This implied that there was plenty of room for rate reduction. As Table 1 shows, both operator B and operator D have reduced their tariffs dramatically. Simultaneously, improving IDD quality was not at the top of their agenda (see Figure 9).

The implication of the above analyses is that price reduction is probably the most commonly used strategy by new entrants to gain market shares. However, when the competition becomes mature, in addition to rate reduction, IDD quality has to be given a higher priority. In other words, quality is probably the final decisive determinant in competitive strategy formulation. For regulators, this implies that the subscribers' overall interest can only be

Figure 7. Overall IDD quality to the U.S.

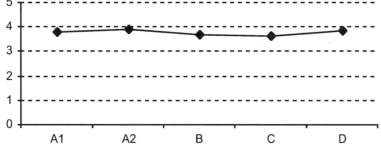

Figure 8. Overall IDD quality to Canada

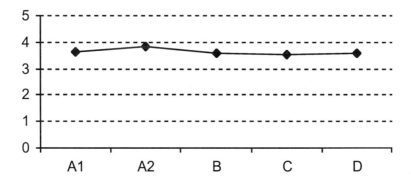

protected by relentless liberalization of the market. However, before competition reaches maturity, a certain amount of monitoring and regulation of IDD quality may be necessary.

Quality: A Global Issue

There are some quality indicators that are beyond the control of the originating operators. The results of the experiment show that these indicators are indifferent among operators in Hong Kong but are different with regard to the destinations of IDD calls. Figure 10 illustrates the analysis of abnormal signals which included congestion tone, abnormal announcements, silence, and disconnection during the IDD calls.

The results show that North China and the Philippines were the two destinations that have the highest rate of abnormal signals at 10.25% and 8% respectively. In fact, these are the two destinations that have the poorest telecommunications infrastructures among the 10 destinations included in the experiment. In China, the telephone mainline per 100 inhabitants was only 6.96% at the end of 1998, which was similar to that of the US in the 1920s (Kan, 1999). For the Philippines, the telephone mainline per 100 inhabitants in the same year was 3.70%. Compared with 66.13% for the US and 63.39 percent for Canada, the telephone infrastructures of China and the Philippines are not well developed (ITU, 1999). The less developed infrastructure will lead to high congestion rate and other quality problems. Additionally, both countries have undergone very limited deregulation in fixed network service provision. In China, China Telecom fully controls and owns the fixed network, while in the Philippines it is Philippines Long Distance Telephone Company (PLDT) that dominates the market. The lack of competition, as has been experienced

Figure 9. Overall IDD Quality and Rate Level to North China

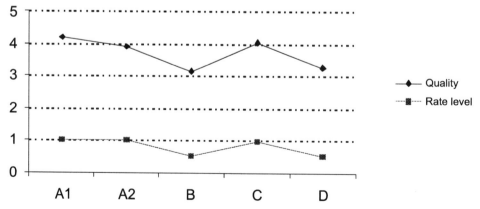

by early-mover countries, will lead to low efficiency and poor quality performance (Redwood, 1988). However, as Figure 10 indicates, victims of a poor
infrastructure and less liberalized market are not necessarily limited to inside
their own borders in the case of IDD service. The fruits of telecommunications
competition can only be fully achieved within the context of a worldwide
development of infrastructure and deregulation.

CONCLUSION

In many ways, Hong Kong has become a "test bed" and showcase (or
policy laboratory) for later deregulators in the Asia-Pacific region (Ure,
1997). This chapter, based on an innovative experimental methodology,
provides an empirical analysis of the effects of telecommunications deregulation in Hong Kong on the IDD operators' strategy formulation. The analysis
suggests that IDD quality is probably one of the most critical factors in
formulating the competitive strategy. Operators may temporarily sacrifice
quality in an immature competitive market at the initial stage, but they will
have to place a higher priority on the quality issue when the market becomes
fully competitive and marginal rate reduction is not feasible. Only then will
IDD subscribers be beneficiaries of full market liberalization in terms of
reduced tariff and improved service quality.

With the incumbent operator's monopoly of the provision of international circuits and leased lines, resale-based competition fails to allow
subscribers to fully exploit the benefits of competition. The application of
efficiency enhancing technology such as Internet Protocol results in inferior
IDD quality. In order to prevent this phenomenon from happening, regulators

Figure 10. Abnormal signals

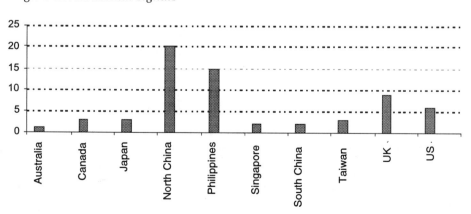

should push for facility-based competition at the earliest possible date. In Hong Kong, the introduction of facility-based competition in IDD service from the beginning of 2000 has dramatically reduced the rental for leased lines. The reduced rental cost will surely, as illustrated in Figure 5, create more room for further tariff reduction and quality improvement.

Finally, the quality of telecommunications services can only be fully exploited within the context of a worldwide deregulation. Poor performance of telecommunications services in a country due to its poorly developed infrastructure and less liberalized operation can affect the quality of service for subscribers at the other end of the line. In this case, international organizations such as the World Trade Organization (WTO) and the ITU should take a more proactive stance to propel telecommunications deregulation globally and to facilitate the development of telecommunications infrastructure in developing countries.

This study has several implications for telecommunications regulators. First, competition is the most powerful driving force for quality improvement. To ensure that customers get the best possible choice, good quality, and low tariffs from their telecommunications service operators, regulators have to take a relentless stance over deregulation. Second, although deregulation is the best instrument for guaranteeing service quality, its effectiveness becomes evident only when competition has matured, as there are other determinants in an operator's competitive strategy, such as tariff, during the transition phase. During this phase, a certain degree of monitoring and implementation of a regulatory scheme over service quality may be necessary. Third, resale-based competition will create high economic barriers for the new entrants. Consequently, customers may not enjoy the full benefits of deregulation. Facility-based competition should be introduced as soon as possible.

REFERENCES

Banfield, J. (1999). World's watchdogs–Many bark but few bite. *Communications International, 26(10),* 22-24.

Berg, S. V., & Lynch, J. G. (1992). The measurement and encouragement of telephone service quality. *Telecommunications Policy, 16,* 210-224.

Brewer, L. T. (1989). Customer needs and quality of service: A major issue. *Telecommunications Policy, 13 (1),* 2-9.

Cable and Wireless HKT. (1999). Hong Kong Telecom Annual Report 1999.

Carney, M. G., (1986). Strategy in the telecommunications market: The effects of liberalization and competition. *Telecommunications Policy, 10(3),* 245-257.

Cook, T. D. & Campbell, D. T. (1979). *Quasi-experimentation: Design and analysis issues for field settings.* Chicago: Rand McNally.

Elbert, B. R. (1990). *International telecommunications management.* Boston, MA: Artech House.

Godfrey, A. B. & Endres, A. C. (1994). The evolution of quality management within telecommunications. *IEEE Communications Magazine, October,* 26-34.

Hong Kong Telecom. (1998, February 20). Hong Kong Telecom press news.

ITU. (1992). *Service quality assessment for connection set-up and release delays.* ITU-T Recommendation E.431.

ITU. (1993). *Telephone transmission quality: Method for evaluation of service from the standpoint of speech transmission quality.* ITU-T Recommendation P.82.

ITU. (1996). *Observations on international outgoing telephone calls for quality of service.* ITU-T Recommendation E.422.

ITU. (1999). *World Telecommunication Development Report.*

ITU. (2000). Background issues paper on IP Telephony workshop, http://www.itu.int/iptel.

Kan, K. L. (1999). Where to go for Chinese telecommunications industry? *Posts and Telecommunications Economic Management,* 10, 8-12.

Lynch, J. G., Buzas, T. E. & Berg, S. V. (1994). Regulatory measurement and evaluation of telephone service quality. *Management Science,* 40, 169-94.

Martin, D. W. (2000). *Doing psychology experiments.* Fifth Edition, Belmont, CA: Wadsworth.

Mullee, T., and Oodan, A. (1994). Telecommunications quality of service– Principles and management. *British Telecommunications Engineering,* 13, 53-61.

OFTA (2000). Office of Telecommunications Authority of Hong Kong. http://www.ofta.gov.hk/index_eng1.html.

Oodan, A.P., Ward, K. E. & Mullee, A. W. (1997). *Quality of service in telecommunications.* London: Institute of Electrical Engineers.

Redwood, J. (1988). Preface for *Privatizing the world,* by O. Letwin (1986), London: Cassell Educational.

Shaw, J. (1997). Telecom*munications deregulation.* Boston, MA: Artech House.

Shaw, J. (2000). *Strategic management in telecommunications.* Boston, MA: Artech House.

Telecom News, (2000, February 23). New T&T provide IPLC international leased line service. http://www.cci.cn.net.

Ure, J. (1997). *Telecommunications in Asia-Policy, planning, and development*. Hong Kong: Hong Kong University Press.

Wong, M. H. (1997). Information age. Hong Kong, Hong Kong Economic Daily Press.

Xavier, P. (1996). Monitoring telecommunications deregulation through international benchmarking. *Telecommunications Policy, 20(8)*, 585-606.

Xu, Y. (1999). Industrial deregulation: The strong propellant for quality improvement–With reference to the experience of British Telecom. *Strategic Change, 8*, 135-42.

Xu, Y. & Pitt, D. C. (1999). One country, two systems–Contrasting approaches to telecommunications deregulation in Hong Kong and China. *Telecommunications Policy, 23*, 235-260.

Chapter X

The Role of New Connectivity Options in Information Infrastructure Development in Sub-Saharan Africa

Fola Yahaya
London School of Economics, United Kingdom

INTRODUCTION

The greatest difficulty in providing telecommunications services in Sub-Saharan Africa has been the establishment of a comprehensive national telecommunications infrastructure. With the majority of the population rurally based, extending the coverage of the public network within African countries continues to be an expensive and time-consuming proposition. Further, demand for such services has rapidly exceeded supply and the infrastructure has necessarily, and for practical reasons, been concentrated in urban areas. However, a global shift in the technological paradigm of telecommunications development has opened up opportunities for African countries to rapidly deploy information infrastructure and facilitate the achievement of universal access objectives.

This chapter examines innovative telecommunications connectivity options, in particular fiber optic submarine cable and satellite systems, emerging on the African continent and asks how they can contribute not only to improved telecommunications, but also to the broader development of information infrastructure within the region. It is argued that if less developed countries and regions are to implement telecommunication networks and information services that will serve their interests, they must prioritize development objectives that rest firmly in their particular economic, political, cultural and social context.

NEW CONNECTIVITY OPTIONS
Satellite Projects

The application of satellite technology to telecommunications transmission appears ideally suited to the Sub-Saharan African region. Satellite systems can be used to provide basic telephony as well as radio and broadcast television with the principle advantages of reliability and durability. Capable of installation wherever necessary, they are considered to be well suited to the African environment (Gifford & Cosper, 1998). For example, small, low-cost earth stations such as those used to provide rural telephony with domestic satellites can provide isolated regions with voice and data communications. However, there is huge international disparity in the availability of satellite services. Most satellite systems serve the northern hemisphere and extend from the east to the west, leaving the southern hemisphere grossly underserved. One of the causes of this unevenness has been the mechanism by which satellite segments are allocated.

The International Telecommunications Satellite Organization (INTELSAT), who up till 1984 operated two thirds of all intercontinental message traffic, keen to maintain its free market ethos, disperses satellite segments on a "first come, first served" rather than an equitable basis. Partly as a result of this bias, and also resource issues, there is now a huge disparity in the satellite communications capabilities of the developed and the developing world. As of 1993, there were some 184 communications satellites in geosynchronous orbit. Of these only a small number had been launched by developing countries,[1] severely limiting the capacity of developing countries to exploit the benefits of satellite technology. This is compounded by the fact that Africa remains the only continent without its own regional satellite system. Thus, though practically all countries in Sub-Saharan Africa have satellite earth stations, the technology has yet to be fully exploited. Rather, the high cost of using satellite telephony has restricted access to a handful that are willing to pay up to US$3 per minute for the privilege.

In an attempt to resolve the lack of indigenous satellite communications capacity the Regional African Satellite Communication System (RASCOM) was established in 1992 to harness satellite communications and to boost telecommunications traffic among African states.[2] RASCOM has rationalized satellite telecommunications in the region by pooling satellite capacity purchased by individual national operators and plans to invite preliminary tenders from international companies who want to join a "build, operate and transfer" (BOT) consortium to install the first pan-African communications satellite. RASCOM estimates that calls from its phone stations would be around 10 US cents a minute, with the cost of building one phone station projected at US$1,000.[3]

RASCOM is far from alone in its ambitions to boost the telecommunications capacity in Sub-Saharan Africa. A number of multinational consortia are planning the deployment of new satellite systems designed to offer services ranging from global mobile services to broadband fixed telephony. Current satellite constellations deploy geostationary orbiting satellites that suffer from a variety of restrictions that these new systems aim to bypass. Propagation time delays arising from the lag between signal transmission and reception are problematic, as is noise deterioration in the form of echoing. Also, the power required to send a signal an average distance of 36,500 km necessitates the use of large terminals for the receipt of signals, thus making handheld mobile communication, for the most part, impractical (Leite, 1996). In an attempt to bypass these problems, new satellite communications systems are being planned and deployed which utilize the latest in satellite technology and have the potential to provide Sub-Saharan Africa with instant infrastructure. The common denominator of all these planned systems is their use of low earth orbiting satellites, which rest at relatively close proximity to the earth and therefore avoid some of the deficiencies that affect their forerunners.

As of 1999, there were three types of low earth orbiting (LEO) satellite systems that were being proposed. The so-called "Little LEO" satellite systems are designed to use low earth orbits to offer worldwide data communications in small tranches, at transmission rates akin to mid-1980s personal computer modems. Among the communications services offered by little LEOs are automated meter reading, remote asset tracking, vehicle messaging, personal messaging and supervisory control and data acquisition. Next are the medium-sized LEOs, which would allow global communications using handheld Global Mobile Personal Communications Service (GMPCS) devices from any location on the planet. Finally, there are the super-LEOs such as Skybridge and Teledesic. Teledesic's 266-satellite system is designed to provide broadband communications to users globally. Backed by Microsoft chairman Bill Gates, the Teledesic system is designed to be accessible via laptop-sized terminals mounted flat on a rooftop and connected to a personal

Table 1. Planned satellite projects relevant to Sub-Saharan Africa, July 1999

Name	Main Investors and industrial partners	Industrial Partners	Estimated Project Cost (US$)	Type of system	No. of satellites	Services	Start date	Relevance to Africa
ACTEL	ACTEL Ltd.	American Mobile Systems	385 million	GEO	2	Mobile telephony, voice and data	2001	Initial coverage of Southern Africa and then pan-African
East	Matra Marconi Space	n/a	1 billion		1	Telecommunications and multimedia	2000	Pan -African coverage
Ellipsio	Mobile Communications Holdings Inc.	n/a	n/a	MEO	10	GMPCS, fixed telephony, fax, data, paging, positioning services	2001	Coverage in Sub-Saharan Africa
Globalstar	Loral Space and Communications and QualComm	Aérospatiale, Alcatel, Daimler Benz, Fimmeccanica and Hyundai, Teital and Ericcson	2.5 billion	Narrowband LEO	48	GMPCS, telex, fax, data, paging, position services	1999	Partners in South and West Africa
ICO*	Inmarsat	Hughes Electronics, NEC, Ericsson, Samsung, Panasonic, Mitsubishi and Wavecom.	3 billion	MEO	10	GMPCS, fixed telephony, fax, data, paging, position/emergency maritime services	2000	Earth Station in South Africa
Inmarsat	Inmarsat International Consortium	n/a	n/a	Narrowband GEO	5	GMPCS, telex, fax, data, paging, position/emergency maritime services	1993	Global organisation providing specialised services
Iridium*	Motorola	Lockheed, Raytheon, DEVCOM, Siemens	3.8 billion	Narrowband LEO	66	GMPCS, fixed telephony, fax, data, paging,	1998	Iridium Africa holds a 1.2 per cent stake
Orbcomm	Orbital Sciences Corp and Canadian telecom provider Teleglobe Inc.	Technology Resource Bhd	500 million	Little LEO	36	2-way messaging, data,global monitoring & positioning	1998	Services available between the tropic of Cancer and Capricorn
PanAmSat	Hughes Electronics	n/a	n/a	Broadband GEO	17	TV, private communications networks, video conferencing paging,	1997	Already have a service provider in Africa
RASCOM	African governments & 40 operators in African countries	Open to tender	1.2 billion	Broadband GEO	2	Fixed telephony, distance education/health, TV, radio, data	2001	African organised
Skybridge	Alcatel	Ericcson	1 billion	Broadband LEO	64	Telehealth/education/commuting Internet access, interactive entertainment	2001	Coverage in Africa
Spaceway	Hughes Communications Inc.	n/a	1 billion	MEO/LEO	20 MEO/8 LEO	Fixed telephony, fax, data Inter/Intranet access, telecommuting, CAD/CAM transmission, videoconferencing	2001	Coverage in Africa
Teledesic	Microsoft and McCaw cellular communications	AT&T	9 billion	Broadband LEO	288	Voice, data, video conferencing, Internet access	2002	Main focus on rural and sparsely populated areas.
VITAsat	NGO	n/a	n/a	Little LEO	2	Global e-mail	1998	Service in North West Africa

Source: Collated from UNESCO World Communication Report, 1997, Fibre Optics News, Satellite Communications and InfoDev, 1998.

computer or network. The system is designed to support millions of simultaneous users, with access speeds more than 2,000 times faster than the 1998 standard of 33 kbps analogue modems.

Submarine Cable Projects

While competition increases apace in satellite communications, African policy makers are also able to choose from a raft of ongoing initiatives to integrate Africa into the global information network through fiber-optic cables. Since the 1980s there have been several proposed projects to encircle the African continent with submarine cable systems. By utilizing a system of diverse routing, the rationale behind these submarine cable schemes is to provide global connectivity with the capability of direct transmission links between African countries.[5] These schemes can be broadly situated within one of two categories: continent-specific projects such as Africa ONE and intra-continental projects planned to link Africa with other continents, such as SAFE, SAT-3 and WASC.

Africa ONE is perhaps the most trumpeted of a raft of fiber-optic cable schemes. Originally developed under the auspices of the ITU by AT&T Submarine Systems, the project consists of a 32,000 km submarine fiber-optic ring that encircles the African continent. At the heart of the Africa ONE concept is its vast "ring-and-branch" configuration. This consists of branches connecting coastal landing points with the main fiber-optic ring, allowing connection to Africa's coastal and landlocked countries as well as its islands (Blake, 1998). The scheme has adopted the latest in fiber-optic technology, utilizing wavelength division multiplexing (WDM). This transmission technique increases fiber-optic capacity by simultaneously transmitting signals over different wavelengths within one fibre (Africa ONE Ltd, 2000). Thus, an important element of the system is the independence of each connecting node.

In older submarine systems, telecommunications traffic is routed uniformly; all traffic passes through the same location irrespective of origin. With wavelength division multiplexing, each country's traffic is represented by a separate colour on the fiber-optic pair, allowing countries to maintain sovereignty over their own traffic (Blake, 1998). This has been seen as a key element in convincing African policy makers of the efficacy of the project's treatment of telecommunications traffic. Architecturally, Africa ONE is proposed as a three-tiered network: the primary coastal tier focusing on populous centres in Africa, a secondary tier connecting signatories through a regional network, and a tertiary tier providing links to existing transcontinental cable schemes. The volume of telecommunications traffic on Africa ONE is projected at some 4 billion minutes in the first year of its operation (2001). The traffic base is then projected to grow to some 28 billion minutes by the year 2014,[6] whereas the total traffic for the continent in 1995 was 4.7 billion minutes. It is estimated that a single fibre pair will provide over 240,000 full bandwidth (64 kbit/s) voice circuits, thus meeting all the cable circuit requirements of African countries up till 2020.

In terms of funding, it is traditionally the carriers who plan to use the submarine cable system that finance the upfront costs of laying the cable and constructing landing points. However, a lack of capacity commitment precludes such an approach in Africa. Instead a build, operate and transfer scheme has been set up, with a private company, Africa ONE Ltd, constructing the project itself and then selling capacity and access via landing points to African public telecommunications operators (PTOs). PTOs will then get the revenues from the circuits they buy immediately and, after a period of 12 years, ownership of the scheme will revert in its entirety to the African carriers (Africa ONE Ltd, 2000). Though trumpeted as the ultimate connectivity solution for the African continent, the project has been plagued by a number of economic and political problems.

Firstly, it has faced the formidable problem of coordinating so many countries of variable size and resources. Secondly, the macroeconomic and

Figure 1. Map of existing and planned submarine cable systems linked to Africa
Source: *Africa ONE Ltd.*

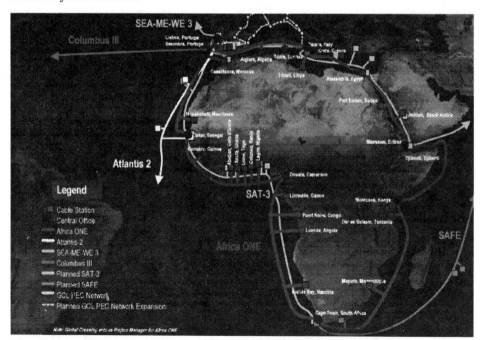

political instability on the continent has militated against effective fundraising. Initially conceived by the ITU in 1993 and officially announced in 1994 by AT&T Submarine Systems Inc., the Africa ONE project seemed stuck in the rut of the conference circuit until the project was sold to Tyco Ltd in July 1997 who promptly abandoned it two months later. However the project was revived in 1999 and is currently being developed by a consortium led by Africa ONE Ltd and including Global Crossing and Lucent.

Criticized by many as being unfeasible and having taken far too long to come to fruition, it remains to be seen whether Africa ONE will improve communications capability on the continent. Even if it is constructed the question remains at what cost to Africans? The project appears to presume that telephone traffic is already there to be tapped. Preliminary estimates are that call charges will be around US$1 a minute, cheaper than current international charges but out of the reach for the vast majority of rurally based Africans (Zsakany & Marshall, 1995). Moreover, there has been little substantive research conducted on the most applicable connectivity option for individual countries. Small landlocked countries, for example, with sparse rural populations may well find other options such as satellite systems much more amenable to developing communications capacity. However, as Figure 1 reveals, there are a number of competing submarine cable projects, planned or operational, that may provide additional telecommunications capacity to Sub-Saharan Africa. These include competing cable schemes with landing points in Africa such as the Fibre Optic Link Around the Globe (FLAG) and Afrilink.

Africa ONE Ltd is far from alone in its attempt to enter the African telecommunications market. Table 2 shows the large number of planned and existing cable schemes that are offering connectivity options to African policy makers. Of the planned intercontinental schemes, by far the largest cable system in operation in Sub-Saharan Africa is SAT-2, which traces a route between the UK and South Africa and down the west coast. SAT-3, though originally designed to increase capacity over the same route, is now likely to be combined with the proposed West African cable (WASC) and SAFE projects.[7]

Sea Me We 3 will also connect to SAFE, thus providing a total circumnavigation of the African continent, though neglecting the east coast. This omission, however, may be rectified by Africa ONE and Afrilink, which may have landing points in all the coastal states. The critical commercial question for any African cable scheme is whether, and how, sufficient traffic can be generated from a region in order to provide a service that is competitive with current and envisaged communications systems. With the significant excep-

Table 2. Fiber-optic cable projects connecting to Africa

Scheme	Key Player	Status	Start date	Capacity	Cost (US$)
FLAG	Bell Atlantic	Operational	1999	10 Gbit/s	1.2 bn
Africa ONE	Global Crossing Lucent	Planned	2002	80 Gbit/s	1.3 bn
SAT-2	Telkom South Africa	Operational	1993	565 Mbit/s	150 m
Sea Me We 2	France Telecom	Operational	1994	n/a	n/a
Sea Me We 3	France Telecom	Installation	1998	40 Gbit/s	737 m
Sea Me We 3 Extension	France Telecom and Singapore Telecom	Planned	1998	n/a	436 m
SAFE/ SAT-3/ WASC	Telkom South Africa	Planned	2000	20 Gbit/s	n/a
Afrilink	Siemens	Planned	n/a	n/a	n/a
Atlantis 2	Embratel	Planned	1999	5 Gbit/s	231 m

Source: *Infodev, 1998; Foley, 1998; Gifford, James and Cosper, 1998*

tion of South Africa, there is widespread acknowledgement that no one single African country generates sufficient volumes of traffic to justify the construction of a single cable link. Thus, cooperation will be the *sine qua non* of these cable projects.

Wireless Technologies

So-called wireless infrastructures are emerging as a potentially useful technology for developing countries. Wireless technology is being increasingly deployed to solve the so-called "local loop" problem. Traditionally, the local loop is the most expensive segment in telecommunications installation (Faulhaber, 1995). This is especially true in Sub-Saharan Africa, where placing copper cables in remote and often inaccessible areas has proved prohibitively expensive. With radio and satellite options for the local loop, widespread deployment of telecommunications can become affordable, and national operators can provide a better service at a much lower cost compared with prevailing rates (Forge, 1995). Wireless local loop technologies (WLL) are cheaper than mobile cellular and can be installed more quickly than fixed line and, as a result, are being deployed by a growing number of countries within the region.

Several benefits are claimed for WLL technologies over alternative access technologies. Firstly, they can be deployed in places where, because of adverse terrain, building density or antiquity, wire and cable are simply not feasible. Second, for certain loop distances and population dispersions, wireless can be more economic than alternative transmission systems. Labour and loop lengths are the two main cost considerations here. The cost of wired systems is critically dependent on the distance between households and the penetration levels achieved, whereas the cost of wireless is broadly independent of those factors. Rather, it is dependent on the cost of installing subscriber units, which tends to decrease over time with increasing economies of scale (Palumbo, 1998). A third factor is that WLL can be installed more rapidly than copper-based systems. Finally, in Africa, where buried copper and even fiber-optic cable is routinely stolen, wireless systems have additional benefits in the sense that, as nothing physical exists between transmission points, they can be easier to maintain and protect than wired systems.

Irrespective of which of the above technologies or connectivity options policy makers choose, it is undeniable that there are now a bewildering number of communications options open to African policy makers to rapidly deploy information infrastructure. However, policy makers should not be seduced by the alluring concept of "instant infrastructure." Rather, the burgeoning number of connectivity options raise serious issues that must be tackled prior to their introduction. Firstly, there must be a recognition that no technology–no matter how advanced or powerful–can single-handedly solve the problem of connecting a continent as vast and as heterogeneous as Africa. These new connectivity options are not designed to supplant existing telecommunications infrastructure, but rather to work in complimentary with the existing domestic infrastructure. Secondly, these projects will be run according to commercial criteria. International operators whose only concern is profit maximization may have little truck with ideals such as universal service. Finally, there is the control dimension: In all likelihood, these projects represent only the beginning of an era of global connectivity that will increasingly see information flows bypassing national boundaries. For countries used to the lucrative revenues from international call transmission and control over their citizens, this period may well be a rude awakening.

At the same time, policy makers in Sub-Saharan Africa are not in the most enviable of positions. Faced with rapid technological changes, resource constraints and a long-term decline in commodity prices as well as international aid flows, their bargaining position would seem to be rather weak. Compounding this problem is that little substantive research has been conducted on the potential synergies and trade-offs that exist between these various connectivity options. For example, to improve international links, should a Sub-Saharan African country invest its limited foreign exchange in underwater fiber-optic cable or should it focus on satellite communications and buy into a GMPCS system?

The highly publicized failure of the Iridium satellite system in March 2000 highlights the importance of investing in appropriate connectivity options. The company, formed in 1991 and backed by an international consortium that included Motorola, launched 66 LEO satellites over the period 1997–1998. However, the ambitious service, which sought to connect people "anytime, anywhere" through satellite phones, failed to attract more than 50,000 users worldwide. Factors including the US$1500-US$3000 handset costs, high call tariffs of US$3, the large size of the phones and their failure to function indoors discouraged the buildup of a large subscriber base. As a result, the company was forced to file for bankruptcy in August 1999, with debts totalling more than US$4 billion. Unable to find a buyer for the company and forced to comply with US law on space debris, each satellite will be de-orbited in 2000, burning up in the earth's atmosphere, leaving 50,000 users bereft of service and providing an ignominious ending to the first in a raft of GMPCS systems.[8] Whether a satellite or submarine cable system is appropriate for a particular African country or which consortium to back is thus a crucial strategic decision. Resolving these issues necessitates firstly an understanding of the economics of these projects and secondly an analysis of the "pros and cons" of each system in relation to each individual country.

A COMPARATIVE ANALYSIS OF PLANNED CABLE AND SATELLITE PROJECTS

Constructing or investing in the technologies mentioned above is unlikely to represent a sufficient condition for developing effective information infrastructures. In order for cable and satellite projects to truly contribute to the construction of the African information infrastructure, further conditions must be met. Firstly, these connectivity options represent only potentialities. If countries fail to upgrade their national networks, users will continue to be frustrated by the availability of world-class international links that are dependent upon an archaic and inefficient domestic counterpart. Secondly, countries need to have domestic service providers in order to effectively exploit the services on offer. A community of local service providers is needed that can respond to users' specific requirements. Finally, the cost of international and domestic telecommunications tariffs for users needs to be reduced to give a truer reflection of actual transmission costs and to increase access to these services.

Whilst, the aggregate benefits of new connectivity options may well appear enticing to Sub-Saharan African countries, but it is impossible to ascertain the true worth of these projects without recourse to an analysis of the economics of the various connectivity options. In terms of submarine cable systems the variables involved are both varied and complex. The main factors to be taken into consideration for those considering connecting to submarine cable projects are length, capacity, number of landing points, network design and capital and operational costs (Blake, 1998). Given that the majority of cable schemes which are connected to, or plan to connect to, Africa are intercontinental, there will typically be only one landing point per country, with landing points most likely being located in coastal areas. Thus, for landlocked countries, access agreements must be negotiated in order to allow participation in these schemes. It is envisaged that countries will access submarine cable schemes via a neighboring country or directly depending on their location vis-à-vis landing points. For small coastal countries that do not generate significant levels of traffic and landlocked countries, the method of connection throws up different cost scenarios. Connectivity to cable schemes for these countries will involve additional costs; thus, for them, the continued use of existing transmission systems may compare favorably with the advantages of newer systems. Evidently, the choice amongst connectivity options must be firmly located in the national context.

In the same vein, choosing between competing satellite telephony systems will involve an understanding of the economic fundamentals of satellite systems. These revolve around two factors: a space segment and an earth segment. The space segment consists of satellites that are typically solar-powered and have a maximum life span of 10 years or less. The earth segment consists of earth station operation centres that monitor and correct satellite movement and position, gateways which connect satellites to the public switched telecommunications network and subscriber terminals. The distinguishing characteristic of the three main satellite types-geostationary or geosynchronous (GEO), medium (MEO) and low earth orbiting (LEO)-is the method in which they orbit the earth.

The GEO satellite appears stationary from earth as it revolves around the earth in exactly 24 hours. Its great distance from earth ensures that it has a large footprint with, in principle, only three GEO satellites required for global coverage. INTELSAT and the other treaty organizations all use GEO satellites. However, their higher orbit means that there are noticeable delays in transmission and large dishes are required to receive satellite signals. LEOs,

Table 3. Satellite system comparison by orbit[12]

System Overview	GEO	MEO	LEO
Spectrum Resources			
Satellites necessary for global coverage	3	10-12	48-840
Altitude (km)	35,680	2,000-10,000	400-1,401
Global roaming	Not available (but possible via connection to PSTN)	Yes	Yes
Frequency coordination complexity	Medium	Medium	High
Telecommunications			
Antennas	Large multibeam	Small	Small
Handheld	No	Yes	Yes
Call handover	None	Infrequent	Frequent
Coverage (footprint)	Very large	Large	Small
Time for signal round trip (seconds)	0.25-0.5	0.1	0.05
Estimated Costs			
Space segment min/US$	~0.20	~0.40	~1.00
Ground segment	Low	Medium	High-medium

on the other hand, due to their lower orbiting altitude, require less power to reach the satellite, hence receptive antennas can be smaller. Whilst this leads to an almost imperceptible time delay in transmission, more satellites are required to provide global coverage. LEOs can be placed as close to 400 km from the earth, transmission delay is therefore imperceptible and signal strength is greater. However, mobile LEO phones cannot be used indoors, are vulnerable to erratic weather systems and may interfere with frequencies used by local emergency services (Wright, 1997).

In terms of pricing and costing, GEOs are typically the most expensive satellite systems to deploy, costing more to build and launch. MEOs and LEOs are smaller and less expensive but consequently more satellites are required and they have a shorter life span. The total cost of a LEO scheme may therefore be higher (Wright, 1997). The business risks are also higher with LEOs as the satellites are less versatile, and if insufficient demand is created for GMPCS services, then operators may face serious financial loss.[10] For these reasons the LEO systems are likely to launch their services in as many countries as possible, banking on rapid growth of call and data traffic and revenues (Wright, 1997).

In summary, the new cable and satellite projects being promoted world-wide constitute an important new dimension in the development of modern information infrastructure in Sub-Saharan Africa. However, each system has advantages and disadvantages that must be placed in a national context in order to optimise infrastructural development objectives. Comparisons between such diverse systems remain fraught with complexity, and a number of key factors must be taken into account when assessing their relative merits. In all likelihood the issue will not be one of straight trade-offs between competing systems, but rather of divining the most effective combination of available connectivity options.

From a systemic and technological point of view it may appear relatively straightforward to decide which connectivity option is superior. Succinctly put, the particular advantages of submarine cable systems are that they offer far greater capacity whilst being less expensive than satellite systems, are unaffected by atmospheric conditions, and are more flexible as operators can divide traffic amongst a host of users and charge for direction and volume. On the other hand the particular advantages of satellite systems accrue mainly to countries with sparsely populated rural areas. Theoretically, universal access can be achieved more effectively with a satellite system. Satellite systems also represent the closest thing to an "instant infrastructure," thus remaining the cheapest option in regions where the volume of telecommunications traffic is slim. Evidently, straight comparisons, in the absence of factoring in the contextual dimension, are of little use to policy makers. Any attempt to arrive at an optimization strategy must encompass a variety of variables. Such variables include: tariff levels and revenue requirements; infrastructure costs and extent of existing infrastructure; demographic characteristics and indigenous demand for communications services; and development priorities and connectivity purpose. In all likelihood policy makers may wish to explore the possibility of deploying both systems, but such decisions will necessitate a greater deal of government involvement.

THE PIVOTAL ROLE OF PUBLIC POLICY

The analysis above reveals that the choices facing policy makers in Sub-Saharan Africa are far from straightforward. Innovative information and communications technology transmission systems constitute an extremely important added dimension to the current arguments on telecommunications restructuring. However, they have thrown up three important dimensions that must be addressed by policy makers:

1. The regulatory dimension, which involves issues such as licensing and regulating operators, landing rights and planning permission.
2. The economic dimension, which focuses on issues such as investment participation, allocation of revenue and interconnection issues.
3. The political dimension, which focuses on issues of access to these new services, regional issues, such as cooperation and sharing of resources, and control issues.

THE REGULATORY DIMENSION

The deployment of new cable and satellite schema is likely to give new impetus to reforms underway in the telecommunications sector in Africa. But governments now face a new challenge in terms of regulation. Already facing difficulties in effectively privatizing national carriers, the situation is being compounded by the rash of foreign private sector consortia bidding to exploit the African market. However, the capacity of national governments to cope is constrained by a number of key factors including: information deficiency; a lack of organizational and management competency; weak political will; little positive experience of regional cooperation; and geopolitical considerations. In spite of this weak bargaining position, African countries must implement a drastic overhaul of tariffs and institute regional cooperation in various guises and new methods of operation for international telecommunications services. In the majority of African countries, the institutional capacity is not suitably developed to allow the effective handling of such complex regulatory issues. How, for example, the new global infrastructures will connect with existing public networks is a key issue that policy makers have yet to address.

A critical area for regulation is the effect these projects will have on the deregulation of telecommunications within the domestic market. Undoubtedly, if countries allow access to these new connectivity options, this represents a *de facto* acceleration of deregulation. All the schemes outlined above require the installation of new infrastructure, thus ownership issues would have to be dealt with. In terms of the accounting rates and the costs of international transmission, though increased capacity for transmission of international calls will inevitably lead to lower prices, such falls will be slow to arrive. Because the cost of call transmission is shared equally by two operators at a previously agreed price or accounting rate. Each operator bears the cost of transmitting its half of the route, with an annual payment being made for any discrepancy between the number of call minutes flowing each way over the route. Thus the operator sending more call minutes than it receives pays for the difference at half the accounting rate. A reduction in costs benefits the operators but does not automatically feed into lower call charges (Forge, 1995).

Overall, cable and satellite projects pose significant challenges to national operators and to regulatory authorities. For example, at a minimum, cable projects are likely to require planning permission and a regulatory framework guarding against discrimination between rival schemes. However, they do not compel a fundamental change in sector policies, nor is it necessary to devise radical licensing schemes. Rather, licensing policies need to be adapted to facilitate the take-up of the services that will be provided over new infrastructures. In conclusion, regulatory intervention is needed to ensure that consumers benefit from the reduced cost of international access; rules are needed to ensure that any exclusivity granted should not restrict the choice of new technologies and services available.

THE ECONOMIC DIMENSION

In terms of the economic dimension, a primary concern for national operators must be the fear of network bypass. Satellite services essentially offer users the opportunity to bypass the public network and link directly with international connections. Such bypass will lead to some loss of revenue for national operators and is to an extent inevitable–the question is how can it be accommodated without significant revenue losses accruing to national operators? Answering this question is difficult due to the nascent nature of the majority of these schemes. In the short term, the threat from satellite systems, for example, may be minimal for a number of reasons. Firstly, international treaties restrict their entry into international fixed voice telephony. Secondly, from an economic standpoint it is unlikely that satellite telephony services can compete with fixed telephony in terms of price. Rather they will likely, in the short term, remain a niche service which, as a result, will attract a suitably high premium (Infodev, 1998). Thus, satellite systems should not be seen as a competitive threat to national operators, rather a complementary service which can aid governments in their endeavors towards achieving universal access targets. Both submarine cable and satellite telephony systems are also likely to generate additional revenue for the national fixed and mobile operators through the interconnection of calls. Moreover, any negative revenue repercussions for national telecommunications operators can be recouped through the levying of appropriate licence fees.

A second important area in the economic dimension is that of creating a climate conducive to private investment. Given the massive sums necessary for upgrading the telecommunications networks in almost all African countries, governments need to encourage private-sector participation. Given the speed at which information and communication technologies are changing, policy makers need to encourage the participation of the domestic, regional and global private sector. In order to do this a host of investor expectations must be satisfied, including: the availability of good market prospects; an attractive business environment; a reasonable, well-defined regulatory framework and/ or strong contractual arrangements; and access to foreign exchange.

THE POLITICAL DIMENSION

In terms of the political dimension, new connectivity options may force policy makers to confront a number of issues, namely that of regional and international cooperation. The political manoeuvrings over RASCOM and Africa ONE have highlighted the political problems of coordination amongst such a diverse number of countries (Mouka, 1998). Given that the majority of African country telecommunications traffic is slim, it is vital that Sub-Saharan Africa unites in an attempt to improve information infrastructure within the region. An example of the efficacy of a united front is negotiations over satellite frequencies. Policy makers in Sub-Saharan Africa could, for example, demand that in return for access to their lucrative markets LEO satellite services offer low-cost public pay phones or subsidized usage for emergency services and local NGOs.[11] Though operators are unlikely to want to grant preferential rates to Sub-Saharan African countries, systems are likely to have extra capacity on satellites operating over less affluent areas and operators will probably have to offer better rates to attract subscribers in those areas (InfoDev, 1998). Realistically, subsidies may be difficult to deliver even if operators were inclined to grant preferential rates as LEO users will roam from country to country and region to region, making it hard to establish who is eligible for subsidy. However, African policy makers should still attempt to set up subsidy programs for rural users of fixed big LEO services.

In the final analysis, though the promoters of new connectivity options have argued that fundamental regulatory changes are unnecessary, there is a host of roles that government must play to optimize any benefit that may accrue from them. The majority of new connectivity options being touted may well reduce the transmission costs of telecommunications within Sub-Saharan Africa. However, national and international operators are likely to want to maintain high tariffs in order maximize profitability, and affordability remains one of the key barriers to the effective use of these systems to improve information infrastructure in the region. African policy-makers must articulate explicit strategies that address the regulatory, economic and political dimensions in order to develop, implement and sustain affordable access.

CONCLUSION

As social shaping theorists such as Bijker and Law (1992) have argued, it is actors who shape technologies in negotiation processes. In Africa, in the absence of effective public policy, the manufacturers and suppliers of information and communication technologies may become the dominant actors in information infrastructure development. It is thus in the interests of African policy makers to combine their negotiating strengths to work on improving the terms of trade for the region as a whole. However easy it is to succumb to Afro-pessimism, African policy makers must realize that the continent as a whole can be much stronger than the sum of its individual parts. A united front is essential at such a crucial stage in the face of the increasing barrage of sales pitches from international players who are far better informed.

This chapter has concentrated on the burgeoning number of new connectivity innovations–such as submarine cable and satellite systems–that have emerged over the last decade. These connectivity options appear to offer seductively simple answers to the slow growth of Sub-Saharan African communications capacity. Yet few have asked the critical question as to what extent they can contribute effectively to the development of information infrastructure in the region. It has been argued that while new technological innovations increase the number of options open to African policy makers to improve communications capacity, there is an urgent need to create the appropriate regulatory environment for economic and political coordination. The choice of which technologies to deploy to modernize and improve the quality and extent of information infrastructure is a crucial one. As the above analysis has revealed, there is no universal solution, rather choices about which system to use are dependent on an in-depth analysis of requirements at the national level.

REFERENCES

Africa ONE Ltd. (2000). *About Africa One*. Retrieved September 7, 2000 from the World Wide Web: http://www.africaone.com/english/about/

about_project.cfm.

Bijker, W.E. & Law, J. (1992). *Shaping technology/Building society: Studies in sociotechnical change*, Cambridge, MA: MIT Press.

Blake, P. (1998, May). Telecom by sea: the ambitious Africa ONE project promises to be the foundation for teledensity growth on the African continent. *Global Telephony.*

Dexter-Smith, J. (1998, June). High frequency communication. African Business. (233): 37.

Faulhaber, G.R. (1995). Public policy in telecommunications: The third revolution, *Information Economics and Policy*. 7(251), 282.

Forge, S. (1995). The Consequences of Current Telecommunications Trends for the Competitiveness of Developing Countries, Washington D.C: World Bank.

Gifford, J. and Cosper, A.C. (1998, April). Out of (and into) Africa. *Satellite Communications*, 34.

InfoDev. (1998, June). *Briefing report on cable and satellite projects.* Paper presented at the Global Connectivity for Africa Conference, 2-3, Addis Ababa, Ethiopia.

ITU. (1997). Challenges to the Network: Telecommunications and the Internet. Geneva: ITU.

Leite, F. (1996). Global Mobile Personal Communications. Geneva: Radio Communication Bureau, ITU.

Mouka, R. (1998, November 3). Africa's grand satellite plan still beset by politics. Communications Week International, 34.

Palumbo, M. (1998, September). Ghana gets into the loop. Global Telephony, 12.

Saunders, R., Warford, J. & Wellenius, B. (1994). Telecommunications and Economic Development. Baltimore: Johns Hopkins University Press.

Wilson, E.J. (1996). The Information Revolution Comes to Africa. CSIS Africa Notes. Washington DC: CSIS, University of Maryland.

Wright, D. (1997). Obtaining Global Market Access for GMPCS. Telecommunications Policy. 21(910): 775-782.

Zsakany, J.C & Marshall, N. (1995, January/February). The Application of Undersea Cable Systems in Global Networking, AT&T Technical Journal, 34-39.

ENDNOTES

1 One by India; three each by Colombia and Indonesia; two each by Brazil, Mexico, and a consortium of Arab nations; and one by China.

2 RASCOM, based in Côte d'Ivoire, has over 40 African countries as members.

3 "African Satellite Telecom Network Set for Launch," *Newsbytes,* 5 December 1997.

4 Both Iridium and ICO had filed for bankruptcy by the end of 1999.

5 The inadequacy of African telecoms linkages results in an estimated annual expenditure on intra country transit fees of US$300 million (ITU, 1997).

6 "Africa One garners support," *Fiber-Optic News,* 20 October 1997.

7 *Fiber-Optics News*, 30 March 1998.

8 See Grimes (2000) "Iridium's 66 satellites to crash," *The Financial Times*, 17 March 2000: 4.

9 Collated from Leite (1996) and Noll (1996).

10 The first LEO scheme to go to market, Iridium, filed for bankruptcy in August 1999 and was judged to have failed for precisely these reasons.

11 "Developing countries seek big LEO subsidies," *Communications Daily*, 9 October, 1996, 16 (197): 2.

12 Collated from Leite (1996) and Noll (1996).

Part Three:

Organizational Challenges and Impacts in Deploying Telecommunications and Networking Technologies

Chapter XI

Management Challenges in Broadband Networking

Murali Venkatesh
Syracuse University, USA

INTRODUCTION

Organizations today face significant challenges in managing advanced telecommunications and computer technology. The digital convergence of applications–voice, video and data all in one "pipe"–confronts the technology manager with urgent new questions on the design and management of systems. Converged applications are new to organizations, as are the broadband technologies that transmit such applications. To a large extent, these technologies are discontinuous with existing solutions. This paper examines the implications of technological discontinuity for organizations in six communities in New York State. From the network manager's perspective, two broad sets of challenges are presented: technological – including specific issues such as bandwidth management and access and backbone issues, and applications– and those related to acquisition of technical support services. Applications prototyping is presented as a response to the technological challenges. The action research project (and the broader research program of which it is a part) underlying this chapter is focused on the public, nonprofit—including government and healthcare institutions, so-called social sector nonprofits, K-12 and higher education—and small business sectors, but lessons learned are broadly applicable.

BACKGROUND

In 1995, a performance-based incentive regulatory plan drafted by the Public Service Commission (PSC), the state of New York and the state's incumbent local exchange carrier (hereafter carrier) required the carrier to commit $50 million to a establish a program: "The stated purpose of the Program was to bring advanced telecommunications to economically disadvantaged areas of New York State" served by the carrier (Annual Report, 1999, p.1). The fund would go to the development of advanced broadband community networks in selected, economically depressed zip codes in "urban/suburban" and "rural" areas. Participation in the so-called Diffusion Program-funded community networks was limited to public, nonprofit and small business *institutions*–city/county government, social sector institutions, K-12, non-formal and higher education, healthcare agencies, and small business units-located in or providing services to these zip codes.

Under the provisions of the program, participants could subscribe to telecommunications services at subsidized rates and receive some support for customer premise equipment or CPE—computer and networking equipment deployed at the user premise. In order to be eligible for these benefits, participants have to connect to the common infrastructure ("backbone"). This requirement was designed to encourage community institutions to find "common ground" and work together to realize community-wide objectives, and was proffered by our respondents as constituting the definition of a "community" network. In order to be successful, proposals had to document broad interest in "cross-functional" connectivity–i.e., schools connected to hospitals and not just to other schools-as well as sustainable, broad-based community support for the project and lasting benefit from it, a sound work plan, and sensitivity to the needs of the disabled.

A competitive request for proposals (RFP) process was used to select communities for a grant. "We were not interested in putting technology in place. User groups had to make a strong case that the investment would make a difference to the community in economic and social terms," a respondent said, explaining the decision to go with a competitive RFP process. Approximately 80% of every grant went to the carrier to implement the infrastructure and provide advanced services; the remainder went to offset CPE costs and incidental training at the customer site. Grant funds could not be used to hire technical consultants or administrative staff. The program has funded over 25 projects in urban/suburban and rural communities over two rounds of grants. The second round is the program's concluding round.

Tariffed telecommunications services (i.e., widely available services governed by rates and rules subject to PSC review) were ineligible in the second round. The carrier would offer eligible (non-tariffed) services as a limited service offering (LSO) to network participants.

This chapter considers key network design and management challenges. The challenges are presented from the institutional customer's point of view (recall that program subsidies were limited to institutions), specifically the network manager's point of view. For this chapter, we draw primarily on an action research project in our community (the MetroNet, described below), supplemented with data from five other communities (Table 1) in New York State. Program-funded broadband community networks will be implemented at these locations later this year. These projects were awarded over $11 million in total funding in the program's second round. The design effort (or phase) started in mid-1998 and concluded in May 2000 in the communities under review. The action research project is part of a larger research program on advanced community network development in economically disadvantaged communities, starting with the communities and projects listed in Table 1.

The MetroNet: The MetroNet was proposed by community leaders and representatives of public institutions in late 1996 in response to the second round RFP. The MetroNet steering committee formed then comprised representatives from small business and city and county government, and from public sector and nonprofit institutions located in or offering services in the eligible zip codes in the community, including healthcare, K-12 and higher education institutions, and the so-called social sector nonprofits–small community-focused organizations providing social support services. The MetroNet

Table 1. Communities and projects surveyed in research

Project	Program Category	Grant Amount
Central New York State (one project, two communities)	Urban/Suburban	$3.8m
Western New York State	Rural	$2.9m
Southern New York State	Rural	$1.5m
Northern New York State	Rural	$1.5m
Eastern New York State	Rural	$1.5m
Number of projects 5		
Number of communities 6		
Total program funding for five projects		$11.2m

proposal was awarded $3.8 million under the program. The author has been a member of the MetroNet steering and negotiation committees since inception and has chaired the technology committee since the project's start in 1996. The author wrote the planning and design sections of the successful MetroNet proposal.

As technology committee chair, the author designed and conducted the planning effort–which comprised user requirements, constraints and resources analyses. Two surveys were disseminated among eligible institutions through the steering committee. One survey elicited application needs–that is, what users would like to use the MetroNet for–and the other, the longer of the two surveys, elicited details on the technology and human support infrastructure and constraints relevant to the respondent site. The surveys were distributed to 300 eligible institutions in the community; 85 completed both surveys, for a response rate of 28%. This was the first such survey conducted in the community. The survey was followed up with individual and focus group interviews with 45 individuals from 16 agencies, using structured and unstructured questions.

Technologically, the MetroNet design (technical specification) is forward-looking and unique in many respects. The MetroNet proposal was the first to recommend digital subscriber line (DSL) as a cost-affordable broadband connectivity solution, multimedia Internet applications (based on findings from the planning effort), and asynchronous transfer mode (ATM) as a backbone and connectivity technology for the larger institutional participants. Subsequently, gigabit Ethernet was added to the list, making it the first gigabit Ethernet LSO in the carrier's entire 14-state service area. As technology chair, the author worked closely with the carrier in recommending design solutions and applications standards.

Late in 1999, the MetroNet project was put out for competitive bid prompted by government participants' concern that, under state law, they could not sign any contract for services that had not gone through a competitive bid process. This process resulted in a competitive local exchange carrier (CLEC) winning a portion of the MetroNet project contract. The carrier and the CLEC will build out their parts of the MetroNet and interconnect the two components. Both components will offer very similar services to participants: DSL, ATM, gigabit Ethernet, and Internet connectivity. The MetroNet is unique among program-funded projects in featuring a CLEC as a service provider; with all the others, the carrier is the sole provider. When implemented, the MetroNet will link between 125 and 150 institutional participants, with the two providers serving roughly 50% each.

By "technology" or "systems" we refer to computer-based information and telecommunications technologies and software applications. We adopt a broad view of management. Broadband technologies are new and complex and discontinuous with existing technologies in the workplace. These discontinuities have complicated technology management. Under the term management we include planning (user needs analysis and analyses of organizational constraints and resources) and design (technical specification), as well as ongoing network performance monitoring and control. We also include: coping with the rapid pace of technology change and technological complexity, managing the human resource as well as professional development and the recruitment and retention of expertise, grappling with technology compatibility and integration as technology evolves, and managing software applications development. This extended list is adapted from Cash, McFarlan and McKenney (1983); not all functions are directly relevant to the present chapter.

We define the term community network or networking as follows:
Whatever the name, community networking is a process to serve the local geographical community–to respond to the needs of that community and build solutions to its problems. Community networking in the social sense is not a new concept, but using electronic communications to extend and amplify it certainly is. (Morino, 1994, cited in Beamish, 1999, p. 352)

In the following section, we describe the research program of which the action research project reported here is a part. We describe the action research project in detail. Then reports on the problems, challenges and issues planners encountered during design deliberations are given, and a section summarizes findings from the action research project. Our action comprised two components: leading the design effort with the carrier, and planning, implementing and evaluating an applications prototyping program in our community. The design process is completed; the prototyping effort is ongoing. Findings from the design process are reported in full; provisional findings from the prototyping effort are discussed. The concluding section outlines recommendations for practice.

BACKGROUND TO THE RESEARCH PROGRAM

Our research program is focused on the broadband community network development process in the six communities listed in Table 1. The program examines several facets of the network development process–network planning, design, and implementation. Post-implementation impacts on the communities will also be assessed as part of the program. Data collection on the planning and design processes has been completed. The design research was conducted in two phases (from mid-1998 to May 2000). In Phase 1, we interviewed 18 planners from the six communities to understand the users' perspective on the design process. Planners, who are also would-be users of the network, were technical (from network management) and nontechnical professionals from eligible institutions in the community. These planners had developed the original proposal and represented the community in design discussions with the carrier. Phase 2 was completed in May 2000. Data was collected from the program selection committee members and carrier staff from engineering, marketing and sales functions. Six selection committee members and eight carrier staff were interviewed. The action research project, which is focused on the design process in our community and provides the bulk of the data for this chapter, ran parallel to both phases of the design research and concluded in May 2000.

Data collection: A variety of data collection methods were used in both phases: mail-in surveys, individual and focus group interviews, archival information (meeting minutes, technical documentation), and informal discussions and e-mail exchange with respondents region-wide. Interviews were conducted face-to-face or via the telephone, using an interview schedule with structured and unstructured questions. Interviews lasted approximately 90 minutes each on average. All face-to-face interviews were audiotaped and transcribed for analysis (instruments used in the data collection are available from the author). The author attended at least one design meeting each at four of the communities, and four design meetings at the fifth. Participant observer meeting notes made by the author were used in the analyses as well.

Data analysis: Our analysis of the data began with findings from our planning effort and with Attewell's (1992) theory of technology adoption. The planning effort in our community indicated that a substantial number of public institutions believed lack of access to know-how was a barrier to technology acquisition. Attewell argued similarly, suggesting that know-how barriers impede adoption of a complex technology like computing. We wrote down these findings, and related assertions in Attewell, in hypothesis form. We then reviewed the data to determine support or otherwise for the hypotheses, identifying patterns and regularities suggested by the content (see Jankowski, 1991, for an account of the approach described here). Overall, we adopted an interpretive, inductive approach to data analysis.

The action research approach: In our community, we used the *action research* approach to study the design effort. The author's meeting notes from 13 design meetings (between mid-1998 and May 2000) provided the data for the analysis reported here. Carrier design staff attended seven of the 13 meetings. Members of the MetroNet technology and steering committees were in attendance at all meetings. Each meeting lasted an average of two hours and featured fifteen attendees on average. Data collected through other methods–surveys, interviews, documentation, and meeting notes from design meetings at the five other communities–were used to supplement the action research data. The action research data–the author's participant observer meeting notes–were analyzed using the interpretive techniques outlined immediately above.

Action research (hereafter AR) "aims to contribute both to the practical concerns of people in an immediate problematic situation and to the goals of social science by joint collaboration within a mutually acceptable ethical framework" (Rapoport, 1970, p. 499).

With AR, the researcher works closely and collaboratively with practitioners in the research situation. The research situation involves a client system; "(a) client system is the social system in which the members face problems to be solved by action research" (Susman & Evered, 1978, p. 588). Among the aims of AR is to change the problem situation and generate social science knowledge about it, while also helping develop the "self-help competencies of people facing problems" (Susman & Evered, p. 588). We use the framework developed by Baskerville (1999) to describe the AR approach and discuss its suitability to the present research.

The AR approach starts with the researcher establishing an agreement with the client system for the research and specifying the theory or theories that will frame it. The researcher and practitioner specify what interventionist actions are possible and permissible and how the research will be conducted and reported, and agree on mutual roles and goals. This is followed by five iterative steps or phases in a cyclical process: diagnosing the problem, planning courses of action for solving the problem, selecting and implementing a course of action, evaluating consequences of the action, and specifying findings from the interventionist action (see also Clement & Van Den Besselaar, 1993; Susman & Evered, 1978).

Setting the stage for AR in the present research: The MetroNet planning data suggested that lack of access to technical expertise was either a significant barrier or barrier to technology acquisition in 60% of the responding organizations. The technology committee was charged with leading the design effort with the carrier and with locating, developing and qualifying community network software applications. It was also agreed by the steering committee that the technology committee would, to the extent possible, work to raise public awareness of technology issues and opportunities to support informed decision-making about technology acquisition. The new services and technologies that were being envisaged for deployment in the MetroNet were expected to seriously challenge the technical know-how available in eligible institutions. Lack of know-how, in other words, emerged as a primary problem.

Action planning: This step identifies the action designed to alleviate the primary problem. The technology committee adopted a two-pronged approach to change: by leading technical discussions with the carrier and representing community interests, and by launching a program of applications prototyping designed to inform technology acquisition decisions by eligible institutions.

We used Attewell's (1992) knowledge-barrier institutional-network approach as the theoretic framework for the research. Attewell argued that lack of technical know-how impedes technology adoption by institutions. We used this view to study user (in the present research, user refers to eligible institutions) participation in the network design process: Who participates and who doesn't and for what reasons? This was, for us, a defining question at the heart of the community network design effort. Findings from the MetroNet planning effort had suggested that lack of know-how could be a reason for nonparticipation in design and, by extension, possibly in the network itself when it is implemented. The larger objective was to enable broad participation in the MetroNet.

Action taking: The planned action is implemented in this step. The technology committee's role in design discussions with the carrier was substantive. We sought information and clarification on choices and researched and proposed emergent solutions for consideration. Our focus was confined largely to design of access to the community network backbone and on applications. The prototyping program comprised a demonstration and a trial component; the latter is active at this writing.

A software application prototype is a mock-up or working approximation of desired features and capabilities. A prototype is incomplete by design; user(s) work with the designer in refining the prototype through an iterative cycle of use and modification until a satisfactory "fit" is achieved. By being a concrete instantiation, a prototype can help potential adopters visualize capabilities that would otherwise be abstract. This is particularly true of broadband technologies, where "bandwidth" is the feature providers like to sell adopters on. But users have trouble visualizing what bandwidth can do for them. Applications prototyping can help concretize abstractions and illustrate advanced applications. Planners clamored for applications like Internet access, but had considerable difficulty visualizing emergent ones, such as videoconferencing. Projecting bandwidth requirements to accommodate as-yet-unknown uses was a challenge. Applications prototyping can stimulate ideas on use (see Gronbaek, Kyng & Mogensen, 1997).

In the communities surveyed, lack of concrete instantiations or prototypes of available technology options tended to exacerbate know-how barriers. Planners were frustrated that they could not visualize the network.
Stylized network diagrams and freehand flowcharts are useful visualization
aids and were used at design meetings. These can be useful at the early stages
of design, to illustrate a technology's possibilities. But they are not as useful
with implementation specifics in actual use settings. Planners felt that
working prototypes would have helped answer many of their questions,
particularly in the later stages of the design process. Prototyping, or "show-
how," can be a powerful complement to and elucidator of know-how.

Based on our experience, two levels of prototyping for show-how are
possible: *demonstrations* and *trials*. Demos are designed to illustrate technology capabilities through generic, sample applications. Our group mounted
two live demos of ADSL and Internet videoconferencing; informal groupwork
and software applications-sharing by three distributed groups was the sample
application. The focus of a demo is on technology capabilities. The demos we
mounted provided "proof of concept" that ADSL bandwidth was adequate for
high-quality video and audio, and that connecting three points over the
Internet during peak usage times did not significantly degrade signal quality.
Members of our group operated the demos, not the user. The demos were
informally evaluated on technical criteria.

Trials, unlike demos, are implemented at the user site and may be left
there for several months to allow extended use directly by the user with actual
organizational work processes. For example, two sites participating in our
trial program are using Internet videoconferencing over ADSL for applicant
screening for Medicaid benefits. The screening process is a crucial and time-
consuming step in the Medicaid benefits certification process. Trials are
formally evaluated on both technical and organizational criteria, the latter
pertaining to impacts of the technology on organizational work. In addition
to technology performance, we will document how the technology impacted
the screening process in terms of efficiency and effectiveness, and acceptance
of the technology by users at the participating sites (i.e., the process specialists), Medicaid applicants, and other stakeholders that impinge on the Medicaid benefits certification process.

The focus of a trial is more on the application and less on technology
capabilities. Demos can show what is possible with technology. Trials apply
those capabilities to actual work processes at the work setting. Trials are time-
consuming and coordination-intensive to implement: We worked with the
carrier, many video vendors for equipment loans, participating sites, the
Internet service provider, and student teams (graduate and undergraduate

students) over a 10-month period before implementation. Our design of the trials roughly parallels the evolutionary prototyping steps identified by Thoresen (1993): system sketch, prototype, test and evaluate.

The timing of such interventions is critical. Our demos occurred early in the planning phase and were useful in stimulating applications ideas in users. Trials were designed to assist with *design* decisions: How well does the technology perform given my specific needs? Does it work with what I have? What step(s) in a work process can it help with? From an organizational learning perspective, trials are likely to be more helpful than demos. Trials can foster learning by doing or learning by using (Rosenberg, 1982), where organizational users may spend months actually using the technology to understand its capabilities and impacts on the organization. Attewell (1992) argues that adopters often have to grow knowledge in-house through actual use of complex technology, like computer-based technology.

> Absorbing a new complex technology not only requires modification and mastery of the technology, viewed in a narrow mechanical sense, but it also often requires (frequently unanticipated) modifications in organizational practices and procedures. (p. 5-6)

We outline below the design of the trial for the Medicaid benefits certification process. The trial implementation is ongoing and will be completed in the next four to six weeks.

Process baseline documentation: We first developed a detailed understanding of the certification process by identifying the process steps, inputs and outputs, functions (departments) involved at each step, time taken at each step, and process stakeholders. The process owner's justification for the technology was carefully recorded, as were stakeholders' expectations of technology impacts. The process owner planned to use IP videoconferencing over ADSL at step 2 in the six-step process:

> **Step 2**: The face-to-face benefits eligibility/certification interview. This is conducted at L____'s unit. The applicant is present; sometimes a representative substitutes for the applicant. The applicant fills out benefits eligibility form during the interview.
>
> L_____, the process owner, said: "This initial interview is very important. We need to get a good interview up front. Typically what happens is this: The applicant has an incomplete form, and we need to ask them for a lot of supplementary information. Medicaid is a very detailed program. Questions begin to multiply like crystals in a vat. It takes 30 to 45 days, sometimes longer, for the information gathering to be completed. On an average, the applicant makes at least two visits to my unit during this process."

"It is very critical to get good information at Step 2, so that we can reduce the delays in certifying applicants for Medicaid benefits. The facility (i.e., the healthcare provider) loses as the process gets delayed. For example, an applicant checks into a nursing home but the certification process is dragging out. When benefits are approved, we only go back up to a point to reimburse the facility for the care. In other words, the facility loses if the process drags out or if the application is denied. Videoconferencing will help us increase the quality of the interview." (Shin, Yun & Shachal, 2000, p. 7 of ms)

Trial implementation: The Medicaid benefits certification process trial is being implemented, linking the process owner's unit (a county government department) and a facility (the leading hospital in the county). Applicants at the facility will be interviewed via video by process specialists located at the county department. The technologies involved (ADSL, IP videoconferencing software, videoconferencing and computing hardware, backend multipoint

Table 2. Stakeholders' expectations of videoconferencing impacts from Medicaid/Chronic Care eligibility and benefits certification process baseline (Shin, Yun & Shachal, 2000)

Stakeholder	Benefits	Operationalization/ Impacts Measure
Patients and patient representatives	• Reduced costs of travel & paperwork • Reduced time off from work in case of representative substitute interview	Quantitative and qualitative Measures
Hospital	• Reduced time and cost of patient accommodations. • Better management of patients • Improved productivity • Reduction of accommodation costs in case of ineligible patients • Swift transition in case of chronic care patients	Quantitative and qualitative measures
County DSS	• Efficient management of Medicaid • Reduced time handling the cases • Increased administrative productivity involved in interview processes • Reduced personnel-related costs	Quantitative and qualitative measures

Copyright Community and Information Technology Institute (CITI), School of Information Studies, Syracuse University

conference unit and gateway) have been tested; the link to the ISP has been tested. Training for process specialists at the county department, for systems staff at the county and the facility, and for selected nursing staff at the facility is underway.

Trial evaluation: Technology performance, usability, and impacts on the process and organization will be documented when the trial concludes. Stakeholders' expectations of technology impacts are critical inputs into the evaluation. These expectations are being operationalized; both quantitative and qualitative measures of operationalized constructs will be used in the evaluation (see Table 2). Both anticipated and unanticipated impacts will be documented. The county department plans to undertake its own independent evaluation at the conclusion of the trial.

CHALLENGES, ISSUES, PROBLEMS

Significant challenges that surfaced during design deliberations centered on: access and backbone connectivity issues, software applications and integration, and acquisition of network and technical support services in a multilayered, multiservice networking environment served by competing service-providers. Note that the networks referenced in this project are "open" environments in that they will implement open protocols: the Internet Protocol (IP) and standards-based ATM, ADSL, and gigabit Ethernet; the last will be deployed only in our community.

Access and Backbone Connectivity

The "access"—also known as the "last mile" or "local loop"—component connects the user premise to the community network "backbone," which consists of switching and other electronics and resides on the carrier's premise. In the case of certain large customers (e.g., the county public library system), the access component could be extended to include internal connectivity between branch offices and "headquarters." That is, branch offices could be linked with "headquarters" with program-subsidized services (e.g., gigabit Ethernet).

Cell Relay/ATM and gigabit Ethernet were the access options. Asymmetric Digital Subscriber Line (ADSL), a copper-based broadband local loop technology, was originally an option. Far higher data rates on the downstream (from the carrier to the user) relative to the upstream (from user to the carrier) qualify ADSL as "asymmetric." But by 1999, ADSL had been tariffed and thus was ineligible for program subsidies; however, ADSL users connecting to the community network backbone are eligible for some CPE support. ADSL is less expensive than the other access options and is appealing to the smaller agencies.

Vendors and service providers have promoted ADSL as a high-speed Internet access service. The carrier was no exception. Three bandwidth levels, all asymmetric, are available, ranging from 90 Kbps to 7 Mbps, according to published data from the carrier. Accordingly, the monthly service charges range from around $40 for the lowest speeds to $110 for the highest; these charges do not include Internet access charges, which are extra. Planners had questions about DSL's ability to support evolving user needs. The DSL services are not scalable. Investigations revealed that the carrier's DSL services could not provide committed information rate (CIR) or assured bandwidth guarantees. While this would not be a problem for Internet access, it did limit videoconferencing applications to the highest bandwidth DSL service available from the carrier–the 7 Mbps downstream and 1 Mpbs downstream service. This service is also the most pricey ($110 or so per month) and is only available to adopters who are under two miles from the carrier's central office. Adopters outside this range have to look at the Cell Relay/ATM of gigabit Ethernet services, which are more expensive.

Unlike ADSL, all three levels of Cell Relay/ATM service (1.5 Mbps, 45 Mbps and 155 Mbps) offered by the carrier are scalable, have no distance limitations and provide CIR guarantees as a service option. Under the program, eligible adopters will only be charged so-called "facilities charges"– which reflect costs of laying the fiber and installing and operating the electronics at the central office, plus admissible overheads – and no "freight" charges – that is, charges associated with hauling the data to the nearest ATM switch. Freight charges can add up very quickly, making Cell Relay/ATM service cost-prohibitive. The subsidy makes the Cell Relay/ATM services very attractive to medium-sized and large institutions; however, ATM is still poorly understood as a technology in the communities surveyed. Potential adopters rightly felt that buying ATM-qualified support staff would be expensive, and equipping existing staff with required skills did not seem feasible because of ATM's complexity and the high training costs. There was widespread lack of understanding of the technology. Some of these misgivings were more perceived than real, but there was significant resistance to ATM.

Gigabit Ethernet was approved as an access technology very recently (early in 2000), and that too, only in our community. Gigabit Ethernet is new to the carrier. In fact, our community is the only market, in all of the carrier's 14-state service footprint, where gigabit Ethernet is being offered as a limited service offering. But despite its relative novelty, it proved immediately popular with the medium-sized and large institutions. Within a month of its becoming eligible as an access option under the program, over 130 institutions signed up or were ready to sign up for the service, which was far in excess of the interest in Cell Relay/ATM. Potential adopters saw gigabit Ethernet as a significant saving over their current solutions. A hospital estimated that replacing their current multiple T1 and T3 services with two 1 gigabit Ethernet "pipes" would save them over $100,000 a year. The gigabit Ethernet monthly service charges, due to some convoluted logic, would be *substantially* less than the Cell Relay/ATM service at DS4 rates (45 Mbps), making it extremely attractive. Potential adopters were also more comfortable with gigabit Ethernet as a technology–they saw it as "Ethernet, but on steroids," as one planner put it. Consequently, many believed correctly that buying technical support skills for gigabit Ethernet would be cheaper compared to Cell Relay/ATM skills.

A major unresolved issue in the communities surveyed pertains to flexible access and service selection via the backbone. As discussed above, the networks under consideration will have the following components: internal connectivity, access, and backbone. Ideally, a user should be able to connect to any resource–the Internet, a virtual private network, or a community resource like a database or video server–via the backbone. It is not currently clear whether, or how, the carrier will support service selection and at what additional costs to the user. For example, a relatively new technology called the L2TP concentrator (for Layer 2 Tunneling Protocol) promises service selection flexibility on the backbone. Using L2TP, an Internet service provider or other service provider can create a virtual tunnel to link a customer's remote sites or remote users with corporate networks. Major vendors such as Cisco and Alcatel support the L2TP method, as do the ADSL Forum and the Internet Engineering Task Force (IETF). Supporting L2TP on the backbone will benefit ADSL, gigabit Ethernet and Cell Relay/ATM users in the communities surveyed.

Software Applications and Integration

A major factor in the design of infrastructure is the "tension" between supporting standard versus emergent applications (The Unpredictable Certainty, 1996). Network managers have to make bandwidth needs estimates based on the applications currently supported as well as emergent applications needs. As we found out, emergent applications introduce uncertainty into network design and management.

During the planning phase in our community, we found a high level of interest among community agencies in cross-functional connectivity (i.e., hospitals connecting to not just other hospitals but to the jail, for example).

Indeed, this emerged as a significant finding from the planning effort and was consistent with the goals of the program and the requirement that participants connect to the common backbone and find "common ground." Interest in cross-functional connectivity was high in the other communities surveyed as well. Videoconferencing, shared database access, and high-speed Internet access were the most frequently mentioned desired applications on the community network. However, this interest appeared to diminish considerably during the design, when monthly service charges had to be factored into calculations of bandwidth need. Quickly, "nice to have" yielded to "must have." Agencies viewed high-bandwidth applications (like videoconferencing) as speculative and were, with a few exceptions, not yet ready to explore their use. They were reluctant to contract for higher bandwidth connections to the backbone (and incur higher monthly charges) for supporting untested applications. Agencies' true utility functions, and priorities, surfaced during these nuts-and-bolts, bottom-line discussions. This point highlights the practical difficulty in selling institutions on broadband connectivity, particularly when applications that would require such bandwidth are not readily available or conceivable.

Community institutions had divergent motivations for participating in the community network. The network, when implemented, would consist of an access component (including internal or customer premise networking tying branch offices to "headquarters") and a backbone component. In general, smaller agencies (nongovernment human service agencies and grassroots institutions with 25 employees or fewer) saw the community network mainly as a high-speed access ramp to the Internet. Many smaller agencies did not have Internet access, and those that did wanted to upgrade from slow modem dial-up access. The larger agencies (government institutions, K-12 schools and higher education institutions, hospitals), on the other hand, were more interested in meeting their internal networking needs through gigabit Ethernet. The larger institutions already had Internet access. Meeting their internal networking needs was higher priority relative to external connectivity. The relative weighting, in bandwidth projections provided by one hospital, was stark: 1,000 Mbps for internal networking (substantially more than present arrangements) versus 1 Mbps for Internet AND community network access (at the same level as the present). This relative weighting, and the priorities they reflected, was echoed by almost all large agencies. Similarly, smaller agencies were quite clear on their priority: high-speed Internet access. "I see no need for agencies to be linked to other agencies. It is more important to be linked to the Internet," one small-agency representative remarked at a meeting.

Divergent participant motivations impact design in significant ways. A technical account of the impacts is beyond the scope of this chapter. However, as an illustration of possible impacts, consider a user who only wants to access the Internet. This user's data are transferred to the Internet service provider at the carrier's central office for the connection. Consider a second user who wants access to the community network for multimedia application-sharing and videoconferencing with another community institution. This user's data will have to be switched differently from the first to protect, among other things, quality of service. In other words, the carrier will have to augment backbone switching capabilities to support service selection and flexible access. The network manager has not only to make sure there would be adequate bandwidth on the access component for multimedia applications, but has to ensure that the backbone is equipped with service selection and performance support features for acceptable quality. At present, none of the projects surveyed includes such capabilities in the design.

Another illustration of the challenges stemming from emergent applications is provided by North Carolina:

While North Carolina involved potential users during the planning for its network, the project has experienced slower-than-anticipated acceptance by some users because of the high cost of using the system. One reason for this lower acceptance is that the system was designed to carry two-way video to multiple sites. However, some of the schools that the state anticipated would use the network wanted to buy only access to the Internet at higher speed than were available over conventional telephone lines, which is a less expensive service to provide. As a result, some users were unwilling to pay for the capacity to send and receive video images, when they would rather have had less expensive data connections. Since the rates the state pays the telephone companies were based on estimates of use that have not been met, these rates, and ultimately the rates charged to users, could go up to allow the telephone companies to recover their investment, further discouraging the use of the statewide network. (GAO, 1996, p. 26-27)

Even if the network manager can be assured of strong demand for high-bandwidth applications in his/her organization, the question remains: What are the costs involved in developing and implementing secure applications? Bernstein and Yuhas (1999) observe: "The cost of software development and systems deployment must be well-estimated initially… most software development is late, fragile, and expensive because the full arsenal of controls is not consistently applied" (p. 2).

Acquiring Technical Support Services

The Services Reference Architecture (SRA; Figure 1) uses the Open System Interconnect (OSI) layering scheme to analyze, from the point of view of a network manager at the participant's site, network and technical support services common to the projects surveyed. The networks referenced in the projects surveyed may be described as open, broadband, multilayered, multiservice environments. The focus of this account is on the emerging services marketplace and the complexities it introduces into the services acquisition process. We only discuss illustrative problems.

The SRA comprises the physical, data link, IP (with a value-added IP extension), "service," and applications layers. Network users (i.e., institutional participants, in this case) will need services at each of these layers. The SRA applies to the program projects surveyed and includes services that we expect will be needed minimally with reference to known applications. The picture is necessarily incomplete. The model draws on the Open Systems

Figure 1. Services Reference Architecture (SRA), showing a sampling of technical support services needs (present and projected) of projects surveyed

Application Layer Services: Network management, application troubleshooting (help-desk functions)

Application Implementation Services: Developing and implementing World Wide Web-enabled applications, security and privacy, integration of data conferencing with World Wide Web applications and videoconferencing, MPEG/JPEG conversion

Value-added Internet (IP) Services: Multicasting, video bridging, switching and gateway services, Internet (IP) telephony

Basic Internet (IP) Services: Management of standard IP services up to and within participant site

Layer 2 Services: Gigabit Ethernet, Cell Relay/ATM, Frame-to-Cell Conversion, LAN Emulation, integration with existing LANs, (re)designing LANs for multi-media applications sharing

Physical Layer Services: DSn over copper and fiber, SONET.

Interconnect (OSI) reference model, which is influential in informing discussion on telecommunications products and services. We developed the SRA to serve as an analytic aid drawing on data from the design research.

Network and technical support services (hereafter services) are critical to the success of any network. An articulated services architecture can help open up the services provisioning environment to competition, enable service providers to achieve transparency in providing services to the enduser, and promote interoperability under the right operating conditions. Services modularity, flexibility in provision and acquisition of services, standards-based support for multivendor solutions, differentiation between lower and upper layer services and the stimulation of open competition and market conditions are among the critical objectives of the SRA. A layered architecture allows service providers, and customers, to differentiate between infrastructure and services, and between "bundled" versus "unbundled" services. Figure 1 describes service acquisition questions at the various layers. The description is functional; actual service provision may span two or more layers. For example, gateway services for cross-operation between multichannel video and H.323 will involve switching (layer 3) functions as well as some presentation layer data format conversion functions (JPEG to MPEG). Vendors may combine services across layers to create new services. Presentation layer functions (data formatting, among others) are subsumed under the "service" layer in the SRA.

The physical layer features carrier-owned copper and fiber infrastructure, on the backbone and access components, that will be used to deploy the networks. These are core services and include physical layer monitoring, local loop qualification, and interfacing with customer-owned fiber (where available). At layer 2, gigabit Ethernet, ATM switching and transmission functions, and layer 2 tunneling introduce new layers of complexity for the network manager. For example, with gigabit Ethernet, the carrier will provide switching on the backbone. But since gigabit Ethernet will be deployed for internal connectivity by the large institutions, services such as LAN emulation, link aggregation, and integration with Fast Ethernet or 10BaseT office LANs will have to be insourced or acquired from an independent provider (this could be an unregulated subsidiary of the carrier). With gigabit Ethernet, we expect significant management challenges to surface as the technology diffuses and organizational need for multimedia applications grows. Given the three Cell Relay/ATM services (1.5 Mbps, 45 Mbps, 155 Mbps), how much bandwidth should an agency contract for? A bandwidth baselining period is recommended to permit estimation of bandwidth need based on actual use; service charges should be suspended during this period. Once the service contract is signed, service performance needs to be tracked against contracted goals. While the carrier was prepared to offer a virtual private network (VPN) service, there were no plans to support flexible service selection using layer 2 tunneling (as noted earlier). Functions and services at layers 1 and 2 may be said to comprise "core" network functions.

Internet access (layer 3) has been problematic. With gigabit Ethernet linking branch sites, larger participants have to decide whether to insource or buy internal management of Internet access in addition to buying the Internet access service. Value-added Internet services would be needed to support, for example, H.323 videoconference switching and bridging (to ISDN sites), multicasting, and IP telephony. Large ISPs may not see a market yet for such value-added services, allowing niche providers to develop.

The "service" layer comprises application implementation and enabling services, such as the design and development of Web-enabled applications (e.g., e-business applications), "marrying" H.323 videoconferencing with Web-enabled applications and office applications, and data format conversion (e.g., JPEG, MPEG) services at the presentation layer. The applications layer includes help-desk functions for end-user support and network management using standard platforms and protocols. Even a significantly expanded set of service offerings by the carrier or the ISP is unlikely to cover "service" and help-desk services. These are usually seen as outside the purview of the core network and have to be acquired from independent providers or insourced. Network management services may follow the functional layering scheme as well. In the communities surveyed, the carrier has been reluctant to monitor beyond layer 2; the ISP will only provide layer 3 monitoring, and that only on the backbone (not on the internal connectivity component). This leaves overall network management to a third party provider (it could be a participating institution); this provider will be responsible for problem isolation and handoff to the appropriate service provider.

FINDINGS AND IMPLICATIONS

In this section, we evaluate consequences of the planned action and report research findings and contributions to theory.

Evaluating consequences of the planned action. The technology committee's efforts in the design deliberations with the carrier were moderately successful. Our efforts helped clarify issues for participants and facilitated their participation in the design process. For example, the carrier had decided on ATM as the backbone technology, and there was not much planners could do about that decision. Carriers like ATM for its scalability and multiservice–voice, video, data–support. However, as they learned "on the job," planners' design concerns broadened to include aspects of the backbone to the extent that these impinged on their monthly charges. Under an initial design proposed by the carrier, a gigabit Ethernet user had to buy an ATM connection to the backbone because the carrier would not support Ethernet on the backbone; this proposal was only recently modified to eliminate the additional ATM connection. It is important that planners look at the big picture, because decisions about the backbone affect services and costs to the user.

The prototyping program has been successful in highlighting applications possibilities for users. The two live demonstrations we had mounted opened many eyes to the applications possibilities of the MetroNet (and, by extension, the other networks examined in this research) and led to the development of the trials. Attendees at the demos wanted to take the next step and try the technologies–ADSL, IP video–out in their organizations with actual work processes.

At the very outset of the projects in late 1996 and early 1997, the carrier organized information sessions at each of the communities surveyed to inform planners about the new services and technologies, but these proved inadequate as instructional vehicles. According to Attewell (1992), such sessions would qualify as vehicles for "signaling" or informing potential users about the existence of an innovation and its benefits. Educating the user to make informed decisions on technology adoption calls for learning-by-using or doing, precisely the objective served by our prototyping program. A demonstration prototype allows the user to observe an innovation in live operation; a trial prototype allows the user to play with an innovation in the actual use context. While signaling is useful during the planning phase, it is less so during design, when users want to know whether and how the innovation would fit with legacy technology and extant organizational work processes. Prototyping is much more materially useful to the user during the design phase—which results in technical specification. Given that know-how barriers were a problem in both rounds, respondents felt that applications demos should have been a part of the information sessions hosted by the carrier.

However, prototypes can only address technology integration questions in a limited way. We illustrate some of these issues under bandwidth management below. Frequently asked integration questions in our community included: Would the newer technologies work with legacy technologies? What "edge" devices (i.e., devices that translated between one technology and another) should one buy? A trial is a trial. Trial sites we are working with are taking small steps to reduce risk; for example, the county is running the videoconferencing application on a dedicated network, which is separate from the office LAN and WAN connection. This is highly recommended during the trial phase; running the trial application on a dedicated segregated network aids fault isolation and problem-solving and insulates critical production applications, but is helpful only to a limited extent in evaluating interoperability and compatibility.

Attewell (1992) argued that mediating institutions come into existence where technology   knowledge is scarce and/or organizational learning around a technology is burdensome: these supply-side institutions specialize in creating and accumulating technology know-how regarding complex, uncertain, dynamic technology. They "stand between" a user and complex technology (hence "mediating"). (p. 7)

Such institutions facilitate adoption. The role of the technology committee was similar to that of a mediating agent in the design. However, the larger objective of broadening user participation in design was not met. Participation in design by the smaller nonprofits/small business units was insignificant, and their participation in the implemented network as users promises to be small as well. As we had surmised, know-how barriers were higher in smaller (versus larger) institutions, but there were other barriers as well that combined with know-how barriers to explain their nonparticipation: lack of compelling applications and resources to support the development of applications and lack of time to attend design meetings.

Specifying learning: This step identifies findings and contributions to theory. Our findings support and extend Attewell's (1992) knowledge-barrier institutional network approach to technology adoption by institutions. We found that know-how barriers were significant in public institutions, and the barriers got steeper as the institutions got smaller and the farther one moved from urban areas.

Our findings extend Attewell's (1992) theory. First, we found that know-how barriers inhibit user participation in network design. Nonparticipation in design, we expect, will negatively affect adoption decisions. Second, know-how barriers apply to specific technology topics (e.g., bandwidth management and the access and backbone issues discussed earlier), technical services acquisition, and applications. Third, know-how barriers can affect professional design staff as well, not just users.

Bandwidth management: A network manager affiliated with a hospital illustrated the bandwidth management challenges stemming from the newer technologies like Cell Relay/ATM, gigabit Ethernet, and ADSL, all of which are designed to work with office LANs:

Internet videoconferencing (using the H-323 standard) is new to us. We are quite familiar with ISDN-based videoconferencing. With ISDN, it is like dial-up, it is not on the office network, so it was easy. We didn't have to worry about bandwidth issues. But now, with the IP video stream shared on the office network and needing at least 400 Kbps or so per stream, we have to look into bandwidth sharing. So far it has not been a problem. But if you are running several sessions at the same time on top of all the office traffic, bandwidth availability may become an issue. The whole world has changed.

Congestion can be controlled on the LAN, but on the Internet, congestion can only be controlled up to a point.

The bandwidth management challenges stemming from high-bandwidth multimedia applications suggest revised criteria for (internal) network design. In the example above, the hospital network was used largely for administrative purposes and was designed for reliability. In order to support videoconferencing, the design criteria would have to be expanded to include support for bandwidth management and congestion control. Furthermore, designers and network managers have to be sensitive to new users and new user criteria for acceptable performance. The hospital planned to use videoconferencing for clinical and distance education purposes, which means new users (patients, physicians, distance students) and new performance criteria (How legible is the text on the sonogram? Is the videoconference session too choppy or grainy to support tele-diagnosis? Are patients comfortable speaking into a screen?) have to be taken into account in the technical design.

We expect bandwidth management challenges to increase as applications like telephony, which are traditionally not run over the LAN, begin to be supported on the LAN, and as videoconferencing and streaming get more tightly integrated with workgroup communication and work processes. Furthermore, as network usage evolves and expands, network managers will feel pressure from customers and constituents to support flexible service selection and WAN and virtual LAN access.

Technical services acquisition: Planners were unfamiliar with open, broadband, multilayered, multiservice networks described by the SRA. "It was all one signal," a respondent remarked, referring to the less complex technologies and services contracting models he was familiar with. Buying services in a complex environment, potentially from multiple competing providers, was new to many.

The emerging broadband environment in the communities surveyed is expected to offer customers two services acquisition options: (1) where all or a bulk of the services across the five layers are provided by a small number of providers (e.g., the carrier provides "core" services on layers 1 and 2, an unregulated subsidiary provides the other services, and an ISP covers layer 3 "commodity" Internet access service), and (2) where services beyond the core (layers 1 and 2) can be bought from many providers in a competitive market. Given the technological complexity and discontinuity in the emerging broadband environment, we expect that, at least initially, customers will opt to purchase services from a small set of providers as a way to cope with change. Later, as their knowledge evolves, customers may opt for an environment where the market orientation is more pronounced to benefit from reduced costs and improved quality from increased competition.

Service providers may wish to move in the opposite direction and augment and consolidate their service offerings to the customer. Initially, the carrier may only be willing to offer core services, but this set is certain to grow as they acquire new skills and capabilities. In the present research, the carrier has plans to get into the ISP business, and an unregulated subsidiary has expressed interest in providing services at the other layers, including value-added Internet services. We expect the services market to mature such that a small set of providers is offering an augmented set of services at very competitive prices, with smaller niche providers providing specific, value-added services. Network managers have to be prepared to grapple with (multiple) providers over bundled versus unbundled services, differential service grades, switching costs, and "front of book" versus "back of book" contracts (see Cross-Industry Working Team in References).

The new "market" may feature new entrants, some of whom may have no track record in offering services in a competitive environment. For example, in one of the communities, the county central public library offered to provide internal (i.e., on the internal connectivity component at large customer sites) management of Internet access for a fee. The library would only be providing a small set of services to a few large customers, but it was an unprecedented step for the institution. Buying services from such a provider may pose problems for some customers. Technology procurement by county government has to satisfy stringent requirements relative to the process by which bids are picked, to keep the process open and competitive. It is not clear whether the service the library was offering to provide would satisfy the "open and competitive" bidding criterion, as it had volunteered to provide the service. The network manager may have to be prepared to deal with providers who may be new to the business, without much of a track record.

Planners had a number of questions on regulatory and contractual issues and questions on the provisions under the program guidelines. What exactly was a limited service offering (LSO)? How do you draw up an LSO? Can you add new participants to the LSO? How do you deal with payment defaulters? If you add new participants to the network after the contract is drawn up, should they not get the same lower monthly rates (for the same services) negotiated under the LSO since the carrier would not have to put in new infrastructure? Other issues included the "demarc," the point at which the network infrastructure is demarcated from the CPE. This was a critical issue as the demarcation point would decide what equipment–and, by extension, what services–would qualify as infrastructure (and thus be eligible for support under the infrastructure segment of the grant, which is significantly larger) as opposed to CPE. The demarc question is particularly important in the context of internal connectivity using gigabit Ethernet.

Applications: Users lacked compelling applications and resources to develop multimedia applications that would require the high bandwidth of the MetroNet; this was a barrier to participation in design and is expected to negatively affect adoption decisions. The application issue is particularly critical in broadband network technologies. Users could readily see their need for high-speed Internet access, but could not justify how they would use the extra bandwidth the MetroNet would make available. High-speed Internet access can be obtained outside of the MetroNet, and for significantly less per month. This suggests an intriguing explanation of technology adoption based on user needs hierarchy (the author wishes to thank a referee for pointing this out). Most users in our sample wanted affordable high-speed Internet access; this need was more pronounced in the smaller institutions, and even the larger institutions were interested in replacing their existing service arrangements (e.g., T1) with cheaper alternatives (e.g., DSL). Applications over and above the Internet were much less well understood, and users were understandably reluctant to contract for bandwidth they were not sure they knew how to use. This could change as user needs evolve and mature and a network of users develops, as seems possible with the videoconferencing application prototype discussed earlier.

The planning effort in our community (and in other communities) revealed a high interest in multimedia applications. The specifics of developing and deploying such applications proved to be expensive and complicated. The relatively new H.323 standard supports desktop video- and data-conferencing over the Internet and the LAN. However, the integration of video and data is complex, involving "hooks" between needed software repositories and hardware resources for seamless access. So while H.323 can augment "talking heads" with data conferencing, taking advantage of its capabilities can be challenging. Recall that access to shared databases was a frequently mentioned "desired" network application. In the communities surveyed, several government agencies providing various forms of public assistance need data from social sector nonprofits and vice versa. It was felt that secure access to such databases could be provided through the community network. The cost issues involved are only beginning to be understood, and it may take many years before such databases-or, more accurately, data warehouses-are operational. Enabling secure access to software applications over the community network and the World Wide Web called for new controls to be incorporated into applications, and this was daunting to many planners.

Among the challenges involved in the development and implementation of emergent applications is the question of standards and integration (or interoperability). A question facing the network manager is: Should I go with the new H.323 standard or with the H.320 standard? Compared with the newer H.323 standard for Internet and LAN videoconferencing, the H.320 standard for ISDN-based videoconferencing was more familiar to users in three of the communities surveyed (ISDN service was ineligible for program funding in the second round). A network of users had developed around the H.320 standard which could be tapped for help; such a help network was unavailable with the H.323 standard. As with the reservations about ATM (discussed above), technical support for H.323 systems can be expensive because it is currently scarce. While H.323 is more versatile and function-rich, it is still evolving as a platform. Uncertainty can delay adoption of an emerging standard, even if it is more versatile relative to an older standard (see Farrell & Saloner, 1985).

Gateways for H.323-H.320 integration are currently available. One of the communities surveyed has a significant installed user base of a proprietary broadband multichannel videoconferencing solution (with a bandwidth of 45 Mbps and used for distance learning) that they want to integrate with the H.323 component of their network. This has proved to be a challenge, since no off-the-shelf package exists. But the bigger question is: Should this community continue with the pricey multichannel videoconferencing system or scrap it in favor of H.323 and use the DS-3 (45 Mbps) pipes currently dedicated to video and some channelized voice for other purposes?

IP telephony is an attractive option given that local telephony costs are a significant contributor to an organization's telecommunications bill; indeed, large organizations in at least three communities expressed strong interest in IP or packet telephony. However, there are major challenges in migrating from circuit-switched to packet-switched telephony, for example: reliability (How reliable is the computer phone, or "softphone"), added costs (dedicated digital handsets are more reliable than the softphone but are currently pricey), powering (remote, as in conventional telephony, versus local), bandwidth management and congestion control (to the extent that packet telephony uses the office LAN), openness of the unified messaging feature (your e-mail and voice-mail systems may not be supported), link to the Centrex service provided by the carrier, and human factors and workload issues (since IP telephony shifts management of telephone service from the central office to the organization, workload issues and skill needs of support staff have to be carefully considered).

One of the advantages of broadband connectivity is that institutional users can be *providers* of content, not just *consumers*. This is also the problem with broadband connectivity. During the planning effort in our community, the larger institutions told us that the MetroNet could help them improve services and information delivery at reduced costs. Providing information and services would justify the expense of the connection, which was significantly more than the standard dial-up Internet connection. To date, nearly four years after the planning effort, no institution has come forward with a network application or has made a commitment to develop a network application for providing services or information. This may change, but the point is, a role change from *consumer* to *provider* usually involves committing substantial resources to design and develop secure applications, and it is not clear when that will happen. Even if the resources were available, organizations that have historically only been *users* of applications would have to think like a provider; most have no conception of how to estimate development costs or the nature of the controls that would have to be applied to manage the applications development effort. Until this happens, the MetroNet promises to be a high-speed ramp to the Internet and a fast backbone for private virtual LANs and LAN connectivity. The "common ground" ideal of the community network originally envisaged for the MetroNet may have to wait until applications are developed to motivate participants to use the MetroNet as a *community* resource.

Know-how barriers and professional design staff: While ATM was familiar to the carrier staff, DSL and gigabit Ethernet were less so, and the carrier staff were learning about them even as we did. The idea of designing collaboratively with the user was also new to carrier staff. This was partly an attitudinal barrier – participative design is not new in the systems arena, but is quite new in public network design. The carrier staff were open to the idea, but were unsure of their new, emergent role as participant designers. This was also a know-how barrier – the carrier staff were unfamiliar with participative design methods and tools. Even if the user can surmount know-how barriers and has the tools to be an informed participant, the carrier staff have to be similarly trained to adopt the appropriate attitudes and methods for the process to be mutually rewarding. An institutional network approach to technology adoption has to be sensitive to the interaction modes and to assumed roles and their malleability, between technology transfer agents and adopters.

Generalizing from findings: As the AR study involves a sample of one, generalizations from findings "must be tempered with an interpretation of the extent of similar settings to which the theory can be expected to apply" (Baskerville, 1999, p. 20). Know-how barriers among users were singled out for comment by planners in all the communities examined in this research and by the program selection committee members we interviewed. Know-how barriers were a significant impediment to design and to project progress in these communities. Know-how barriers had been a significant problem in the program's first round as well, so much so that second round RFP was modified to emphasize applications: Proposers had to describe how they would use the network and leave technology decisions to the carrier. The first round RFP asked proposers to specify both applications and the technology, and this had proved disastrous. Proposers could not provide this information. A program selection committee member noted: "Either they asked for things the carrier couldn't do, or they simply didn't know what to ask for. There was widespread lack of understanding and knowledge of technology specifics."

Our findings suggest that know-how barriers are pervasive in the context of broadband networks, applications and services. This is problematic for community network development, because of the implications for user participation in design. If knowledge barriers get steeper as the organization gets smaller, then smaller organizations are not likely to participate in the design process. The resulting design is likely to be biased in favor of the larger organizations that could and did participate to shape the design outcomes. Furthermore, participants may be forced to defer to the carrier on decisions that, ideally, should be participative.

RECOMMENDATIONS AND CONCLUSION

Attewell (1992) has argued for the examination of "the role of learning and technical knowledge in the diffusion of advanced ... technologies" (p. 6). Gabel and Mueller (1999) argue similarly with respect to broadband technologies: "(D)ue to the high cost of information, there are few early adopters of access facilities. Until a substantial critical mass of users exists that create an inexpensive market of information, users may find themselves committed to inferior, but well accepted technology" (p. 4). The technological complexity and discontinuity of the emerging broadband environment impose an organizational learning burden on the institutional adopter. Lack of, or lack of access to, know-how impaired planners' ability to make informed decisions in the communities surveyed.

Our recommendation is for network managers to work with applications prototypes to develop understanding of technology *before* adoption decisions are made. Unlike systems prototyping, broadband applications prototyping requires the cooperation of entities external to the user organization: the carrier, the ISP, equipment vendors, software applications designers, implementors and evaluators. But because trials are time-consuming to design and implement, organizations considering adoption may want to form a consortium or buying group and negotiate a trial from the vendor as part of the process. Trials are but one tool for organizational learning, through learning by using. For best results, trials have to start with a formal baselining effort and conclude with formal evaluation; also, they have to be undertaken in a *programmatic* fashion for continuous learning to occur. In the emerging broadband environment, organizations have to be prepared to learn continuously as part of an aggressive, strategic response to fast-paced technology change. Vendor-provided information could be a part of an organization's learning program, but has to be balanced by objective and firsthand evaluations of technology under actual work conditions.

Network management will be the key as broadband networks become more widespread and interconnected. Interconnecting two or more broadband networks raises challenging questions for the network manager: How will quality of service be protected for delay-sensitive applications like voice and video? How will the gateway service be priced? Who will manage the gateway? How will local IP addressing be affected when two intranets are connected? Our future research will document these network management challenges as the number of participants grows and as both the internal connectivity within large agencies as well as inter-backbone connectivity for regional broadband networking expand in the communities under scrutiny in the present research.

REFERENCES

Annual Report. (1999). Diffusion Program annual report.

Attewell, P. (1992). Technology diffusion and organizational learning: The case of business computing. *Organization Science*, 3(1), 1-19.

Baskerville, R. L. (1999). Investigating information systems with action research. *Communications of the Association for Information Systems*, 2 (19), 1-23.

Beamish, A. (1999). Approaches to community computing: Bringing technology to low-income groups. In D.A. Schon, B. Sanyal, & W.J. Mitchell (Eds.), *High technology and low-income communities: Prospects for the positive use of advanced information technology* (pp. 349-368). Cambridge, MA: The MIT Press.

Bernstein, L., & Yuhas, C.M. (1999). *Basic concepts for managing telecommunications networks: Copper to sand to glass to air.* New York: Kluwer Academic/Plenum.

Cash, J.I., McFarlan, F.W., & McKenney, J.L. (1983). *Corporate information systems management: Text and cases.* Homewood, IL: Irwin.

Clement, A., & Van Den Besselaar, P. (1993). A retrospective look at PD projects. *Communications of the ACM, 36* (4), 29-37.

Cross-Industry Working Team (XIWT). (1999). *Building the information infrastructure: A progress report.* Retrieved from the World Wide Web: http://www.xiwt.org.

Farrell, J., & Saloner, G. (1985). Standardization, compatibility and innovation. *Rand Journal of Economics, 19,* 70-83.

Gabel, D. & Mueller, M. (1999). *Household financing of the first 100 feet?* Available from http://ksgww.harvard.edu/iip/doeconf/gabel.html.

General Accounting Office. (1996). *Telecommunications: Initiatives taken by three states to promote increased access and investment,* GAO/RCED-96-68.

Gronbaek, K., Kyng, M., & Mogensen, P. (1997). Toward a cooperative experimental system development approach. In M. Kyng & L. Mathiassen (Eds.), *Computers and design in context* (pp. 201-238). Cambridge, MA: The MIT Press.

Jankowski, M.S. (1991). *Islands in the street: Gangs and American urban society.* Berkely, CA: University of California Press.

Rapoport, R.N. (1970). Three dilemmas of action research. *Human Relations, 23,* 499-513.

Rosenberg, N. (1982). *Inside the black box: Technology and economics.* Cambridge: Cambridge University Press.

Shin, D.H., Yun, G-Y., & Shachal, O. (2000). *Medicaid/Chronic Care eligibility & benefits certification process baseline.* Community & Information Technology Institute (CITI) Working Paper, School of Information Studies, Syracuse University.

Susman, G. I., & Evered, R.D. (1978). An assessment of the scientific merits of action research. *Administrative Science Quarterly, 23,* 582-603.

The unpredictable certainty: Information infrastructure through 2000. Retrieved from the World Wide Web: http://www.nap.edu/readingroom/

books/unpredictable.

Thoresen, K. (1993). Principles in practice: Two cases of situated participatory design. In D. Schuler & A. Namioka (Eds.), *Participatory design: Principles and practices* (pp. 271-289). Hillsdale, NJ: Lawrence Erlbaum Associates.

Chapter XII

The Internet, the State Library, and the Implementation of Statewide Information Policy: The Case of the NYS GIS Clearinghouse

Sharon S. Dawes
University at Albany, State University of New York, USA

Sharon Oskam
New York State Library, USA

ABSTRACT

Geographic Information Systems (GIS) are used by government, researchers and businesses in a wide range of domains including economic development, environmental management, education, health, human services, infrastructure management, and disaster response. Most experts agree that the most expensive part of a GIS program is the creation of spatial data. Some estimate that as much as 80% of the cost of any application is attributable to the expenses of acquiring and geocoding information (Thapa & Bosler, 1992). Often the information needs of different GIS applications overlap and data created by one organization can be used by others. Data

This chapter originally appeared in the *Journal of Global Information Management*, Vol. 7(4), 27-33.

sharing can therefore help reduce costs of GIS application develop-ment and yield considerable benefits and efficiencies. To achieve this purpose, the State of New York has implemented a GIS Coordi-nation Program which features an Internet-based GIS Clearing-house operated by the New York State Library (Dawes & Eglene, 1998). In this program, the Library acts as a critical implementer and value-added facilitator of an important new state information policy that has influence over spatial data development, exchange, and use at all levels of government and in the private and not-for-profit sectors. The Clearinghouse provides the conceptual frame-work and operational platform for a fully functioning data coopera-tive which is the heart of the New York State GIS Data Sharing Policy. The library-based clearinghouse has become the essential portal to many newly identified information resources. It organizes the data descriptions, provides a publicly available and easy-to-use means of access, promotes sharing, points the way to education and other services, and generally makes possible the vision of a living data resource.

LIBRARIES AND GIS INFORMATION RESOURCES

Library services related to GIS are a recent development and have been the subject of some research and much experimentation during the 1990s, mostly as an extension of traditional library functions. Much of the literature focuses on providing GIS services directly to library patrons (see for example, Boisse & Larsgaard, 1995; Abbott & Argentati, 1995). Soete (1995) notes key decisions that library planners must make about GIS services: what kind of service, how to build collections, staffing, learning and education programs, partnerships, data storage methods, and costs. In making these decisions, libraries need to attend to both general public (Gluck, 1996) and nontraditional (Argentati, 1997) user needs, to building relationships with other GIS experts (Cobb, 1995), and to providing convenient means of access to spatially referenced information, as well as primary and secondary literature on GIS (Longstreth, 1995). Others emphasize the shift that GIS represents from "documents" to "data sets," and discuss the importance of collecting, describing, and accessing spatial data (Lamont, 1997; Hunt & Joselyn, 1995) through use of the national standards for geo-spatial metadata (Domartz, 1995).

Very recently, the Internet has become a major factor in the provision of spatial data and software to library patrons. A variety of Internet-based tools now offer both access to remote data and interactive analysis (Bergen, 1995; English & Margulies, 1995). The advent of interconnected networks also makes libraries a player in the development of the National Information Infrastructure (NII; Lutz, 1995). Three major examples of NII-type GIS resources are the National Spatial Data Clearinghouse operated by the Federal Geographic Data Committee (Domartz, 1995), the federal Government Information Locator Service (Moen, 1995) and cooperative efforts between libraries and government agencies in the U.S. Global Change Data project (Hill, 1995).

In 1997, *The Journal of Academic Librarianship* published a special issue devoted to the questions and choices libraries now face (Hernon, 1997). These include the level of staff expertise in GIS, the geographic and temporal coverage of library GIS holdings, and the range and depth of service to patrons. Emerging networks of relationships and information sources pose an interesting choice for libraries: Should they focus on direct provision of GIS information and services or should they serve as guides to information housed elsewhere (Stephens, 1997)? The effort described here shows how libraries might do both. It builds on the traditions of librarianship, but also illustrates how a nontraditional role for the library can add considerable value to the entire infrastructure of publicly available information.

EVOLUTION OF THE NEW YORK STATE (NYS) GIS COORDINATION PROGRAM

In the early 1990s, New York State lagged behind most other states in term of GIS coordination and was one of only four states without a formal or ad hoc coordinating body (Healy, 1994). However, New York State benefited from many geographic data resources, deep pockets of GIS expertise, and a number of localized coordination efforts. The central issue facing New York was how to organize and sustain a collaborative effort across all levels of government and with the private sector that would take advantage of the analytical power of GIS to improve government services, drive down costs, and stimulate economic development. Significant barriers to GIS data sharing in NYS were identified in a 1995 study by the Center for Technology in Government (CTG; Kelly et al., 1995, pp. 29-36):

- Lack of awareness of existing data sets led to duplicate data development and failure to pursue projects for which agencies did not have their own data.

- Lack of or inadequate metadata did not allow potential users to easily determine the suitability of a particular data set for a particular purpose.
- Lack of uniform policies on access, cost recovery, revenue generation, and pricing resulted in an inconsistent mixture of free access and fee-based pricing.
- Lack of uniform policies on data ownership, maintenance, and liability made agencies reluctant to share their data freely.
- Lack of incentives, tools, and guidelines for sharing left agencies to reinvent the rules for each new sharing project.
- Absence of state-level leadership prevented New York from leveraging a considerable array of uncoordinated assets and from participating in the national movement to create a spatial data infrastructure.

To demonstrate some possibilities for addressing these problems, CTG, in cooperation with many state and local agencies, produced an Internet-based prototype spatial data clearinghouse that contained a metadata repository and search capability. Selected spatial data sets maintained by a variety of state and local agencies were described using portions of the Federal Geographic Metadata Standard and loaded into the prototype database. By using the search and query capabilities of the prototype clearinghouse, a user identified a data set of interest and linked to the full metadata document to obtain a fuller understanding of its properties. The distribution section of the metadata contained instructions for obtaining the data set. Those instructions, supplied by the metadata provider, could include online file transfers, electronic order forms, or instructions for ordering by phone or mail. The prototype clearinghouse was well received within the GIS community. Experience in building and using it led to specific recommendations (DiCaterino, 1995) for building a permanent system.

In a parallel development, the state legislature established a temporary state GIS coordinating council charged with reporting to the governor and the legislature recommendations for improved coordination of GIS in New York State. Among the council's highest priority recommendations was the creation of a permanent GIS coordinating body and the establishment of a clearinghouse for spatial information (Temporary GIS Council, 1996). Accordingly, the NYS GIS Coordination Body was established as a standing program of the newly established New York State Office for Technology (OFT) and charged with a host of policy-oriented goals-and the development of a spatial metadata and information clearinghouse at the New York State Library.

The first statewide policy on GIS was issued by OFT in September 1996 (NYS OFT, 1996). It established a framework for the development of a statewide GIS program and created a broadly representative GIS Coordinating Body drawn from state and local government and the private sector. Working groups and advisory committees were initiated to focus sustained attention on such issues as data sharing, education, communication, and private sector concerns.

The Data Sharing Policy and Cooperative

The Data Coordination Working Group of the Coordinating Body developed an overall Data Sharing Policy for GIS (NYS OFT, 1997). This policy directs that a NYS GIS Data Sharing Cooperative be established in order to provide an organized mechanism to share GIS data easily. It further directs that all NYS agencies join the cooperative by signing the *NYS GIS Cooperative Data Sharing Agreement,* created by the Legal Working Group. Through the cooperative, public agencies gain access to GIS data of all the members at virtually no cost. Agencies do not need to own data to join the cooperative; however, as members of the cooperative, they are obligated to contribute corrections and enhancements that they make to any data set obtained through the cooperative. Each data set has only one primary custodian designated by the Coordinating Body. The designated agencies are responsible for the maintenance of these data sets as well as their distribution to other agencies needing to use them (Johnson, 1997). A comparable data sharing agreement for local governments and not-for-profit organizations was released in February 1998 and all local governments were invited to join. Agreements with federal government agencies and several other states have also been signed. Data sharing agreements between public agencies and consultants are currently under development. More than 150 agencies had signed agreements by mid-1999.

EVOLUTION OF THE NYS GIS CLEARINGHOUSE AT THE STATE LIBRARY

The NYS GIS Clearinghouse, created and established on the World Wide Web (*http://www.nysl.nysed.gov/gis/*) by the New York State Library, is the lynchpin of the data sharing cooperative. It includes a metadata repository describing GIS data sets held by many different organizations as well as information about how to obtain the data; in selected cases the data resides in the clearinghouse itself. It also has extensive information about New York's GIS Data Sharing Coordination Program and information on and links to GIS education and training opportunities, other state and federal GIS resources, GIS user groups throughout New York, and GIS-related listservs.

The Metadata Repository, an enhanced version of the Center for Technology in Government prototype, was created within the clearinghouse to allow producers of geographic data to describe the data sets they have available so that users can identify existing data before they attempt to create new data sets. Data producers describe their data sets using the Federal Geographic Data Committee Standard for Digital Geospatial Metadata. It includes information about who produced the data, the geographic area covered, the data set category or theme, scale, accuracy information, and how to obtain the data sets. Users access metadata by doing a search online. A list of data sets is returned as the result of a search and the complete metadata record for each of these data sets can be viewed to determine the relevance of the data to the user's need. Users can then contact the data owners to obtain the data they want.

The Metadata Repository and all the ancillary services are available to anyone who visits the clearinghouse on the Internet. In addition, members of the Data Sharing Cooperative can have direct access to selected data sets at the NYS Department of Transportation and several other organizations that have made their GIS data available through the Internet.

Why the Library?

The New York State Library (NYSL) has made special GIS services available free of charge or at minimal fees since 1992 when the Association of Research Libraries and ESRI entered into a partnership to bring GIS technology into libraries (Strasser, 1995). The library's early involvement in GIS services for its patrons brought its expertise and services to the attention of state agencies involved in GIS and gave the library a substantive role in the discussions of the temporary GIS council and the subsequent GIS coordinating body.

The library, with its expertise in collection management, cataloging, and description of information resources, also had key information management skills that existed in no other public agency. More importantly, NYSL was the logical place to host the clearinghouse because of its neutrality in the territorial environment that can sometimes occur in state government and because it carried no negative "history" with any state agencies. The library staff are seen as capable information professionals without an agenda to push. None of the state agencies that are GIS users wanted to see the clearinghouse become the program of another operating agency, since they believed that the clearinghouse might confer special status and give the impression that the agency which operated it is "the leading" GIS agency in the state. Since the library's mission is information dissemination and services to the public, not

GIS applications, it was not considered a rival and, in fact, was regarded as the best choice at a very early stage.

NYSL was enthusiastic about hosting the clearinghouse because it coincided with a priority goal to increase statewide access to electronic information. Library administrators also felt that NYSL involvement with the Coordination Program and the clearinghouse built on existing experience with GIS and could take the library to another level of service to the people of the state. Lastly, GIS data was viewed as another form of government information. NYSL has been disseminating government information since the 1800s through its New York State Document Depository Library Program; it is also a Regional Depository for United States Government information and a central repository for New York State Government information. Hosting the clearinghouse allowed the library to augment its role as a provider of government information by implementing the clearinghouse within the Government Documents Unit.

When the library first agreed to host the clearinghouse, it was not clear what kind of support the site would need in terms of staff or equipment. There is no designated funding for either the Coordination Program or the clearinghouse to hire staff or purchase equipment and software. The concept of "recycle, reuse," which is the basis of the Data Sharing Cooperative, was therefore carried over into establishment and maintenance of the clearinghouse Web site. The library added the clearinghouse site to its existing Web site server and managed it with existing software or with software downloaded without charge from the Web.

This same concept of "recycle, reuse" was also applied to staffing. The associate librarian responsible for the Government Documents Unit within NYSL became the coordinator for the site. Her responsibilities include overall supervision of the site at NYSL, outreach to state agencies and local governments, promotion of the coordination program and clearinghouse, and liaison to members of the Data Sharing Cooperative. Technical expertise comes from the associate librarian for automation, a computer programmer/ analyst and a senior librarian. Neither the senior librarian nor the computer programmer/analyst had prior experience with Web development or GIS. They used tutorials available via the Web and materials available at the library to gain the necessary expertise to update and maintain the site. Their responsibilities include general maintenance of the site such as updating pages, creating new pages, and verifying information and links on the site.

NYSL staff also developed the New York State Metadata Entry System, which is a modified version of the form available from the Federal Geographic Data Committee (FGDC), through which users can enter metadata records into the Metadata Repository, where they will be searchable through a Z39.50 search engine. Clearinghouse technical staff also work closely with the agencies and local governments that are storing their data on the clearinghouse to ensure that it is accessible and that any necessary instructions or tools are included in the description of the data set. Currently, the equivalent of two full-time professionals work on the administration and maintenance of the clearinghouse site.

Initially NYSL agreed to host only the Mmetadata Repository, but it soon became apparent that the ideal situation would allow users to download some data directly from the clearinghouse. To facilitate this exchange of information, NYSL offered to house data on its server for those agencies or local governments that either did not have a Web site or were not able to handle the volume of requests for their data. In order to house the growing number of data sets, the library has purchased a new, larger server along with extra disk space.

THE VALUE OF THE CLEARINGHOUSE

The key goal of the clearinghouse is to promote use and reuse of spatial data. Use of the clearinghouse and the data sets available through the clearinghouse has therefore been of paramount importance both to NYSL and to the GIS Coordinating Body. In addition to publicizing the establishment of the site within the New York State GIS Coordination Program and via the NYS GIS listserv (GISNY-L), the clearinghouse was registered with all the major search engines of the Web to increase its visibility. Visits to the site are logged on the front page; nearly 50,000 visitors were counted in its first two years. Usage of the site has increased steadily as it has become well known throughout the state, with peaks occurring when there have been major additions to the site, such as the addition of data sets from the Department of Transportation, the Office of Real Property Services, the Adirondack Park Agency, and the Department of Health.

It is vital for clearinghouse staff to be able to monitor not only the number of visitors to the site, but what pages are being visited regularly. These statistics are kept on a monthly basis and are sorted by the different pages on the site. As can be expected, the most popular pages are those related to what data is available and where the user can obtain it. The most frequently and regularly visited pages are those relating to the Data Sharing Cooperative. These pages include general information on the Data Sharing Cooperative concept, frequently asked questions, and information on the participants and their data inventories. The Metadata Repository pages are also visited on a regular basis, with the browseable index to the metadata being very popular.

The site map, a chart of the major categories of information on the site including links to the pages related to those categories, is quite popular. It offers users a quick way to see all areas covered on the site and to go directly to the desired topic. The related sites page and the education and training pages are also visited very frequently.

As the key to implementation of the statewide spatial data sharing policy, it was imperative that NYSL develop a way to monitor the usage of the data sets available through the clearinghouse. Daily statistics are kept on information such as what data set is being downloaded, how often it is being downloaded, and who is accessing the data. These statistics are sent weekly to the primary data custodian and also to the chair of the Coordinating Body. This information is of vital interest because, for the first time, the actual cost-benefit of reusing data can be quantified. A key assumption behind the clearinghouse is that it is more cost-effective to reuse existing data. These statistics now offer hard data to begin to test and refine that assumption. It was also essential to develop a log with information on who is accessing the data because, as part of the data sharing agreement, users who download data and make improvements to that data are required to send those enhancements back to the primary custodian of the data set. The primary custodian can then make improvements to the original data set, which then benefits all future users of the data.

The clearinghouse continues to expand in its scope and vision. In September 1998, the clearinghouse became a gateway to the Cornell University Geospatial Information Repository (CUGIR). CUGIR is the repository for data from the Department of Environmental Conservation as well as data on topics relating to agriculture and the environment. Through the clearinghouse Z39.50 gateway, users are able to search for metadata from both the NYS GIS Clearinghouse and CUGIR.

With the cooperation and assistance of many of the state agencies, the clearinghouse has added many new features to its original design. Clearinghouse staff have developed a clickable county data map of New York State. Through this map users can click on any county in the state to display a list of the data sets available for that county or links to metadata records in the New York State Metadata Repository. More recently, clearinghouse staff have been working on a digital image map of the state. This map displayed digital raster graphics (DRGs) of New York State. The CD-ROMs containing the DRGs were loaned to NYSL from the New York State Department of Health and were loaded onto the library's servers. The map shows each county within the state and is divided into quadrangles matching those stored on the library's servers. Users can click on a specific quadrangle and view the actual image.

They also have the option to download the image and data files that go with it. This map will be the basis for continued expansion into the display of digital orthophotos on the clearinghouse.

Strengths and Weaknesses of the Clearinghouse

The single greatest strength of the clearinghouse is that it has done what it was intended to do: provide "one-stop shopping" on GIS in New York State. It is designed to allow users to find and obtain data and other resources quickly and efficiently. The clearinghouse gives users the ability to identify and access spatial data sets and in some cases download them directly. It eliminates the excessive time and effort previously spent attempting to identify and locate, or in some cases recreate, existing geospatial data.

In just its first year, the clearinghouse accomplished its fundamental goal to become the focal point for the statewide GIS Coordination Program. It is the cornerstone for implementing a statewide policy for the transfer of GIS data easily among state and local governments and others at minimum or no cost. It is the one place that users can go to find out what data sets are available in the state and to download data directly from the site or from custodial sites.

The many electronic forms make it simple for users to create and submit metadata online, update personal or organizational information, or correspond with clearinghouse staff. The listings of user groups and Coordination Program participants provides a way for GIS users across the state to communicate and network with each other and with members of the Coordination Program. The clearinghouse also provides links to GISNY-L and other GIS-related listservs to keep its users informed. The education and training pages offer links to educational opportunities both on-site and online, as well as GIS-related publications and resources.

The constant expansion of the site is another strength of the clearinghouse concept. A great deal of effort goes into exploring ways to improve the site, whether through new features, such as the image map, or suggestions from users, such as new user groups or links to new resources. Many of the improvements made to the site are based on ideas from members of the cooperative or requests from its users which contribute to the effectiveness of the site in meeting user needs. Because it is a virtual, rather than a physical, resource it is possible to make changes and enhancements quickly and to respond readily to user needs and suggestions.

The success of the site was recognized in May 1998 when the clearinghouse received the Urban and Regional Information Systems Association's (URISA) Exemplary Systems in Government Award in the National Spatial Data Infrastructure-Data Partnerships Category.

The clearinghouse is not without weaknesses, however. The lack of formal funding for the Coordination Program and clearinghouse is a double-edged sword. On the one hand, lack of formal funding fosters greater cooperation and collaboration between clearinghouse staff and other state agencies and local governments to continue to make the site viable. However, without dedicated funding, the site is dependent on the continuing support of library administration in terms of dollars and human resources. State agencies have been very cooperative in sharing their resources, but the clearinghouse would become more institutionalized and could develop more user services if it had dedicated staff and funding.

While state agency participation is high, the much more minimal involvement of local governments and the private sector can be viewed as a weakness not only of the clearinghouse, but of the entire Coordination Program. Local government information has traditionally been difficult to find and make accessible (Durrance, 1988). In this case, local governments have viewed the Data Sharing Cooperative with some skepticism and have been slower to join. There are opportunities for local governments to showcase their GIS projects on the clearinghouse, but few have done so in the first two years. This reluctance is accounted for by two main reasons. First, some local government GIS programs are reluctant to make their data freely available and are advocating for the ability to charge user fees. Second, while GIS professionals in local governments are often enthusiastic about the cooperative, they still need to educate their administrators and elected officials about its value and implications before formal data sharing agreements can be signed. The clearinghouse and communications workgroups have recently been combined with greater representation from both the private sector and local government. With increased representation, and more experience, the interests of these groups may be more fully addressed.

The relatively slow accumulation of metadata records in the Metadata Repository (about 200 at the end of 1998) has been a concern. The original metadata records from the Center for Technology in Government's prototype were converted at the start and some records were added quickly, mainly by Westchester County and the New York State Department of Transportation. To encourage agencies to describe their data holdings, the clearinghouse offers its users multiple choices for submitting metadata and there is always the opportunity to talk with clearinghouse staff about how to convert in-house or legacy systems. The Coordination Program has also received a grant from the Federal Geographic Data Committee (FGDC) to assist in the development of metadata. The grant includes funds for training and technical assistance for state and local governments in the form of paid interns to assist agencies in preparing metadata records. During 1999, five interns were placed in state and local government offices. Eight metadata training sessions were held across the state with more than 400 participants. The benefits of this effort have been immediately realized: the number of metadata records doubled to about 400 by mid- 1999, and data owners show increased interest in creating metadata in the future. While the Metadata Repository does not yet truly represent what GIS data is available in New York State, these efforts are clearly helping the inventory grow. The ultimate goal is for all State and local government agencies that hold GIS data sets to create metadata records and submit them to the Clearinghouse.

Future Directions for the Clearinghouse

The New York State GIS Clearinghouse has come a long way in the two years since its inception, but a number of new initiatives are underway.

One goal is to make all major GIS data sets for New York available online. This will mean more follow-up with agencies that are Data Sharing Cooperative members, but have not made their data available electronically (either through the clearinghouse or on their own accessible sites linked to the clearinghouse). It also means more promotion and outreach to local governments and not-for-profits that have not yet joined the cooperative since they hold many of the important GIS data sets.

Another goal involves digital orthophotos. Although these photos have existed for many years, advancing technology has brought them into prominence. Clearinghouse staff have already created an image map which allows users to access and download DRGs generated by the United States Geological Survey (USGS). In the coming year, the Department of Transportation's digital quadrangles for New York State will also be available through the image map on the clearinghouse. The ultimate goal for the clearinghouse is to have digital orthophotos for all of New York State available online, in an easily distributed format.

The clearinghouse is also being used to help New York address year 2000 concerns. Key data sets have been targeted by the New York State Disaster Preparedness Commission and are being delivered to the clearinghouse. These data sets pinpoint the locations of hospitals, schools, armories, state and other facilities with fuel supplies, and utility service areas that could be used in an emergency. Clearinghouse staff are working with the primary custodians of these files to ensure that the data is geocoded and is as accurate as possible. Metadata is also being created and added to the metadata repository for these high-priority data sets which will be made available for direct downloading through the clearinghouse.

The clearinghouse staff are also exploring the capability of providing simple GIS viewing online. This option would allow users to pull GIS data into a map server and be able to see an actual map and perform simple GIS operations such as zooming in and out or querying the database.

CONCLUSION

The mission of the New York State Education Department, as identified by the Board of Regents, is to "raise the knowledge, skill, and opportunity of all the people of New York." NYSL's work in making GIS data available is helping to exploit the considerable resources of this exciting new technology for the benefit of New Yorkers and others who use the New York State GIS Clearinghouse.

The clearinghouse provides the conceptual framework and operational foundation for implementing New York State's GIS Data Sharing Policy. This policy pertains to data sets in active use by government agencies for a myriad of public purposes and, as such, most of them change frequently and are not candidates for traditional library collections. The state library, therefore, serves as the gateway to rich data sources held by an extensive network of primary data custodians. It organizes the data descriptions, provides easy public access, promotes sharing, and links to education and other services. By playing this lynchpin role, the library enhances the ability of scores of other organizations to use information to do their own jobs better. Although much remains to be done to completely achieve the state's vision, this nontraditional role played by the New York State Library is clearly a success-for the library, for state government, and for the GIS community.

REFERENCES

Abbott, L.T. and C.D. Argentati (1995, July). "GIS: A new component of public services," *Journal of Academic Librarianship* 21(4), 251-256.

Argentati, C.D. (1997, November). "Expanding horizons for GIS services in academic libraries," *Journal of Academic Librarianship*, 23(6), 463-468.

Bergen, P.E. (1995) "Interactive access to geographic information systems and numeric data on the World Wide Web," *Journal of Academic Librarianship* 21(4), 303-308.

Boisse, J. A. and M. Larsgaard (1995, July). "GIS in academic libraries: A managerial perspective," *Journal of Academic Librarianship*, 21(4), 288-291.

Cobb, D.A. (1995). "Developing GIS Relationships," *Journal of Academic Librarianship,* 21(4), 275-277.

Dawes, S. and Eglene, O. (1998). *New models of collaboration: GIS coordination in New York state.* Center for Technology in Government, Albany, NY.

DiCaterino, A. (1995). *The New York state spatial data clearinghouse technical report.* Center for Technology in Government, Albany, NY.

Domartz, M. (1995). Finding and accessing spatial data in the National Spatial Data Infrastructure, in *Geographic Information Systems and Libraries: Patrons, Maps, and Spatial Information,* p.31-40. University of Illinois Graduate School of Library and Information Science, Urbana, IL.

Durrance, J.C. (1988). "Providing Access to Local Government Information: The Nature of Public Library Activity," *Government Information Quarterly,* 5(2), 155-167.

English, J. and Margulies, J. (1995). Expanding library horizons through use of the Internet. Growth of the Internet, Past and Future, *Computers in Libraries,* 15(8), 41-45

Gluck, M. (1996) Geospatial needs of the general public: Text, maps, and users' tasks," in *Geographic Information Systems and Libraries: Patrons, Maps, and Spatial Information,* p. 151-172. University of Illinois Graduate School of Library and Information Science, Urbana, IL.

Healy, D. (1994). *Survey of State GIS Coordination Bodies, Summary Results and Recommendations.* National States Geographic Information Committee, Calais, VT.

Hernon, P. (1997). "GIS as a Service Option," *Journal of Academic Librarianship,* 23(3), 235-237, May.

Hill, L.L. (1995) Spatial access to, and display of, global change data: Avenues for libraries," in *Geographic Information Systems and Libraries: Patrons, Maps, and Spatial Information,* p. 125-150. University of Illinois Graduate School of Library and Information Science, Urbana, IL.

Hunt, L. and M. Joselyn (1995). Maximizing accessibilitly to spatially referenced digital data.

Johnson William (1997). The NYS GIS Data Sharing Cooperative: An innovative new model for data sharing and partnerships." Retrieved from the World Wide Web: http://www.nysl.nysed.gov/gis/coop_gis.htm

Kelly, K., and Pardo, T. A., Dawes, S. S., DiCaterino, A. and W. Foderingham (1995). Sharing the costs, sharing the benefits: The NYS GIS Cooperative Project. *Center for Technology in Government,* Albany, NY.

Lamont, M. (1997). Managing geospatial data and services, *Journal of Academic Librarianship,* 23(6), 469-474.

Longstreth, K. 1995. GIS collection development, staffing, and training, *Journal of Academic Librarianship,* 21(4), 267-274.

Lutz, M. (1995, June). Making GIS a part of library service, *Information Technology and Libraries,* 14(2), 77-78.

Moen, W.E. (1995). The Government Information Locator Service: Discovering, identifying, and accessing spatial data, in *Geographic Information Systems and Libraries: Patrons, Maps, and Spatial Information,* p.41-67. University of Illinois Graduate School of Library and Information Science, Urbana, IL.

NYS Office for Technology. (1996, September). Technology Policy 96-18. Retrieved from the World Wide Web: http://www.irm.state.ny.us/policy/tp_9618.htm.

NYS Office for Technology. (1996, July). Technology Policy 97-6. Retrieved from the World Wide Web: http://www.irm.state.ny.us/policy/tp_976.htm.

Soete, G.J. (1997). *Transforming Libraries: Issues and Innovations in Geographic Information Systems,* Volume 2. Association of Research Libraries, Office of Management Services, Washington, D.C.

Stephens, D. (1997, November). Managing the Web-enhanced geographic information service, *Journal of Academic Librarianship,* 23(6), 498-504.

Strasser, T. (1995, July). Desktop GIS in libraries, technology and costs: A view from New York state, *Journal of Academic Librarianship* 21(4), 278-282.

Temporary Geographic Information Systems Council. (1996). Geographic Information Systems: Key to competitiveness. Submitted to Governor George E.Pataki and the New York State Legislature, Albany, NY.

Thapa, K., and J. Bossler (1992). Accuracy of spatial data used in Geographic Information Systems. *Photogrammetric Engineering and Remote Sensing.* 58(6), 835-841.

Chapter XIII

Organizational Impacts of New Communication Technology: A Comparison of Cellular Phone Adoption in France and the United States

Patricia J. Carlson and Beverly K. Kahn
Suffolk University, USA

Frantz Rowe
Universite de Nantes, France

ABSTRACT

This study tests the multicultural applicability of Huber's technological imperative framework by comparing the effects of the adoption of a new telecommunication technology, cellular phones, on the behavior of the sales force in several industry sectors in France and the U.S. The study investigates three areas of interest. First, the study finds that, though the sales strategies are the same in both countries, the actual behavior of the sales force to attain these strategic goals differs. Second, a comparison of these differences with the variables in Huber's theory shows that the differences in the variables are consistent with the sales representative behavior

This chapter originally appeared in the *Journal of Global Information Management*, Vol. 7(3), 19-29.

in the two countries. Third, the study asks what effect the use of cell phones has had on sales force behavior. Analysis on all the data combined shows the predicted results of new technology adoption— a shortening of decision-making time occurs in both countries. When the data is stratified by country, however, changes in variables in the U.S. support Huber's theory, those from France do not. These results indicate a cultural bias in the generation of theory that has important implications for cross-cultural research.

INTRODUCTION

Organizations in recent years have been inundated with new information technologies that change the nature of communication and affect such important organizational variables as organizational structure, standardization, and formalization (Hirscheim, 1985; Huber, 1990; Markus & Robey, 1988; Orlikowski & Robey, 1991). This study investigates the effects of the adoption of one type of telecommunication technology, cellular phones, in two different cultures (France and the United States).

As the world becomes more accessible through telecommunication and other technology, our concern about the universal application of theories to diverse cultural groups intensifies. Each researcher who develops theories may be influenced by his or her own cultural biases. It is important to know if this occurs. It is also important to validate theories in multicultural situations. When theories are validated in diverse cultural settings, they lend themselves to the establishment of universal traits that can then be used to predict behavior with added certainty in other settings. This study sheds light on the important area of cross-cultural research through the study of multi-cultural adoption of technology.

The study also tests another question of interest to researchers with a cross-cultural orientation. This question concerns the validity of theories across cultures. Theories specifically developed to apply to multiple cultures are assumed to be valid in many cultural settings. In this way, researchers have investigated the adoption and use of technology assuming adoption across cultures to be the same (Rogers, 1995). It is also usually assumed that theories developed within one culture are applicable in that culture. Thus, organizational researchers have investigated the ways technology affects organizations within one culture (Damanpour & Evan, 1984; Huber, 1990; Yates & Orlikowski, 1992). What about the applicability of theories developed in one culture to other cultures? Do these theories remain valid? Huber (1990) has developed a theory that states that technology affects organizational variables in a specific manner. Testing Huber's theory in two cultures gives us the opportunity to test a specific instance of technology adoption across cultures. This study is a test of Huber's framework in two different cultures. Its purpose is to determine whether Huber's variables (both dependent and independent) are relevant in a multicultural environment.

LITERATURE REVIEW

This study investigates the relationship between the adoption of information technology and organizational change in two cultural settings. It draws upon two bodies of established literature: the cross-cultural research literature and the organizational change/technology adoption literature. These sets of literature are examined below.

Cross-Cultural Research

The understanding of cross-cultural diversity is critical to the development of international business strategies and to the management of multicultural organizations (Cox & Blake, 1991). While the need for both cross-cultural and multi-cultural studies is high, their implementation attains a level of complexity that has resulted in a dearth of these studies. This situation is the result of two converging forces. First, the research is methodologically difficult, and second, researchers cannot agree on whether comparisons across cultures are meaningful and valid.

The methodological difficulties involved in doing cross-cultural and multi-cultural studies include language barriers, differences of interpretation due to cultural biases, and questions about the transferability of measures (Riordan & Vandenberg, 1994). Other obstacles include the North American positivist approach with its emphasis on rigorous quantitative methods, which sharply contrasts with the need to accommodate context found in international studies (Adler, Campbell, & Laurent, 1989; Graham & Gronhaug, 1989). Adler (1984) suggested using collaborative multi-cultural teams to meet these challenges. Cost, time commitment, and methodological challenges have also been identified as impediments to cross-cultural management research (Adler, 1984; Arndt, 1985; Brislin, Lonner, & Thorndike, 1973; Wind & Perlmutter, 1973).

Comparisons across cultures have traditionally followed either an emic or an etic approach. Research concerning the applicability of concepts across cultures is dominated by this debate which focuses on the two concepts of cultural uniqueness (the emic approach) and cultural comparability (the etic approach). The cultural uniqueness side of the debate advances the idea that concepts, theories, and practices cannot be applied universally because of cultural differences, while the cultural comparability view contends that there are universal traits that affect mankind (Berry, 1969; Hofstede, 1980; Lammers, 1977).

Cross-cultural studies in information systems (Abdul-Gader & Kozar, 1995; Straub 1994; Rowe & Struck, 1996) have supported both the universal trait and the culture specific points of view. In one of these studies, a scale for computer alienation was tested in Saudi Arabia and the United States (Abdul-Gader & Kozar, 1995). This scale was found to predict computer adoption in both countries, thus, illustrating an etic approach. Straub (1994) found that the rates of adoption of e-mail and fax in the U.S. and Japan were influenced by a local trait. This trait is the number of distinct characters composing the written language of the respective nationalities. Shore and Venkatachalam (1996) introduced another level of analysis by showing that the effect of national culture on technology adoption is contingent, in some cases, on other variables. Rowe and Struck (1996) took the debate to another level and found that cultural analysis and social theories are alternatives in understanding telecommunication choices.

The present study assumes an "etic" approach. "Etic" approaches depend on surfacing universal traits for validation. Some classification schemes for the differences among cultures have been established and validated. They represent traits that are relevant across multiple cultures. For example, Hofstede (1980, 1993) has defined the degree of difference along four dimensions for defining values associated with national cultures. These dimensions are: behavior toward people higher or lower in rank (power distance), behavior toward the group (individualism/collectivism), behavior of collecting things such as money or of concern with caring and quality of life (masculinity vs. femininity), and uncertainty avoidance. Two main differences between French and American values on this scale concern power distance and risk avoidance. The French are stronger in both of these characteristics than the Americans. Another model was developed by Adler (1984) which identified fundamental problems that permeate all aspects of cross-cultural management research. The present research is an extension of this type of investigation-to determine whether members of diverse cultural groups react similarly to the adoption of new technology. Our study takes the view that, though multicultural research is complex and demanding methodologically, it is a valuable contribution to science since it represents a unique opportunity to compare traits across cultures and gain insight into their universality.

Organizational Change

This research focuses on the relationships between information technology and organizational change. Recently researchers have striven to enlarge our understanding of the perspectives underlying these studies (Kling, 1980; Hirscheim, 1985; Crowston & Malone, 1988; Orlikowski & Robey, 1991). Three main approaches have been identified: the organizational imperative, the emergent perspective, and the technological imperative.

Organizational Imperative: Damanpour and Evan (1984) develop a view of the historical dynamics between information technology and organizational change. According to this perspective, in the diffusion of a given technology, there is some organizational imperative-i.e., the diffusion depends on organizational structures, top managers' choices, or the existence of someone promoting the new technology. Over time the use of the technology begins to shape organizations and transforms them in a deterministic fashion. This view, then, states that the organizational imperative prevails first, then the technological imperative (Adler & Borys, 1989). Evidence supporting this perspective shows that the adoption and use of data networks is conditioned by past habits and organizational characteristics, but, after a period of time, which depends on competitor's anticipation of technology strategies, the use of the technology brings about drastic organizational changes (Rowe, 1994b). This view would be tested by gathering data from organizations with the same sets of organizational imperatives, requiring them to be in the same culture. For this reason, this view was not tested in the current study.

Emergent Perspective: The emergent perspective is adopted by Yates and Orlikowski (1992), who develop the concept of communication genre. They use the memo as an example and provide a first approach by suggesting that conditions influencing media use and the consequences of media are tightly coupled in the process of structuration (Giddens, 1984). Rejoining Barley's study (1986) on computerized tomography, Yates and Orlikowski do not just mix the technological and organizational imperatives, but contribute to the emergent perspective (Pfeffer, 1982). According to the emergent perspective, "the technology presents an occasion for structural change but does not determine which of a large variety of alternatives actually emerges from the process of structuring" (Markus & Robey, 1988, p. 588). This use of structuration theory seems very helpful to build a better understanding of the changes, but is not predictive, in the sense that it tells nothing about when and why a structural change can occur. That means that it is difficult to define independent and dependent variables. For this reason, the emergent perspective was not used in this study.

Technological Imperative: The technological imperative rests on the assumption that the technology will influence the organization. Huber (1990) developed a theory that proposes that the adoption of new technology creates a potential for change in organizational structures. The theory considers that, once adopted, new technology deeply alters the way decisions are made in an organization. Huber (1990) argues, in the context of communication technology, that advanced communication technologies compensate for the insufficient or excessive levels of some organizational attributes such as centralization. The theory postulates that the advanced technologies will affect organization design, organizational intelligence, and decision making in certain predictable ways, with the final result of the adoption being the shortening of the decision-making process and the improvement of the quality of decisions. This theory postulates that "universal" variables operate independently of the organization, and thus of the cultural context. For this reason, Huber's theory is tested in this study.

The Technological Imperative

The technological imperative theory, (Huber, 1990) gives the opportunity to test whether technology adoption as predicted by a U.S. researcher applies to its adoption in another country, France. Huber's theory is described in detail below.

Huber sets forth the beginning of a conceptual theory predicting the effects of adopting advanced information technology. The theory predicts that adopting advanced information technology leads to increased information accessibility. This increased information accessibility leads to changes in organization design. Both the increased information accessibility and the changes in organization design increase the speed and effectiveness with which information can be changed into intelligence and intelligence into decisions. The net result, then, of adopting advanced information technology is a shortening of the decision-making cycle time. Huber's theory (1990) suggests that organizations adopting advanced information technologies should expect the following types of changes. Five key changes in organization design at the organizational level predicted by the theory are:

1. *Centralization-Decentralization*: More uniform distribution, across organizational levels (For a highly centralized organization, use of advanced technologies leads to more decentralization, and vice versa for highly decentralized organizations).
2. A greater variation across organizations in the levels at which a particular type of decision is made (This proposition applies to comparison across organizations and was not included in the present study).

3. *Levels of Management:* Reduced number of organizational levels involved in authorizing proposed organizational actions and fewer intermediate human nodes (levels of management) within the organizational information processing network (reduced number of organizational levels involved in processing messages).
4. *Formalization:* No change in organizational formalization, which may be manifested by the number of written communications.
5. *Standardization:* Reduction in organizational standardization (number of strictly defined procedures).

Additionally, there are key changes in decision making. First, there is reduced time to authorize organizational actions and reduced time required to make decisions. Second, higher quality decisions should result. (This is not tested in the study).

STUDY OVERVIEW

Telecommunication technology includes many types of devices that are more and more necessary to continued competitiveness. The asynchronous nature of some telecommunication devices, such as electronic mail, voice mail, and pagers permits users to save time previously wasted in "telephone tag." The synchronous nature of other devices, such as cellular telephones, allows users to communicate more easily and reduce the constraints imposed by temporal availability and geographic location. In fact, with mobile telecommunication devices, an individual's ability to communicate no longer depends on his/her proximity to an office equipped with the appropriate media. Instead a person can potentially call or be reached anywhere in order to respond to an event. This ability to transcend geographic barriers makes cellular phones more than a substitute for end-to-end wired telephones, but the real nature of the effect of cellular phones on organizations remains unknown. This research investigates that effect in two different cultures-France and the United States.

Sales organizations were targeted due to their wide use of cellular phones. The mobility of sales representatives made them ideal candidates for our study. The study first gathered data about the sales strategies in both countries, to determine whether the underlying goals of the sales departments in both countries are similar. This would affect the use and impact of cellular phones. The sales strategies are very similar for the two countries. The study then shows the differences in the ways the sales departments in the two countries attained their goals. This is reflected by the behavior of sales representatives. Finally, the study measures the organizational variables in Huber's theory to determine which of these variables might be instrumental in influencing the effects of the adoption of cell phones.

The study highlights the actual impacts of the adoption of cellular phones. Several key variables reflecting the impact of cellular phones were identified, based primarily on the research of Huber (1990) and Rowe (1994a). These variables will be referred to as the technological imperative (TI) variables. The four independent variables are:

- *Centralization-Decentralization:* Change in the degree of centralization,
- *Levels of Management:* Change in the number of management levels,
- *Standardization:* Change in the number of strictly followed formal procedures, and
- *Formalization*: Change in the number of written documents used.
  The one dependent variable is
- *Decision-making Time:* Change in the length of the decision-making process.

These TI variables relate to the behavior of sales representatives. A change in centralization/decentralization would affect the number of times the representatives visit their home base. A change in formalization would change the number or type of paperwork the representatives perform. A change in standardization would give representatives more or less freedom to follow different procedures and might affect the number of meetings they attend.

METHODOLOGY

The study was designed to test whether cellular phones have an effect on decision making in the organization and to test which of the variables described by Huber might be influential in any changes in decision making. The French study was funded by a prominent French telecommunications organization. The objective of the study was to determine the impact of the use of cellular phones on sales and marketing departments in organizations. The French part of the study was carried out first. The U.S. study was carried out a year later by two American researchers.

This study was based on a questionnaire that was developed in France. The questionnaire consisted of both open-ended and close-ended questions. Only data from close-ended questions are described in this paper. Relevant questions are in the Appendix (in English). In both countries, the questionnaire was administered to the person in charge of sales in each firm. A trained research assistant administered each questionnaire in person. This questionnaire was paired with an additional one administered to the individual in charge of telecommunications. This provided the means to evaluate the organization-wide perspective of mobile communication devices and their impact. Specific methodological information for each study is given separately below.

The Mann-Whitney nonparametric test was used to compare differences between the U.S. and France. This statistical test is analogous to and less restrictive than the t-test and is appropriate for the data in the sample (i.e., two independent samples of ordinal data). Our sample size in the stratified analysis is of sufficient size for the Mann-Whitney test.

The French Study. In France, the study focuses on mobile services provided by both public and private operators. Cellular telephone services contribute about 80% of France Telecom revenues from mobile services, at the time of the study. Three types of cellular services fall into the definition of this study:

1. the analog service provided both by France Telecom and Societe Francaise de Radiotelephone, a private sector competitor,
2. the pan European GSM digital service that the same companies initiated in France in 1992, and
3. the closed user mobile trunk service.

Similar services are offered throughout Europe and the United States.

The survey field research was carried out in 1994 using a representative sampling of 39 of the 1,000 largest firms in France, primarily in and around Paris. It was preceded by a pilot study during which the questionnaire and the methodology were validated (Rowe, 1994c). All the firms had more than 1,000 employees and were from the industry sectors of manufacturing, services, transportation, and construction. The questionnaire was written in French and the interviewing was conducted in French.

The U.S. Study. Analog cellular phone services in the U.S. are offered by both the large nationwide companies, such as AT&T, Sprint and MCI, and local companies. During the period of the study, digital service was rare in the U.S. Competition in these service areas is open in the U.S.

The study in the U.S. was carried out to replicate the French study in 1995 in a large metropolitan city on the East Coast of the U.S. This is approximately a year after the French study. A total of 46 firms participated in the survey. The firms were chosen based on size and to be representative of the types of firms present in this metropolitan area. Most companies are in the service sector, which is dominated by the financial, insurance and health care areas. The average number of employees was approximately 2,500.

The questionnaire used in the American study was a translation of the French questionnaire. Comparable U.S. companies replaced French companies mentioned in the survey. It was translated by a bilingual individual and reviewed by other bilingual individuals to verify that the two surveys conveyed the same information.

Multicultural Comparability. The sample in each country was approximately the same size. The companies are primarily very large, reflecting the size of each country, and are located in large metropolitan areas. While the industry sectors are slightly different, they both include a large service sector. The sales strategies in the two countries are not different, making any differences in industry sectors irrelevant for the study.

A stratification of the sample in each country revealed a significant difference in the number of years of cellular phone usage (see Figure 1). This data analysis determined that there is an association between country and length of time the company has used cellular phones. The French have used cellular technology longer. Correlations were conducted to determine whether the country, length of time the technology has been used, or their interaction was the major effect. In all correlations, most of the effect was caused by country.

RESULTS

The study results are based on similar sales strategies, which gives a basis for multicultural comparison. Sales strategies and the sales representative behavior in implementing the sales strategies are discussed in the comparison of sales policies and practices section below. Huber's theory of the effects of the adoption of new technology is tested on both the combined data from both countries and on the data stratified by country, and is discussed in the effect of adoption section below.

Comparison of Sales Policies and Practices

Since our data details the acquisition, use and impact of cellular phones in sales and marketing, the study first investigates the sales strategies in France and the U.S. Sales managers selected the most important sales strategy from a list: improving the quality of service, increasing sales, reducing costs and reducing delays. The results for France are described by Rowe (1994a). The present study extends the results to the U.S. Sales strategies in France and the U.S. are not significantly different. Figure 2 also shows that the strategies in both countries are similar. In addition, Figure 2 illustrates that the most important strategy in both countries is to improve the quality of service, which should provide the means to achieve increased sales, the second most important strategy.

The study then investigates the actual behavior of sales representatives in both countries. Cellular phones have provided sales representatives with the ability to be on the job from almost anywhere. This behavior is reflected in two areas. First, it is shown by the frequency with which representatives return to their home base and, second, it is shown by their reasons for the return and the activities carried out once they return to home base. As shown in Table 1, there is no significant difference between France and the U.S. in the frequency with which sales representatives return to their home base. Sixty-seven percent of the sales representatives return to their home base several times per week; of that total, 22% return at least once per day. The remaining 33% of the sales representatives return less often, usually several times per month.

The reasons the sales representatives return to home base are significantly different in the two countries (see Table 1). The origin of the differences is shown in Figure 3. (Note: The reasons for returning to the home base are ordered in Figure 3 to resemble a bell curve where the differences between the U.S. and France can be easily seen. This ordering was then used in Table 1.)

Figure 1. Years of organizational cellular phone usage

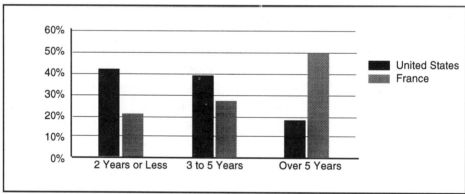

Figure 2. Sales strategies in the U.S. and France

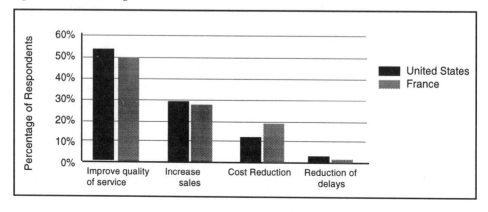

Table 1. *U.S. vs. France sales representatives behavior*

SALES REPRESENTATIVES' BEHAVIOR	P VALUE
Frequency of return to home site	.91
Returned to attend meetings	.02
Returned to complete administrative work	.04
Returned to evaluate work	.32
Returned to retrieve additional information	.63
Returned to pick up orders	.00
Returned to upload data	.00

It is clear that representatives in both countries return with comparable frequency to evaluate work and get information.

The differences arise in the other categories. In France, the representatives return with high frequency to perform procedural tasks connected with sales orders (pick up sales orders and upload data). In the U.S., representatives return with high frequency to take care of paperwork (administrative tasks) and meet with people. This means that, in France, sales people engage in more activities that involve standard procedures (Huber's standardization variable). The U.S. sales representatives have more meetings and do more administrative work, usually involving written documents (Huber's formalization variable). This reflects sales representatives' current behavior. In the next section the impact of this behavior on Huber's TI variables is described.

Effects of Cellular Phone Adoption
on the Total Sample

All the data from both countries is combined in Figure 4 to show the direction of change in all five TI (technological imperative) variables. Except

Figure 3. *Reason sales representatives return to the office in U.S. and France*

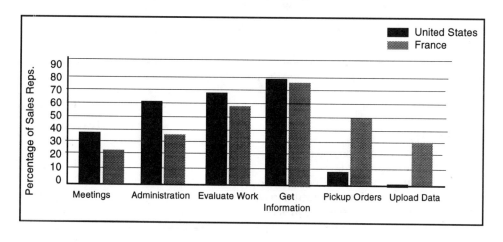

for decreasing the time for decision making, most subjects indicated that no change resulted from the adoption of cellular phones. The shortening of the decision-making time is beneficial and the effects of changes in the other four TI variables on the organization may be profound and, in some cases, undesirable. Example adverse changes in these dependent variables can include: changes in the degree of centralization of decision making which would be disruptive for an organization, reductions in the levels of management which would cause low morale, and a reduction in the number of standard procedures which could also be confusing for organizational members and lead to layoffs. Huber (1990) predicts that changes in these variables will cause the shortening of the time for decision making. It would be desirable to have decision-making time reduced without the concomitant changes in the other four variables and the ensuing negative impact.

Without any further country specific analysis, the conclusion could be drawn that, in this study of cellular phones, decision time is shortened without the potentially disruptive effects of changes in other organizational variables in both countries. This is beneficial since disruption of organizational functions could be considered an unnecessary side effect in obtaining shorter decision cycles. However, differences between the countries were analyzed and show characteristics that change these initial conclusions. Therefore, this data does not support the theory explained in Huber's work (1990). These country-specific differences are analyzed in the following section.

Figure 4. Effect of adoption on whole sample

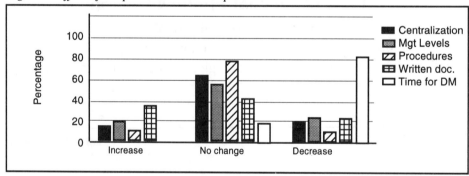

Table 2. Effect of cell phone adoption-French vs. U.S. practices

CHANGE IN	MANN-WHITNEY SIGNIFICANCE
Centralization of decision making	0.394
Number of management levels	0.469
Amount of used strictly defined procedures	**0.004**
Amount of written documentation used	**0.030**
Length of the decision-making process	**0.000**

Country-Specific Effects

Sales representative behavior in both countries is different. This behavior reflects differences in the TI variables. The source of these differences needed to be investigated and, therefore, each country was studied separately and then comparison techniques were used to highlight differences between the U.S. and France.

When the TI variables are examined for specific characteristics of each country, interesting differences appear. Though the impact of the adoption of cellular phones on the whole sample showed a change only in the area of the time of decision making (see Figure 4), Mann-Whitney U statistical tests analyzing these same variables discover significant ($p<.05$) differences between the countries. Differences in standardization, formalization and decision-making time (see Table 2) are identified. Table 2 shows differences in the responses for the two countries concerning the effect of using cellular phones on the speed of decision making, use of standard procedures and use of written documents. The decision making time was shortened as a result of the adoption of cellular phones. This was also shown in the analysis of the total sample. The differences in the other TI variables are further analyzed below in our discussion which highlights significant differences in these variables between France and the U.S.

Centralization/Decentralization and Management Levels

There is no significant difference between France and the U.S. in centralization/decentralization of decision making. Additionally, there is not significant difference in the number of management levels, which represents organizational downsizing. These variables do not support Huber's theory in either the U.S. or in France. Huber predicted that the adoption of advanced technologies would move an organization towards the center of the centralization-decentralization spectrum and reduce the number of management levels.

In our study there was no movement in centralization/decentralization for 65% of the total respondents (with the U.S. at 60% and the French at 72%). In the U.S., there was a greater move towards decentralization (24% of the U.S. respondents compared to only 12% of the French). The difference in France occurred with a larger group showing no change.

The management levels in both countries showed even less change than the centralization/decentralization variable. In over 90% of the total responses there was no change in the number of management levels.

Figure 5. Changes in sales representatives behavior: Use of standard procedures

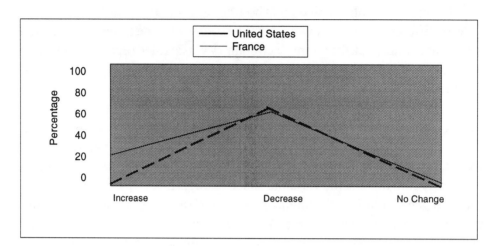

Standardization

Several graphs were produced to further investigate these differences. The graph in Figure 5 shows that most of the respondents in both countries indicated no change in the number of standard procedures. The differences between the countries occur in the "increased" and "decreased" categories. Practically none of the U.S. respondents indicate that the number of standard procedures increased but about 15% of them indicate that the use of standard procedures has decreased, while the results for the French companies is just the opposite-practically no one in France indicated a decrease in procedures while about 20% of them indicated an increase. This situation is consistent with the country-based differences in the reasons sales representatives return to their home base. It indicates a fundamental difference in standardization between the two countries in the manner in which they achieve their sales goals. The result for the U.S. is also consistent with Huber's theory indicating a decrease in standardization.

Formalization

Changes in formalization are significantly different between the U.S. and France. The change in the number of written documents, shown in Figure 6, illustrates where differences occur between France and the U.S. Again, as for standardization, most respondents indicated no change. But for formalization, the differences between countries show up in "no change" and "decrease" categories. More U.S. participants indicated no change and more French participants experienced a decrease in formalization. This is also consistent with the reasons sales people return to home base in each country and indicates a fundamental difference in formalization between the two countries in the ways the sales force carries out the sales strategy (see Figure 2). The result in the U.S. is consistent with Huber's theory. Huber predicted no change in this variable.

Decision-Making Time

Last, the level of change in decision making is significantly different in France and in the U.S. (see Figure 7). The French companies reported a larger decrease in decision making time than the U.S. companies. France and the U.S. also differ significantly in the number of years of cellular phone usage (see Figure 1). French companies have used cellular phones longer than their U.S. counterparts.

In order to explore this variable in more depth, we conducted a stratified analysis by year using the Mann-Whitney test. We included all three variables where the two countries are significantly different. The results of the test controlling for the number of years of utilization of the cellular phone

Figure 6. Changes in sales representatives behavior: Use of written documents

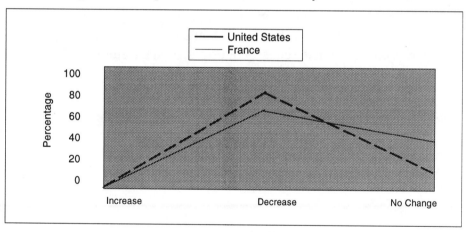

Figure 7. Changes in decision making time

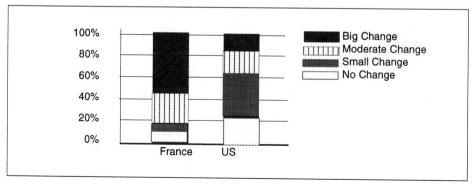

technology identified only a significant difference in the decision-making variable. (The significant results are shown in Table 3.) For this variable, the data show that differences between the countries are most pronounced early in the adoption cycle. By the time phones have been used for five years or more the magnitude of the differences between countries appears to lessen and both countries have attained a shorter decision-making cycle. These results are confirmed in Figure 7.

IMPLICATIONS TO MANAGEMENT AND RESEARCH

The results of the study have strong implications for management and for the research community. Based on the study, managers should strongly consider adopting new technologies such as cellular phones, since these technologies will reduce the decision-making time for their organization without concomitant organizational disruptions. Any reduction in decision-making time can be translated directly into shorter turnaround for orders, better customer service, and other time-related advantages.

The results of the study, however, should provide a cautionary note for managers who are not in the country of origin, or in the cultural group, of the

Table 3. Significantly different impacts in U.S. and France (stratified by time)

Variable Controlled by Length of Time Cellular Technology is in Place	Mann-Whitney
Decision time	.0
Less than 2 years	.025
3 to 5 years	.014
Over 5 years	.042
Use of standard procedures	.004
Less than 2 years	.576
3 to 5 years	.235
Over 5 years	.402
Use of written documents	.030
Less than 2 years	.130
3 to 5 years	.702
Over 5 years	.636

researcher who established the theory that explains the effects of certain actions. In fact, the present study shows that, even though the end result may be identical, the ways the result are achieved may be different from one cultural unit to another.

Researchers are clearly shown, given the results of the study, that each theory requires careful testing in different cultural groups. Cultural bias is one of the insidious hazards of intercultural research and it is an area that has not been investigated until recently. Researchers are cautioned about generalizing from one culture to another, using theories from one culture in another culture, and, finally, about assuming that because the end results support a particular theory, that the mechanisms of the theory explain the results in all cultures.

CONCLUSION

In general, the results of the study with the data from both countries combined support the predicted effects of the technological imperative theory. This theory predicts a high impact of adopting advanced information technologies on the shortening of the decision-making process in organizations. While the technological imperative theory was supported in its prediction of a shortening of the decision-making process, the change in the independent variables was not as predicted. For this reason, with all the data combined, the study opens the possibility that changes in decision making can be achieved without the negative effects of changes in management levels (downsizing) and changes in centralization and decentralization. This is good news for organizations that wish to attain the benefits of new technology without the accompanying disruption.

With the results of each country considered separately, however, the analysis shows a different picture. The theory predicted changes in independent variables more accurately in the U.S. than in France. In fact, the theory was not supported for any variables except the dependent decision-making variable in France. This means that the mechanisms that affect shortening of decision-making time are those mentioned in the theory in the U.S., but that other variables, or changes in the same variables but in different directions, caused the shortening of decision-making time in France. These results confirm those of Shore and Venkatachalam (1996) which support the effects of national culture on technology systems.

While more work is necessary to clearly separate the effects of extraneous variables (such as industry sector and differences in the capabilities of the technology) from the effects of cultural differences, the results of the present study point to the enormous potential of cross-cultural and multicultural studies of technology adoption. More studies of a longitudinal nature in similar industry sectors will elucidate this important area of research.

REFERENCES

Abdul-Gader, A. H., & Kozar, K. A. (1995, December). The impact of computer alienation on information technology investment decisions: An exploratory cross-national analysis. *MIS Quarterly*, 535-559.

Adler, P. & Borys, B. (1989). Socio-dets and techno-dets: Determinants of the diffusion and implementation patterns of automated machine tools. *Journal of Engineering and Technology Management 6*(2), 161-86.

Adler, N.J. (1984). Understanding the ways of understanding: Cross-cultural management methodology reviewed. R.N. Farmer (Ed.) *Advances in International Comparative Management,* JAI Press, Greenwich, CT, Volume 1, 31-67.

Adler, N.J., Campbell, N. & Laurent, A. (1989). In search of appropriate methodology: Outside the People's Republic of China looking in. *Journal of International Business Studies*, 20(1), 61-84.

Arndt, J. (1985). On making marketing science more scientific: Roles of orientations, paradigms, metaphors, and puzzle solving. *Journal of Marketing*, 49(3), 11-23.

Barley, S. (1986). Technology as an occasion for structuring: Evidence from observations of CT Scanners and the social order of radiology departments. *Administrative Science Quarterly,* Vol. 31, 78-108.

Berry, J.W. (1969). On cross-cultural comparability. *International Journal of Psychology*, Vol. 4, 119-128.

Brislin, R.W., Lonner, W.J. & Thorndike, R.M. (1973). *Cross-cultural Management Research Methods,* New York: Wiley Publishing.

Crowston, K. & Malone, T. (1988). Information Technology and Work Organization, Helander, M. (Ed.). *Handbook on Human Computer Interaction.* North-Holland, 1051-67.

Cox, T.H. & Blake, S. (1991). Managing cultural diversity: Implications for organizational competitiveness. *Academy of Management Executive,* Vol. 5, 45-56.

Damanpour, F. & Evan, W. (1984). Organizational innovation and performance: The problem of organizational lag. *Administrative Science Quarterly,* Vol. 29, 392-409.

Giddens, A. (1984). *The Construction of Society: Outline of the Theory of Structure*, Berkeley: University of California Press.

Graham, J.L. & Gronhaug, K. (1989). Ned Hall didn't get a haircut; or why we haven't learned much about international marketing research in the last 25 years. *Journal of Higher Education,* Vol. 60, 152-57.

Hirscheim, R. (1985). *Office Automation: A Social and Organizational Perspective*, Wiley Publishing.

Hofstede, G. (1993). Cultural constraints in management theories. *Academy of Management Executive,* Vol. 7, 81-94.

Hofstede, G. (1980). *Culture's Consequences: International Differences in Work Related Values*, Beverly Hills, CA: Sage Publications.

Huber, G. (1990). A theory of the effects of advanced information technologies on organizational design, intelligence and decision making. *Academy of Management Review,* 15(1), 47-71.

Kerlinger, F.N. (1973). *Foundations of Behavioral Research,* 2nd edition, New York, NY: Holt, Rinehart, and Winston, Inc.

Kling, R. (1980). Social analysis of computing: Theoretical perspectives in recent empirical research. *Computing Surveys,* Vol. 12, 61-110.

Lammers, C.J. (1977). *The Contributions of Organizational Sociology,* Leyden Institute for Sociology, University of Leyden, The Netherlands.

Markus L., & Robey D. (1988). Information technology and organizational change: Causal structure in theory and research. *Management Science* 34(5), 583-599.

Orlikowski, W. & Robey, D. (1991). Information technology and the structuring of organizations. *Information Systems Research*, Vol. 2, 143-69.

Pfeffer, J. (1982). *Organizations and Organization Theory,* Marshfield, MA: Pitman.

Riordan, C.M. N. & Vandenberg, R.J. (1994). A central question in cross-cultural research: Do employees of different cultures interpret work-related measures in an equivalent manner. *Journal of Management,* 20(3), 643-672.

Rogers, E. (1995) *Diffusion of Innovations*, 4th edition, New York, NY: Free Press.

Rowe, F. (1994a). *Diffusion des mobiles et changement organizational.* Working Paper, Department Economy & Management, Telecom, Paris, France, October.

Rowe, F. (1994b). Data network productivity and competitive behavior. *Technological Forecasting and Social Change,* 46(1), 29-44.

Rowe, F. (1994c, August). New media diffusion and changing organizations: car phones versus pages. *Proceedings of the Second World Conference on Management,* Dallas, Texas.

Rowe, F. & Struck, D. (1996, September). Cultural values and telecommunication media use. *Second Conference on International Network Manage-*

ment, HEC, Lausanne Switzerland, 23-24.

Shore, B., & Venkatachalam, A.R. (1996). Role of national culture in the transfer of information technology. *Journal of Strategic Information Systems,* Vol. 5, pp.19-35.

Straub, D. (1994). The effect of culture on IT diffusion: E-Mail and FAX in Japan and the U.S. *Information Systems Research*, 5(1), 23-47.

Wind Y. and Perlmutter, H.V. (1973). On the identification of frontier issues in multinational marketing. *Columbia Journal of World Business*, 12(4), 131-144.

Yates J. & Orlikowski, W. (1992). Genres of organizational communication: An approach to studying communication and media. *The Academy of Management Review,* 17(2), 299-329.

APPENDIX: SELECTED PORTIONS OF THE QUESTIONNAIRE (IN ENGLISH)

Company name: (optional)

1.   How would you describe the strategy of the sales/marketing area?
    a. cost reduction
    b. quality of service (advice, service after sales)
    c. reduction of delays in delivery of service or product
    d. increasing sales, even at the expense of increasing costs

2.   How often do traveling sales people come back to their home site?
    a. _____% come back once or more per day
    b. _____% come back several times a week
    c. _____% come back several times a month
    d. _____% come back less than once a month

3.   Please indicate the three main reasons for which sales people come back to their home site.
    a. pick up orders
    b. exchange general information
    c. evaluate ongoing work
    d. meet colleagues
    e. accomplish administrative tasks
    f. upload data
    g. other (please specify)_____

4.   How do sales people contact their home site when they are traveling? (circle as many as apply)
    a. public phone
    b. phone from customer office
    c. cellular phone
    d. other (please specify _____)

5.   Over the last three years has the number of management levels in the sales/marketing area changed?
    a. increased
    b. decreased by one level
    c. decreased by at least two levels
    d. no change

6.   Over the last three years has the importance of following strict procedures changed?
      a. importance has increased
      b. no change
      c. importance has decreased

7.   Over the last three years has there been a change in the number of written documents the sales force handles?
      a. increase
      b. no change
      c. decrease

8.   Are any of the following centrally controlled in the company (circle all that apply)
      a. people who can have mobile communication devices
      b. local, national, international subscription
      c. monthly expenses or number of calls
      d. outgoing or incoming calls
      e. other constraints (for example, calls can be made only during sales calls, etc.)

9.   What are the major reasons for choosing mobile communication devices? (please circle all that apply)
      a. status symbol for the user
      b. project an image of leading edge technology for the company.
      c. Improve the circulation of information in the company
      d. reduce the number of management levels or do away with specific functions
      e. make optimum use of time while away from the home base
      f. increase sales
      g. other (please specify)_____

10.   Does the use of mobile communication devices affect the number of times the people using them come in to the home base?
      a. it increases the number of times they come in
      b. it decreases the number of times, but only by a little
      c. it considerably decreases the number of times they come in
      d. it eliminates the need for them to come in
      e. it has not affected the time they come in

11.   Do you think that the use of cellular phones has changed the number of management levels in the organization?
      a. yes, it has increased the number
      b. yes, it has decreased the number
      c. no, it has no effect

12. Do you think the use of cellular phones influences the number of times traveling sales people come back to their home base?
    a. yes, it increases the number of times
    b. yes, it slightly reduces the number of times
    c. yes, it considerably reduces the number of times
    d. yes, it makes it unnecessary for them to come in at all
    e. no, it has not affected the number of times

13. In your opinion, what is the effect of cellular phones on users?
    a. it increases their INDEPENDENCE in relation to the rest of the employees
    b. it increases their DEPENDENCE on their supervisors
    c. it increases their DEPENDENCE on their subordinates
    d. it has no effect

14. Do you think the use of cellular phones has influenced the centralization or decentralization of decision making in your organization?
    a. yes, it has greatly increased the centralization of decision-making
    b. yes, it has slightly increased the centralization of decision-making
    c. no effect
    d. yes, it has greatly increased the decentralization of decision-making
    e. yes, it has slightly increased the decentralization of decision-making

15. Do you think that the use of the cellular phones has changed the amount of time sales people spend following strictly defined procedures?
    a. yes, it has decreased the time spent
    b. no, it has had no effect

16. Do you think the use of cellular phones has shortened the decision-making process in this organization?
    a. yes, much change
    b. yes, a moderate change
    c. yes, but very little
    d. no, not at all

17. Have any of the following changes occurred in the decision-making process because of the use of cellular phones? (circle all that apply)
    a. certain management levels are short circuited
    b. decisions are made at lower levels
    c. additional decision-making groups have appeared
    d. no change

About the Authors

EDITOR

Gerald Grant

Gerald Grant is Assistant Professor of Information Systems at the School of Business, Carleton University, in Ottawa, Canada. His areas of specialization are strategic management of IT, telecommunications management, and e-business. He previously taught at McGill University, Montreal, Canada and in the Department of Computer Science and Information Systems at Brunel University, Uxbridge, United Kingdom. He obtained his PhD in Information Systems from the London School of Economics and Political Science, University of London.

CONTRIBUTING AUTHORS

André L. Brandão

André L. Brandão received his BSc degree in electronics engineering from the University of Campinas (Unicamp) in Brazil, 1985, and MSc degree in communications and signal processing also from Unicamp, 1990. He received his PhD degree from the University of Leeds, UK, 1995 with emphasis in communications. He has worked as an engineer for the Brazilian Telecommunications (Telebrás) for more than 10 years. He joined Nortel Networks in 1999, where he is presently working in software development for base station transceiver systems in Ottawa, ON, Canada. His main current interests are in advanced radio link resource management for third-generation mobile systems and digital signal processing.

Rob Brennan

Rob Brennan (brennanr@teltec.dcu.ie) received a BSc in applied physics from Dublin City University, Ireland, in 1992 and a MSc in computational science from Queens University Belfast, UK, in 1994. He then worked from 1994 to 1997 on standards-based messaging and directory systems development for ISOCOR B.V. Since 1997 he has been a research officer at Teltec Ireland, a telecommunications research institute funded by the Irish government, working within the Intelligent Networks group. He is the chair of the OMG IN/CORBA finalization task force and an editor of the original specification proposal. In 1998 he began a PhD degree in next generation telecommunications services with Dublin City University. His research interests are in the areas of distributed systems, performance, hybrid internet/telephony services and agent technology.

Patricia J. Carlson

Patricia J. Carlson is Associate Professor of Computer Information Systems at Suffolk University in Boston, Massachusetts. Her PhD in Management Information Systems was awarded by the University of Minnesota. She has published in such journals as *MIS Quarterly, Journal of Management Information Systems, ACM Computer Communication Review*, and *Journal of Business Ethics*. Her research interests include organizational communication, change management, electronic commerce, and business ethics.

Thomas Curran

Thomas Curran (currant@eeng.dcu.ie) received a PhD in electronic engineering from University College Dublin in 1982. He then joined Dublin City University, where he is currently an assistant professor in the School of Electronic Engineering. During the course of his career he has undertaken extensive consultancy activities of a planning, design and marketing nature in diverse areas such as PBX, X.25 and data networks, networking multiplexors, public network management and switching systems. He has participated in ECMA and ETSI standards bodies covering frame relay, private telecommunication network, broadband and IN. His current research interests relate to IN, IP telephony, performance management and network design. Since its inception in 1991 he has been director of the Teltec Ireland center at Dublin City University.

Sharon S. Dawes

Sharon S. Dawes is Director of the Center for Technology in Government at the University at Albany/State University of New York.

Ping Gao

Ping Gao is a senior researcher at Faculty of Information Technology, University of Jyväskylä, Finland. Prior to late 1997 he was a senior analyst in an official consulting institution affiliated to the Ministry of Posts and Telecommunications, China. He received a PhD degree from Xi'an Jiaotong University, China. He is an expert on Chinese telecommunications industry. His research interests include telecommunications regulation, policy and markets.

Brendan Jennings

Brendan Jennings (brendan.jennings@teltec.dcu.ie) received a BEng in electronic engineering from Dublin City University (DCU), Ireland, in 1993. Since 1993 he has been a PhD candidate (part-time) at DCU and a researcher with the Intelligent Networks Group at Teltec Ireland, performing consultancy work and research in the areas of SS.7, performance management, service creation and agent technology. His main research interest relates to SS.7/IN performance management, an area in which he has published a number of technical papers in international conferences and research journals. Since 1998 he has been project manager of the European Union ACTS project MARINER (AC333), a collaborative research project that is addressing the use of agent technology for resource allocation and load control in Intelligent Networks.

Beverly K. Kahn

Beverly K. Kahn is an Associate Professor of Computer Information Systems in the Sawyer School of Management at Suffolk University. She received her PhD from The University of Michigan. Dr. Kahn's research concentrates on information quality, information resource management, database design, data warehousing and cross-cultural application of information technology and systems. Her publications have appeared in leading journals such as *MIS Quarterly, Journal of Management Information Systems, Communications of the ACM* and *Database*. Dr. Kahn is a Research Affiliate of the Total Data Quality Management program at Massachusetts Institute of Technology.

Thomas Kunz

Thomas Kunz received a double honors degree in Computer Science and

Business Administration in 1990 and the DrIng degree in Computer Science from the Technical University of Darmstadt, Federal Republic of Germany, in 1994. Before joining the Department of Systems and Computer Engineering at Carleton University, he spent three years as Assistant Professor in the Computer Science Department at the University of Waterloo. His research has focused on various problems in mobile computing and distributed systems. At Waterloo, he was involved in the design and implementation of Poet, a Partial Order Event Tracer. He also started, with two colleagues, a project on client-server computing in wireless networks. Some of the research problems addressed in this area are the management of subscriber location, improving TCP over wireless links by transparently offering supplementary services, and the design and development of adaptive mobile applications. His current main research interests are adaptive mobile applications, wireless communication systems, and ad hoc networks. Dr. Kunz published well over 50 technical papers in journals and conferences. He is a member of ACM and the IEEE Computer Society.

Kathy S. Lassila

Kathy S. Lassila has more than 15 years of IS/IT industry experience and is currently Assistant Professor of Computer Information Systems at the University of Southern Colorado. She has a PhD from the University of Colorado at Boulder and an MBA and BA in Economics from the University of Wisconsin. Her work has been published in the *Journal of Management Information Systems*, *Topics in Health Information Management*, and *Journal of Information Systems Education*, and presented at numerous conferences. Dr. Lassila's current research interests are in the effective deployment and use of information technologies, and the organizational impacts of information systems.

Kalle Lyytinen

Kalle Lyytinen is a professor in Information Systems at the University of Jyväskylä, Finland, and currently the Dean of Faculty of Information Technology. He serves on the editorial boards of several leading IS journals including *Information Systems Research, Organization and Information, Requirements Engineering Journal*, and *Information Systems Journal*. He has served also as the Senior Editor of MISQ. He has published more than 80 articles and edited or written seven books or special issues. His research interests include information system theories, system design, system failures and risk assessment, computer supported cooperative work, and diffusion and regulation of complex technologies. He is the leader of the STAMINA group which studies regulation and standardization in the telecommunications industry.

Conor McArdle

Conor McArdle (mcardlec@teltec.dcu.ie) received his BEng degree in electronic engineering from Dublin City University, Ireland, in 1997. At present he is a researcher with Teltec Ireland. His focus during the past three years has been on the introduction of CORBA and agent-based technologies into the Intelligent Networks. He has been involved in the standardization work for the OMG's IN/CORBA specification and in the development of Teltec's IN/CORBA gateway prototype. He is also participating in the MARINER EC ACTS project and is currently studying toward a PhD in the area of performance issues and load management for large-scale distributed telecommunications systems.

Sharon Oskam

Sharon Oskam is Associate Librarian for Government Documents and Coordinator of the New York State GIS Clearinghouse at the New York State Library.

Arogyaswami J. Paulraj

Arogyaswami J. Paulraj (paulraj@isospanwireless.com) founded Isospan Wireless, Inc. in 1998 and serves as the Chairman & CTO. He is also a professor of electrical engineering at Stanford University, where he supervises a research group that pioneered the area of space-time techniques in wireless communications systems. Prior to joining Stanford in 1992, Dr. Paulraj was the Chief Scientist for Bharat Electronics, India, Director of the Center for Development of Advanced Computing, India, and Director of the Center for Artificial Intelligence and Robotics, India. During 1983-85, Dr. Paulraj was a visiting professor at Stanford University. Previous to that, Dr. Paulraj led the development of military sonar systems for the Indian Navy. Dr. Paulraj received his BE degree from Naval Engg. College (India) and PhD degree in 1973 from the Indian Institute of Technology (Delhi). Dr. Paulraj has won a number of awards for technology development in India. He is a fellow of the IEEE.

Lance Pickett

Lance Pickett is a Process Manager with WorldCom in Colorado Springs, Colorado. He graduated from the University of Southern Colorado with a BS in Computer Information Systems and a minor in Business Administration.

His responsibilities at WorldCom include coordinating day-to-day processes among billing platforms, applications, and organizations, resolving billing problems, and preventing future billing problems through detailed analysis of improvement initiatives. His prior experience includes project management for Colorado government entities, and research and consulting for an Internet start-up company. He is currently pursuing an MBA and working toward a senior-level management position at WorldCom.

Frantz Rowe
Frantz Rowe is a Professor at the Universite de Nantes in Nantes, France, and at ENST, Paris. He received his MS from the University of California at Berkeley and his PhD from the University of Paris. He has published in journals such as *ISDN Networks and Computer Systems, Technological Forecasting* and *Social Change, Transportation Research* and numerous French journals in management and sociology. He is the Editor-in-Chief of *SystÉmes d'Information et Management*, the leading journal in the French IS community. His interests focus on communication technology use and performance. He is a member of the executive team of his university, where he is in charge of its IS policy.

Bill St. Arnaud
Bill St. Arnaud is Senior Director of Network Projects for CANARIE Inc., Canada's advanced Internet development organization and has led the development, coordination and implementation of the national optical R&D Internet network - CA*net 3. Prior to his appointment at CANARIE, St. Arnaud was a consultant and chief engineer at Switzer Engineering where he developed and patented encryption devices for transmitting high quality video for TV broadcasts, project manager at Motorola where he was involved in the nationwide deployment of a Police wireless communications system, president and founder of TSA Proforma - software and LAN company that developed networked trading systems for brokers and traders which was sold to Eastern Datacomm and ABC Communications (Hong Kong) in 1988, consultant for a number of high tech start ups, and Project Director for Vision 2000. He is a member of the editorial board of Optical Networking Magazine, is a member of the STAR TAP advisory committee, a Glocom Fellow of the Center for Global Communications, Steering Committee for the SPIE Technical Group on Optical Networks. He is a frequent guest speaker at conferences on the Internet and optical networking and a regular contributor to several networking magazines. He obtained his BEng from Carleton University.

Hemanth Sampath

Hemanth Sampath (hemanth@rascals.stanford.edu) is a PhD candidate in the department of Electrical Engineering at Stanford University. He received the MSEE from Stanford University in 1998 and the BSEE (Honors) from the University of Maryland at College Park in 1996. He is also working as a Senior Member of Technical Staff at Isospan Wireless, Inc. His research interests are in the area of signal processing for communications and smart antennas.

Zixiang (Alex) Tan

Zixiang (Alex) Tan is an assistant professor at Syracuse University (http://istweb.syr.edu/~tan). Dr. Tan has published actively on telecommunications regulations, policy, and industry in journals such as *Telecommunications Policy* and *The Communications of the ACM*. His coauthored book, *China In the Information Age-Telecommunications and the Dilemmas of Reform*, was jointly published by the Center of Strategic and International Studies (CSIS)/ Praeger Publishers in 1997. Dr. Tan obtained his doctorate in Telecommunication Policy and Management from Rutgers University.

James Y.L. Thong

James Y.L. Thong is Assistant Professor in the Department of Information and Systems Management at the Hong Kong University of Science and Technology. He received his PhD in Information Systems from the National University of Singapore. His research interests include IT adoption and implementation, IT in small business, computer ethics, and IT personnel management. He has published in *Information Systems Research, Journal of Management Information Systems, Journal of Organizational Computing and Electronic Commerce, Omega, Information & Management, Information Processing & Management, Journal of Information Technology, and European Journal*.

Murali Venkatesh

Murali Venkatesh is Associate Professor at the School of Information Studies, Syracuse University, and Director of the Community & Information Technology Institute (CITI), which he founded. CITI is a technology transfer and applied research and development entity within the School specializing in broadband and Internet technologies, applications and services. Murali's PhD (1991) is from Indiana University, Bloomington, with a dual major in MIS and Telecommunications. His research interests are the institutional adoption of advanced telecommunications technologies, with a focus on the public and non-profit sectors.

Fola Yahaya

Fola Yahaya has a degree in Economics, a master's degree in International Business and has recently completed a doctorate from the London School of Economics in Information Systems. He has worked extensively in the field of information infrastructure development, undertaking consultancy assignments for a number of organisations including the United Nations Development Programme and the UN Institute for Technology. Prior to his doctoral studies he spent a year working in the United Nations Regional Bureau for Africa as an economic consultant focusing on private sector issues.

Xu Yan

Xu Yan is Assistant Professor in the Department of Information and Systems Management at the Hong Kong University of Science and Technology. He received his PhD in telecommunications regulatory policy from the University of Strathclyde, UK, in 1997. His research and teaching interests include corporate management, competitive strategy, and regulatory policy of telecommunications. He has provided consulting services to the Ministry of Posts and Telecommunications of China, British Telecom, Nortel, and International Telecommunications Union in past years. He has also published extensively in renowned international journals such as *Telecommunications Policy*.

Index